IDENTITY, CULTURE AND THE POSTMODERN WORLD

Madan Sarup

Edited by Tasneem Raja, with a Foreword by Peter Brooker

EDINBURGH UNIVERSITY PRESS

© Madan Sarup, 1996

Edinburgh University Press Ltd
22 George Square, Edinburgh

Typeset in Caslon
by Pioneer Associates Ltd, Perthshire, and
printed and bound in Great Britain

A CIP record for this book is available
from the British Library

ISBN 0 7486 0779 X

CONTENTS

FOREWORD

I first met Madan when, with a colleague, I approached him to write a chapter for a book on the politics of teaching. When we arrived at his house, his first thought was to ask us if we knew anything about plumbing because, he said, he thought his water tank was leaking. We climbed to the loft to look, but of course knew no more than he did. Perhaps we thought we did, or should. Madan had no such airs. He was gentle, direct, learned, even bookish, and in a way innocent – in the way of the genuine intellectual, who asks the simple, important question. But Madan wouldn't have used the word 'intellectual' of himself. He said always that he was interested in 'ideas'; that was how he put it. And he assumed that other people had ideas too, that they were interested and therefore interesting.

We met occasionally at lectures, talks and seminars after that (I could only envy the way he made full use of the many venues for discussion and debate in London when he retired), and we met socially with old and new friends. He asked people about themselves, charming their ideas and stories from them. It made him a wonderful asset at parties, just as I was sure his manner and curiosity and knowledge had made him a wonderful teacher.

In the last year or so, Madan started asking more about himself. He was an instinctive and principled democrat, he knew and spoke against the unthinking and institutionalised racism of British society, and he remained, I think, a Marxist. But he began to reflect on his personal formation, to ask who he was speaking for and from what place; whether indeed there could be a settled and secure place between his youth in India (which he now revisited) and himself in England. The idea and material for the present book came from this thinking as he reflected on the themes of home, belongingness and identity in relation to new theory and the narrative of his life. The resulting book was unfinished, but it displays all the command of theory and the pedagogic skills of his earlier work, joined now by something new, as he ventured in a montage of voices to present a fuller personal and theoretical record: the life of ideas combined with images of a life. He knew it would be false to present this as a unity, and might even have recognised an appropriateness in the book's incompleteness. As such, it was one last idea in action, and this makes it, for me, all the more moving and true. There's always work to be done, ideas to explore, people to listen to, a world to change, as Madan knew and taught us all.

Peter Brooker

BEGINNING AND THE END

A stimulating lecture by Peter Dews (on *The Ideology of the Aesthetic* by Terry Eagleton), followed by a convivial evening discussing it with friends Chris and Steven, was the prelude to this book. It was a couple of days after the lecture that Madan decided to write on 'identity', and during the summer of 1993 he completed the autobiographical section (these are the passages in italics at the end of alternate chapters). In writing this book, he was searching for a theoretical, as well as his personal, identity.

This was a particularly painful time for him in more than one way, as he was becoming aware of changes in his body. In September, a week before the conference in Madrid where he was invited to present a paper, he unexpectedly suffered a stroke. The stroke, according to him, was due to his lack of enthusiasm for travel. Fiercely independent, he made a fair recovery. Once again, there were other changes.

Like a thoughtful teacher, he prepared those around him. He would talk movingly of death – in the theatre, in films, of friends, of neighbours, and even his own. One evening, he seemed preoccupied: 'There are some things I will never be able to do again; I know I will never be able to run up the hills any more. I am grieving for my own death.'

Even as we waited for the ambulance, minutes before he died, he referred to himself as a 'fragmented subject'. But to many who knew him, his intellectual strength and commitment to his writing were anything but fragmented. I was astonished to find that the two features of the human subject – perpetual mobility and incompletion – carry on beyond physical death. The heterogeneous process of identity, the differences rather than the similarities, the gaps and the holes rather than seamless webs, are as much a feature of the dead as they are of the living. Madan would have been very interested in the continually changing relationship which he has to those who grieve for him.

I have edited and presented the book as I hope Madan would have wanted. In many ways, even though we had discussed much of the work, I have felt inadequate and unprepared for the task. I accept the inadequacies on my part and hope that it still remains a very worthwhile book.

Tasneem Raja

ACKNOWLEDGEMENTS

(These are the acknowledgements found with the manuscript, which at the time were not quite completed and are here included for their poignancy.)

I have learnt that what books communicate often remains unknown even to the authors themselves, that books often say something different from what they set out to say, that in any book there is a part that is the author's and a part that is a collective and anonymous work. I am greatly indebted to many writers whose work I use, quote or discuss and who are fully acknowledged in the notes. I would like to thank in particular: Ariella Altzman, Maud Blair, Tamara Jacubowski, Eileen Jebb, Martin Klopstock, Brian Matthews, Desa Phillipi, Tasneem Raja and Gudrun Schwinge.

AN INTRODUCTION: WRITING THE SELF

I spend most of my time reading and writing, and often wonder how my identity interacts with my writing. Who am I and why do I write?

My early books were based on a Marxist approach. All the people I admired were Marxists, and it was exciting learning the theory. More importantly, I'd always had the feeling that the world was unfair and unjust, and I so much wanted to do something to make it better.

Now, the strange thing is, retrospectively, that though I saw things from a Marxist perspective, I did not see myself as a black person. This meant, among other things, that I did not seriously analyse issues of 'race'. I remember an evening when I invited a colleague home for supper. After a few hours, she gently commented: 'This is a white man's house'. I was stunned. But it was true; there was not one object or sign which showed that I had come from India, yet I had a high respect for Indian culture and a concern for the exploited peoples of the Third World. I still wonder how and why this aspect of my being had been repressed.

Gradually, my views and attitudes changed. I began to see things according to my commitment to Marxism. I read widely and then wrote a book on anti-racist education. I would argue that my identity changed and I remember that a German friend of mine was not happy with this redefinition. 'You are not black,' she would say, 'you have white culture.'

Could I call myself an Indian intellectual? Well, yes, I was born in India, so I am an Indian intellectual. But my cultural background is almost entirely English. But, because I am not able to identify with Great Britain, the imperialist power, I do not like being called 'Black British'. And 'Indian British' definitely sounds odd, unlike 'Indian American'.

I don't know when I became seriously interested in psychoanalysis.

I can't give a precise date because, in a sense, I have always been interested in it. I joined a study group, and after some years I wrote a book about Lacan's theories. I learned to interpret films and plays and my own life from a psychoanalytic viewpoint. During this time, I was aware that there had been a general intellectual shift from politics to psychoanalysis. Many friends whom I had first met in a *Capital* reading group, I met again in Lacanian circles.

Recently, I have felt very saddened by the events in eastern Europe. I am painfully aware that the heroic struggles of men and women at the beginning of the century have been rejected by the younger generation. I had naively thought that books outlived the individuals, but I learned that this is not the case with most authors. I had strongly identified with my writing for a Marxist sociology of education. I felt that my books were a justification of my life. I then learned that my books were unobtainable, that they were all out of print. I felt that these happenings changed my identity.

As I have just said, at one time I thought of myself as a Marxist (I still do); I then became interested in 'race' and later on in Lacanian psychoanalysis. I have not rejected any of my other concerns, but have tried to integrate them. It is often said that one way of finding out about one's identity is to ask: who does one write for? Does one write for one's self ? I don't think so. We are, as Sartre said, always in a situation. I have heard some writers say that they write 'for themselves'. But I do not believe them. Every writer writes for someone. Sometimes I think that I write and keep on writing to gain recognition from . . . ; but I can tell you about that later.

PASSPORT PHOTOGRAPHS

Who am I? Shall I look at my passport to find some clues about my identity? I have three passports, all British, but the first two have had the right-hand top corner clipped and have been stamped 'cancelled'. In the first one, I am a young man with a lot of hair and a confident smile. My height is 5 ft 8 in. and I am a schoolteacher. In my second passport photograph, most of the hair has gone. I have a white beard and a serious expression. My height now is 1.73 m and I am a college lecturer. In the third, current passport, the smaller red one, I am bald. Again, I have a serious expression, but now my face is heavily lined. My friend asks: which is the real you? Of course, people see me in many different ways: a 'Paki', a 'father figure', 'an old man'. (I've noticed that being old for Asians is not associated with becoming more conservative, as it is in the West, but with being more under-standing.)

I want to have a closer look at my new red passport, which is in front of me. It is smaller than the old blue one; on the cover, at the top, are the words 'European Community' and underneath is written 'United Kingdom of Great Britain and Northern Ireland'. On the back of the inside cover are my names, my nationality and my date and place of birth. The inside of the passport contains visa stamps which permitted me to stay in India and Pakistan for a certain num-ber of days. The Indian visa states that it is not valid for restricted or protected areas; these visas permit entry to and through defined territories.

The passport refers to my nationality (British citizen). I think of it as a formal category because it does not express how I feel about it. I am not proud to be 'British'; it reminds me of the scars of impe-rialism, the days of the Raj. I feel more sympathetic to the idea of being a citizen of the European Community, but here too I feel ambivalent: I would rather be a citizen of a federal European Com-munity, but friends remind me that the concept of 'Fortress Europe' is a Eurocentric strategy to maintain the power and the privilege of the 'First World'.

What a passport does is to show you who you are so that you can be recognised in a bureaucratic sense. But of course, you are more than a photograph plus a few statements about yourself. Even if a passport is supposed to be proof of your nationality, it says nothing about you as a person. I want to suggest that identity is to do with more than one's passport, more than one's appearance; that it is to do with who one thinks one is, what one believes and what one does. Some would say that to get to know someone's identity you have to talk to them, to find out about how they think and feel about themselves.

There exist many theories that inform us that identity is deter-mined. They include socialisation (role theory), ideology (the state apparatuses that Althusser describes), discourse theory (the early Foucault), discipline and the technologies of the self (the later Foucault). In all three theories, institutions play a crucial determining role: there is the family, the school, the place of work and, increasingly, the media. There is no doubt that identity-construction is increasingly dependent on images. Other factors which we must consider include how what is here called 'commodity aesthetics' determines the direc-tion that an individual's being takes. Commodity aesthetics is largely aesthetics based on our perception of the body, and on processes of sexualisation. I want to stress that our identities are not entirely determined: there are counter-identifications at work as well.

I want to argue that we do not have a homogeneous identity but that instead we have several contradictory selves. Moreover, I believe that two important features of the human subject are perpetual mobility and incompletion. I have been told that, for many young black Americans, Malcolm X is an example of someone who was constantly striving to change himself. In the face of great adversity, he refused to acquiesce or compromise, and became the voice of militant opposition. In a sense, identity is a process; it is heterogeneous.

But now let's begin. I want to focus on three key ideas: the meaning of home, the journey of the migrant and the crossing of the border.

1

THE HOME, THE JOURNEY AND
THE BORDER

THE MEANINGS OF HOME AND THE POLITICS OF PLACE

Wherever I go, I come across people meeting together to hear, read and discuss questions about identity: personal identity, social identity, national identity, ethnic identity, feminist identity, and so on. In Raymond Williams's *Keywords* (1983), there is idealism, ideology, image, but no reference to identity. Now it has become a key word; there are conferences, lectures, books and articles on every aspect of identity that one can think of. There are talks and discussions on the meanings of home and place, displacement, migrations and diasporas. Distinctions are made between immigrants, economic migrants, refugees and exiles. There is also a great deal of interest in the self, subjectivity, and in recent developments in the theory of the subject. How does one represent oneself? There is talk about different positionalities. Identity can be displaced; it can be hybrid or multiple. It can be constituted through community: family, region, the nation-state. One crosses frontiers and boundaries. I am not complaining about all this interest in identity; indeed, I am fascinated by it.

A migrant is a person who has crossed the border. S/he seeks a place to make 'a new beginning', to start again, to make a better life. The newly arrived have to learn the new language and culture. They have to cope not only with the pain of separation but often also with the resentments of a hostile population.

While writing, I often keep thinking of home. It is usually assumed that a sense of place, or belonging, gives a person stability. But what makes a place home? Is it wherever your family is, where you have been brought up? The children of many migrants are not sure where they belong. Where is home? Is it where your parents are buried? Is home the place from where you have been displaced, or where you are now? Is home where your mother lives? And, then, we speak of 'home from home'. I am moved when I am asked the phenomenological question 'Are you at home in the world?' In certain places and at certain times, I am. I feel secure and am friendly to others. But, at other times, I feel that I don't know where I am.

What exactly does the word 'home' mean when it is used in everyday life? We speak of homecoming. This is not the usual, everyday return; it is an arrival that is significant because it is after a long absence, or an arduous or heroic journey. If some food is home-made, it connotes something cooked individually or in small batches. It is not something mass-produced; it is nutritious, unadulterated, wholesome. We often say to visitors 'Make yourselves at home': this means that we want people to act without formality; we would like them to be comfortable and relax. 'It was brought home to me' means that I was made to realise fully, or feel deeply, and that what was said reached an intimate part of me. We also say 'It is time you were told some home truths'. These are truths about one's character or one's behaviour that may hurt you. Home truths are unpleasant and hurtful and can only be expressed in a caring environment, where people are concerned about you. A home truth is something private. Many of the connotations of home are condensed in the expression: Home is where the heart is. Home is (often) associated with pleasant memories, intimate situations, a place of warmth and protective security among parents, brothers and sisters, loved people. When I think of home, I do not think of the expensive commodities I have bought but of the objects which I associate with my mother and father, my brothers and sisters, valued experiences and activities. I remember significant life events, the birth of the children, their birthday parties. Particular objects and events become the focus of a contemplative memory, and hence a generator of a sense of love. Many homes become private museums as if to guard against the rapid changes that one cannot control. How can the singing of a particular song or the playing of a piece of music have such an emotional charge? I play a tape of 'La Paloma'. Why am I in tears?

But what are we to make of homesickness? In Freud's fascinating essay 'The Uncanny', he remarks that the fantasy of being buried alive induces the feeling of uncanny strangeness, accompanied by 'a certain lasciviousness – the fantasy, I mean, of intra-uterine existence'. He continues: 'It often happens that neurotic men declare that they feel there is something uncanny about the female genital organs. This *unheimliche* place, however, is the entrance to the former *Heim* of all human beings, to the place where each one of us lived

once upon a time and in the beginning. There is a joke saying that
'Love is home-sickness'.[1]

Of course, I realise that the notion of home is not the same in
every culture, and I know that the meaning of a metaphor used in the
1930s is not the same as its meaning in the 1990s. Nevertheless, I
want to suggest that the concept of home seems to be tied in some
way to the notion of identity – the story we tell of ourselves and
which is also the story that others tell of us.

But identities are not free-floating; they are limited by borders and
boundaries. When migrants cross a boundary, there is hostility and
welcome. Migrants (and I am one) are included and excluded in
different ways. While some boundary walls are breaking down, others
are being made even stronger to keep out the migrant, the refugee
and the exile. A distinction I have found useful is that between
space-based action, an action which a person can move on from, and
space-bound action, which is limiting to the agent.

Any minority group, when faced with hostile acts, does several
things. One of its first reactions is that it draws in on itself, it tight-
ens its cultural bonds to present a united front against its oppressor.
The group gains strength by emphasising its collective identity. This
inevitably means a conscious explicit decision on the part of some
not to integrate with 'the dominant group' but to validate their own
culture (their religion, language, values, ways of life).

Another feature of groups is that sometimes grievances are displaced; in some situations, for example, political interests can only be
articulated in, say, religious terms because no other vehicle for
expression is available. In Britain, a group of people in the Secular
Society are militantly anti-religious, and they are hostile to Hindu,
Muslim, Sikh and Christian groups for their religious views. But, for
members of many ethnic-minority groups, their religion is an aspect
of their culture, a valuable support in a hostile environment.

Some people don't feel at home where they are; they are unhappy
and they look back. Millions of people in the world today are
searching for 'roots': they go back to the town, the country, or the
continent they came from long ago. They try and learn something of
that culture, that history. These are the people who in some way have
found it difficult 'to form roots', to become firmly established. By
learning about their 'roots', they (hope to) gain a renewed pride in
their identity.

It is nearly always assumed that to have deep roots is good. For example, Melanie Klein, the psychoanalyst, writes that if the good object is deeply rooted, temporary disturbances can be withstood and the foundation laid for mental health, character formation and a successful ego development.[2]

It's been said that people with a good memory don't remember anything because they don't forget anything; similarly, perhaps, the person with roots takes them for granted, while the person with no roots whatsoever is vividly aware of them, like some phantom ache in an amputated limb.[3]

Roots are in a certain place. Home is (in) a place. Homeland. How do places get produced? Why has there been a 'resacralisation' of place? The first point to note is that places are not static, they are always changing. We must remember how capital moves, how places are created through capital investment. Capital is about technological change and the expansion of places. Places should always be seen in a historical and economic context.[4] In recent years, money capital has become more mobile. Places are created, expanded, then images are constructed to represent and sell these places. Of course, there is always some resistance ('class struggle in space') to this process.

In contrast to this Marxist view, there is a phenomenological approach. Heidegger, for example, believed that place is the locale of Being.[5] He was very aware that time and space have been transformed through technological change. He shared with Marx a dislike of the market and was antagonistic to the fetishisation of commodities. In Heidegger's view, there were authentic and inauthentic places. He thought about 'dwelling', about place and placelessness. He was aware of rootedness and thought of those people who had lost their rootedness in place.

There is an enormous richness in the ambiguity of the meaning of the word 'place'. I want to emphasise that places are socially constructed, and that this construction is about power. Capital moves about the globe and creates a hierarchy of places.

While the political-economy approach emphasises technical rationality, the Heideggerian phenomenological approach stresses experience. It could be said that both Heidegger and Marx see the world, but that Heidegger does not want to address the external, material aspects of it.

Now, some readers may say that this argument is based on a binary opposition: modernism (Marx) versus tradition (Heidegger), and that there are many other positions. Though we know that place is often associated with tradition, we often forget that tradition, too, is always being made and remade. Tradition is fluid, it is always being reconstituted. Tradition is about change – change that is not being acknowledged.

THE JOURNEY OF THE MIGRANT

We are born into relationships which are always based in a place. This form of primary and 'placeable' bonding is of quite fundamental human and natural importance. This insight is beautifully expressed in a moving and thought-provoking book about the problems which emigrants have to face: language, nostalgia, loss, search for identity. Eva Hoffman's biography *Lost in Translation* is in three parts: Paradise, Exile, The New World.[6] The first part is about Eva's childhood in Cracow, Poland. She writes about her Jewish parents' suffering during the war, her family and friends, her schooling. A fascinating evocation of a happy childhood, Eva's account describes her perceptions and memories in a vivid, sensuous manner. This part ends with a description of her parents' disaffiliation and the emigration of her family, when she is thirteen, to Canada.

In the second part of the book, Eva focuses on her alienation and her problems with the English language. She remarks: 'the problem is that the signifier has become severed from the signified. The words I learn now don't stand for things in the same unquestioned way they did in my native tongue.' Gradually, Polish becomes a dead language, the language of the untranslatable past. She finds her Polish words don't apply to her new experiences . . . and the English words don't hook on to anything. This part of the book is a thoughtful discussion about life in a new language (the subtitle of the book) and her anxieties about identity:

> 'This is a society [an American says] in which you are who you think you are. Nobody gives you your identity here, you have to reinvent your self every day.' He is right I suspect, but I can't figure out how this is done. You just say what you are and everyone believes you? But how do I choose from identity options available all round me?[7]

In part three, Eva gives an account of how she gradually begins to feel at home in 'The New World'. At first, she shares with her American generation an acute sense of dislocation and the equally acute challenge of having to invent a place and an identity for herself without the traditional supports. Feelings of anomie, loneliness and emotional repression drive Eva to therapy. She is asked: why do so many Americans go to psychiatrists all the time? She replies:

> It's a problem of identity. Many of my American friends feel they don't have enough of it. They often feel worthless, or they don't know how they feel? . . . maybe it's because everyone is always on the move and undergoing enormous changes, so they lose track of who they've been and have to keep tabs on who they're becoming all the time.[8]

At the end of the book, Eva acknowledges that she is being remade, fragment by fragment, like a patchwork quilt . . . she is becoming a hybrid creature, a sort of resident alien. For me, the book raises many interesting questions. How do frames of culture, for example, hold the individual personalities in place? How are places imagined and represented? How do they affect people's identities? How do the worlds of imagination and representation come together?

Eva Hoffman's book makes it clear that identity is changed by the journey; our subjectivity is recomposed. In the transformation, every step forward can also be a step back. The migrant is here and there. Exile can be deadening, but it can also be very creative. It can be an affliction but it can also be a transfiguration – it can be a resource. What I am trying to say is that identity is to do not with being but with becoming.

EXILES, STRANGERS, FOREIGNERS

Edward Said has remarked that when some people think of exiles they think of those famous American and British writers who sought a change in the creative surroundings: 'Joyce and Nabokov and even Conrad, who wrote of exile with such pathos, but of exile without cause or rationale.'[9] Perhaps, instead, one should think of the uncountable masses, those exiled by poverty, colonialism and war. Many words in the exile 'family' can be divided between an archaic or literary sense and a modern, political one: for example, banishment/deportation; exodus/flight; émigré/immigrant; wanderer/refugee.

All migrants, refugees, exiles come to the frontier. The frontier does not merely close the nation in on itself, but also immediately opens it to an outside, to other nations. All frontiers, including the frontier of nations, are, at the same time as they are barriers, places of communication and exchange. Frontiers, argues Geoffrey Bennington, are places of separation and articulation (acts or modes of joining); boundaries are constitutively crossed or transgressed.[10]

There are many sorts of travellers; some live on the borderline, the border between two states. The states could be feeling and thought, private and public, or Polish and English. One often hears the remark 'They have a foot in each camp'. These may be migrants who don't want to give up their own culture or assimilate with the new group. The borderline is always ambivalent; sometimes it is seen as an inherent part of the inside, at other times it is seen as part of the chaotic wilderness outside.

I wasn't sure which word to use (émigré, migrant, refugee, outsider or alien?) until I read Julia Kristeva's *Strangers to Ourselves*.[11] She too was once a stranger when she arrived in Paris from Bulgaria in 1966.[12] Her book, an examination of the history of foreigners in Europe, deals with the stranger, as well as the idea of strangeness within the self, a person's deep sense of being, as distinct from external appearance and one's conscious idea of oneself. She shows how the foreigner is thought of in different ways at different times, and she states that the modification in the status of foreigners that is imperative today leads one to reflect on our ability to accept new modalities of otherness.

THE RIGHTS OF A FOREIGNER

Who is a foreigner? The one who does not belong to the group, who is not 'one of them', the other. The foreigner can only be defined in negative fashion. The foreigner is the Other. Kristeva writes:

> The foreigner is the other of the family, the clan, the tribe. At first he blends with the enemy. External to my religion, too, he could have been the heathen, the heretic. Not having made an oath of fealty to my lord, he was born on another land, foreign to the kingdom or the empire.[13]

With the establishment of nation-states, the foreigner is the one who does not belong to the state in which we are, the one who does not have the same nationality. Today, legally, a foreigner refers to a person who is not a citizen of the country in which he or she resides.

Kristeva discusses how the spreading of the French Revolution's ideas over the continent triggered the demand for the national rights of peoples, not the universality of humankind. The situation now seems to be that only those people recognised as citizens of a sovereign state are entitled to have rights.

But what happens to peoples without a homeland? How are those who are not citizens of a sovereign state to be considered?[14] It is not surprising that there is some sympathy for the resurgence of nationalism, whereby those who lost their residence attempt to reconstruct their homeland.

Many people have noted the paradox that it is through legislation that we improve the status of foreigners, and yet it is precisely with respect to laws that foreigners exist. Kristeva remarks that it is philosophical and religious movements, going beyond the political definitions of man, that often grant foreigners rights that are equal to those of citizens. These rights, however, may be enjoyed only within some future Utopian place.

One of the main problems in modern societies is the conflict between the rights of man and/or the rights of the citizen. It seems that one can be more or less a man to the extent that one is more or less a citizen, that he who is not a citizen is not fully a man. Between the man and the citizen there is a scar: the foreigner.

What, then, are the rights of a foreigner? It is argued by Kristeva that foreigners are deprived of the following rights (in contrast to those that citizens enjoy in contemporary democracies). First, the foreigner is excluded from *public service* in all periods and in all countries (barring a few exceptions). Second, the right to own *real estate* is variously handled but is generally denied to non-natives. Third, though foreigners have some civil rights they are denied political rights. The denial of the right to vote actually excludes foreigners from any decision that might be taken with respect to them. Foreigners do not participate in the legal process that leads to the adoption of laws. In short, to enter the territory of the country, to maintain a residence there, to work there, sometimes even to speak out . . . the foreigner must ask permission from the appropriate authorities.

It is not surprising that there are some people who either do not wish to or cannot either become integrated or return where they came from. The arguments on both sides are well known. It is often said that foreigners eventually remain loyal to their country of origin and are harmful to national independence. But others say that foreigners share in the building of economic independence and consequently should enjoy the political rights that endow them with the power of decision.

Foreigners, then, are people who do not have the same rights as indigenous people. They seem to have two roles: they can be positive, revellers in the tribe's hidden significance, or negative, intruders who destroy the consensus. In a sense, the foreigner is a 'symptom': psychologically, s/he signifies the difficulty we have of living as an other and with others. Politically, the foreigner underlines the limits of nation-states. Kristeva perceptively remarks that we are all in the process of becoming foreigners in a universe that is being widened more than ever, that is more than ever heterogeneous beneath its apparent scientific and media-inspired unity.[15]

On the one hand, it is interesting to leave one's homeland in order to enter the culture of others; but, on the other hand, this move is undertaken only to return to oneself and one's home, to judge or laugh at one's peculiarities and limitations. In other words, the foreigner becomes the figure on to which the penetrating, ironical mind of the philosopher is delegated – his double, his mask.

STRANGERS AND STIGMA

Consider the following quotation:

> woman is the other of man, animal the other of the human, stranger the other of native, abnormality the other of norm, deviation the other of law-abiding, illness the other of health, insanity the other of reason, lay public the other of the expert, foreigner the other of state subject, enemy the other of friend.[16]

All visions of artificial order, states Zygmunt Bauman, are by necessity inherently asymmetrical and thereby dichotomising. In dichotomies, the second term is but the other of the first, the opposite (degraded, exiled, suppressed) side of the first and its creation. Dichotomies are exercises in power and at the same time their disguise. They split the human world into a group for whom the ideal order is to be erected, and another which is for the unfitting, the uncontrollable, the incongruous and the ambivalent.[17]

There are friends and enemies. And there are strangers. Friends and enemies stand in opposition to each other. The first are what the second are not, and vice versa. Like many oppositions, this one is a variation of the master opposition between the inside and the outside. The outside is negativity to the inside's positivity. The outside is what the inside is not. The enemies are the wilderness that violates friends' homeliness, the absence which is a denial of friends' presence.

The repugnant and frightening 'out there' of the enemies is both the addition to and displacement of the cosy and comforting 'in here' of the friends.

Obviously, it is the friends who define the enemies; it is the friends who control the classification, and the assignment. While friends are associated with cooperation, enemies, on the other hand, are associated with struggle. The opposition between friends and enemies is one between being a subject and being an object of action. This opposition sets apart beauty from ugliness, truth from falsity, good from evil.

Now, the stranger is neither friend nor enemy; we do not know, and have no way of knowing which is the case. The stranger is one member of the family of undecidables. This term is associated with the work of Jacques Derrida.[18] Let me explain: undecidables discussed by Derrida include the pharmakon, the hymen and the supplement. In French, the word 'supplement' has a double sense: to supply something which is missing, or to supply something additional. The pharmakon is a Greek word which means remedy and poison. The hymen is another ambivalent Greek word standing for both membrane and marriage, which for this reason signifies at the same time virginity – the difference between the 'inside' and the 'outside' – and its violation by the fusion of the self and other.

Strangers are, in principle, undecidables. They are unclassifiable. A stranger is someone who refuses to remain confined to the 'far away' land or to go away from our own. S/he is physically close while remaining culturally remote. Strangers often seem to be suspended in the empty space between a tradition which they have already left and the mode of life which stubbornly denies them the right of entry. The stranger blurs a boundary line. The stranger is an anomaly, standing between the inside and the outside, order and chaos, friend and enemy.

Strangers, Bauman argues, are anomalies who can be dumped into tribal reserves, native homelands or ethnic ghettos. Keeping strangers at a mental distance through locking them up in a shell of exoticism does not, however, suffice to neutralise their inherent, and dangerous, incongruity. An otherwise innocuous trait of the stranger becomes a sign of affliction, a cause of shame. The person bearing this trait is easily recognisable as less desirable, inferior, bad and dangerous. There is cultural exclusion of the stranger. S/he is constructed as a permanent Other.[19]

Stigma (undecidables) is a convenient weapon in the defence

against the unwelcome ambiguity of the stranger. The essence of stigma is to emphasise the difference of the undecidables; and a difference which is in principle beyond repair, and hence justifies a permanent exclusion.[20] Many strangers try to erase the stigma by trying to assimilate. The harder they try, however, the faster the finishing-line recedes. Unlike an alien or a foreigner, the stranger is not simply a newcomer, a person temporarily out of place. S/he is an eternal wanderer, homeless always and everywhere.

The nightmare is to be uprooted, to be without papers, stateless, alone, alienated and adrift in a world of organised others. Fellow members of one's own group are thought to be human and trustworthy in ways that others are not. One's own group provides a refuge.

In terms of their biographies, contemporary individuals pass a long string of widely divergent social worlds. At any single moment of their life, individuals inhabit simultaneously several such divergent worlds. The result is that they are 'uprooted' from each and not 'at home' in any. One may say that the stranger is universal because of having no home and no roots. The stranger's experience is one that most of us now share. Amid the universal homelessness, individuals turn to their private lives as the only location where they may hope to build a home. In a hostile and uncaring world, what can one do?

MARKING THE BOUNDARY

To conclude, I want to suggest that identity is a construction, a consequence of a process of interaction between people, institutions and practices and that, because the range of human behaviour is so wide, groups maintain boundaries to limit the type of behaviour within a defined cultural territory. Boundaries are an important point of reference for those participating in any system. Boundaries may refer to, or consist of, geographical areas, political or religious viewpoints, occupational categories, or linguistic and cultural traditions.

Some theorists, like Kai Erikson (drawing on Durkheim), have written that the only material for marking boundaries is the behaviour of its participants. According to this view, a deviant represents the extreme variety of conduct to be found within the experience of the group.[21] Within the boundary, the norm has jurisdiction. Durkheim, asserted, first, that a social norm is rarely expressed as a firm rule; it is really an accumulation of decisions made by a community over a long period of time. Second, the norm retains its validity only if it is regularly used as a basis for judgement. Each time a deviant act is punished, the authority of the norm is sharpened, the declaration is made where the boundaries of the group are located. This is the way in which it can be asserted how much diversity and variability can be contained within the system before it loses its distinct structure. In short, deviants and agencies of control are boundary-maintaining mechanisms.

This thesis was first applied by Durkheim to deviance. I want to suggest that the deviant has been replaced by the immigrant. In traditional folklore, there were demons, witches and devils. Now we have visible deviants: the foreigners. In Europe today, it is largely black migrants who perform the function of marking the boundary. Harsh sanctions are taken against migrants who, feeling threatened, often emphasise their cultural identity as a way of self-protection. They are forced into segregated areas and their sense of alienation is reinforced. The newcomer is seen as an intruder. There is a common assumption that there is only one norm; the dominant norm is the correct one, and others must adjust.

I want to suggest that the social system appoints many incomers to spend a period of service testing the boundary. Migrants mark the outer limits of group experience; they provide a point of contrast which gives the norm some scope and dimension. At present the norm stresses similarity, but what would happen if the norm changed and stressed difference? What would happen if there was a recognition of the diversity of subjective positions and cultural identities?

NOTES

1. 'The Uncanny' (1919), in Sigmund Freud, *Art and Literature*, vol. 14, The Pelican Freud Library (London: Penguin Books, 1985), p. 368.
2. See Juliet Mitchell (ed.), *The Selected Melanie Klein* (Harmondsworth: Penguin Books, 1986).
3. Christopher Hampton, *White Chamelion*.
4. See, for example, David Harvey, *The Condition of Postmodernity: An Enquiry into the Origins of Cultural Change* (Oxford: Basil Blackwell, 1989).
5. Martin Heidegger, *Being and Time* (New York: Harper and Row, 1962).
6. Eva Hoffman, *Lost in Translation: Life in a New Language* (London: Minerva, 1991).
7. Ibid., p. 160.
8. Ibid., p. 263.
9. Edward Said, quoted by Timothy Brennan, 'The National Longing for Form', in Homi K.Bhabha (ed.), *Nation and Narration* (London: Routledge, 1990), pp. 44–70 (p. 60).
10. Geoffrey Bennington, 'Postal Politics and the Institution of the Nation', in Homi K. Bhabha (ed.), *Nation and Narration* (London: Routledge, 1990), pp. 121–37.

11. Julia Kristeva, *Strangers to Ourselves* (London: Harvester Wheatsheaf, 1991). I am indebted to Kristeva's study for much of what follows in this section.

12. 'To work on language, to labour in the materiality of that which society regards as a means of contact and understanding, isn't that at one stroke to declare oneself a stranger/foreign (*étranger*) to language?', Kristeva asks defiantly in the first sentence of Semeiotike. It is, then, in her own exiled and marginalised position as an intellectual woman in Paris in the late 1960s that we can locate the formative influences on Kristeva's work. See Toril Moi (ed.), *The Kristeva Reader* (Oxford: Basil Blackwell, 1986), p. 3.

13. Kristeva, op. cit., p. 95.

14. The forced movement of unhappy, courageous people around the world continues remorselessly. In the newspapers, as I write, there have been pictures of desperate faces peering out of bus windows, eyes full of the appalled realisation that they are probably seeing their home countries for the last time. I am referring to reports (*The Guardian*, 19 December 1992) of the 400 Palestinian deportees living on a bleak hillside in the no-man's-land between Israeli-controlled South Lebanon and the Lebanese army, neither being allowed by Israel to return, nor by Lebanon to go on.

15. Kristeva, op .cit., p. 104.

16. In this section, I have drawn on Zygmunt Bauman, *Modernity and Ambivalence* (Cambridge: Polity Press, 1991), p. 8.

17. A French writer, Hélène Cixous, has made the following list of binary oppositions: activity/passivity; sun/moon; culture/nature; day/night; father/mother; head/emotions; intelligible/sensitive; logos/pathos. These correspond to the underlying opposition 'man/woman'. She argues that these binary oppositions are heavily imbricated in the patriarchal value system. Each opposition can be analysed as a hierarchy where the 'feminine' side is always seen as a negative, powerless instance. For one of the terms to acquire meaning, she claims, it must destroy the other. The 'couple' cannot be left intact; it becomes a battlefield where there is a struggle for signifying supremacy. In the end, victory is equated with activity, and defeat with passivity. See Hélène Cixous and Catherine Clément, *The Newly Born Woman* (Manchester: Manchester University Press, 1986), p. 63.

18. Jacques Derrida, *Disseminations* (London: Athlone Press, 1981), pp. 71, 99.

19. A well-known example of the construction of the Other is the discourse of Orientalism – a style of thought based on the distinction made between the Orient and the Occident. It is only by examining Orientalism as a discourse that we can understand the systematic discipline by which European culture was able to manage – and even produce – the Orient. Orientalism is not just a European fantasy about the Orient, but a created body of theory and practice. It is a relationship of power. See Edward Said, *Orientalism* (London: Penguin Books, 1985), and his recent book, *Culture and Imperialism* (London: Chatto and Windus, 1993).

20. Erving Goffman, *Stigma: Notes on the Management of Spoiled Identity* (London: Penguin Books, 1968).

21. Kai Theodor Erikson, *Wayward Puritans: A Study in the Sociology of Deviance* (New York: Wiley, 1966.1).

2

IDENTITY AND NARRATIVE

CONSTRUCTING OUR LIFE-STORIES

Identity has a history. At one time it was taken for granted that a
person had a 'given' identity. The debates around it today assume that
identity is not an inherent quality of a person but that it arises in
interaction with others and the focus is on the processes by which
identity is constructed.

There are, broadly speaking, two models of identity. The 'traditional' view is that all the dynamics (such as class, gender, 'race')
operate simultaneously to produce a coherent, unified, fixed identity.
The more recent view is that identity is fabricated, constructed, in
process, and that we have to consider both psychological and sociological factors. Of course, these overlap; there are psychological
aspects to the sociological factors, and sociological aspects to the
psychological factors. Neither of these models can fully explain what
most people experience. Identities, our own and those of others, are
fragmented, full of contradictions and ambiguities.

One element of identity-construction is the process of labelling.
People attach certain labels to others, and the labels often (but not
always) begin to have an effect. But our identities are not only influenced by events or actions and their consequences in the past, but
also how these events/actions are interpreted retroactively. We do
define ourselves to some extent, and yet, at the same time, we believe
that there are determining forces outside the individual.

The 'outside' of our concept of self could be called, perhaps, our
'public' identity, and the 'inside' of our identity our 'private' identity.
I do not mean by this that private identity is psychological and that
public identity is sociological, but that the former is how we see ourselves and the latter is how 'others' have typified us. I often wonder
whether, or to what extent, we can choose (aspects of) our identity.
Do we perhaps change aspects of identity when we realise that there

is some advantage in doing so? Does personal interest, perhaps, prod us to take the initiative?

In this section, I want to argue, first, that any study of identity must be localised in space and time. We apprehend identity not in the abstract but always in relation to a given place and time. Second, the study of identity must be based on something called 'evidence' and we must be aware of our methods of perception. Is an objective perception of identity possible? Is any observer bound to create something of what s/he observes? Here I am referring to the great structuralist insight, that unmediated perception of objects is impossible. The classical subject–object dichotomy has been deconstructed. The interpreter is no longer outside the act of interpretation; the subject is now part of the object.

When considering someone's identity, there is necessarily a process of selection, emphasis and consideration of the effect of social dynamics such as class, nation, 'race', ethnicity, gender and religion. I think we all link these dynamics and organise them into a narrative: if you ask someone about their identity, a story soon appears. Our identity is not separate from what has happened. Usually, these dynamics of class, gender, etc., are not explicitly mentioned in the story. The working-out of these dynamics and their interrelationships are not mentioned because they are taken for granted. It is often assumed that there is an agreement about these 'abstract' things. Discussion of these dynamics is considered unnecessary in an emphatic relationship. When we are talking about ourselves, we tend to emphasise what happened and what we did; we focus on the concrete effects, rather than the possible 'theoretical' causes. Nevertheless, these issues are implied in the story.

A (traditional) story has a discernible form: a beginning, a middle and an end. When asked about our identity, we start thinking about our life-story: we construct our identity at the same time as we tell our life-story. I want to underline the transformative power of telling one's story. Let me give an example of what I mean. Most critics have seen the play *Oedipus* as being about father–son rivalry and desire for the mother. Some have said that the story is about property and inheritance.[1] I want to stress that the play is about a person's search for identity.

It is well known that in folk stories the hero travels on a journey from home arriving unknown at a new and future home where he performs a difficult task (for instance, he rescues the people or the princess from a dragon or monster). He is then rewarded with the kingdom and the hand of the princess in marriage. Oedipus goes through the same three adventures as the fairy-tale hero: he kills the old king; he solves the riddle of the Sphinx and rids the city of plague; and he receives the hand of the queen.

Oedipus leaves the security of his home in Corinth to encounter hurdles and cross boundaries. This journey takes him out of youth into maturity, out of anonymity into recognition, from unmarried to married status, from lone individual in doubt as to his name and parentage into the possession of property and power. As the play proceeds, Oedipus takes on the role of investigator.[2] But it only gradually emerges that he is telling his own story.[3] After wandering in great mental and physical stress, Oedipus arrives at a little wood outside Athens. The local people (the chorus) question him, and he then recounts his story.[4] What Oedipus does is to reconstruct his own history through the process of narration.

I want to suggest that we are all, rather like Oedipus, detectives looking for clues, little pieces of the jigsaw puzzle (stories, memories, photographs) about our parents and our childhood. The story gradually unfolds. But it does not only unfold; to some extent we construct our story, and hence our identity.

When we talk about our identity and our life-story, we include some things and exclude others, we stress some things and subordinate others. This process of exclusion, stress and subordination is carried out in the interests of constituting a story of a particular kind. We are always asking: how did that happen? What happened next?

In the first section, I'm going to introduce briefly some of the main concepts that are used in the analysis of narrative and drama. I am doing this because I think that the concepts are useful in thinking about the life-stories that people construct. Moreover, listening to people's biographical narratives is in many ways similar to the work of psychoanalysis. There are, for example, gaps, exclusions and repetitions in the narrative. And the narrative has to be interpreted.

In the second section, I will give an account of an autobiography, a work that tries to relate (oral) history and psychoanalysis. It is the story of a psychoanalysis of a writer who wants to write the history of his own childhood.

COMPONENTS OF A NARRATIVE

But, first, let me remind you of some of the necessary components of a narrative. Each narrative has two parts: a story (*histoire*) and a discourse (*discourse*). The story is the content, or chain of events. The story is the 'what' in a narrative, the discourse is the 'how'. The discourse is rather like a plot, how the reader becomes aware of what happened, the order of the appearance of the events.

A narrative is a communication: hence, it presupposes two parties, a sender and a receiver.[5] Each party entails three different personages. On the sending end are the real author, the implied author, and the narrator (if any); on the receiving end, the real audience (listener, reader, viewer), the implied audience, and the narrate.

Authors (and we all tell narratives) select those events that they feel are sufficient to elicit the necessary sense of continuum. But, of course, a narrative can never be totally 'complete'. An interesting point about narrative existents (the characters) in drama is that they must remain the same from one event to the next. If they do not, some explanation (overt or covert) must occur. In drama, it seems that some principle of coherence must operate, there must be some sense that the identity of existents is fixed and continuing.

At the risk of contradicting myself, I want to say that the identity of a character in a play does often (slowly) change; for example, in the process of self-realisation. In everyday life, we are quite prepared to accept the fact that identities change: 'She's not the same person'; 'He's a different man now'; 'She's never been the same since . . .'.

The author or storyteller can arrange the incidents in a story in a great many ways. S/he can treat some in detail and barely mention or even omit others. Each arrangement produces a different plot. There are also events to be considered. Events are either actions (acts) or happenings. An action is a change of state brought about by an agent; a happening is when a character is the affected and not the effector. In traditional narratives, events are linked to each other as cause to effect, effects in turn causing other effects, until the final effect.

A major event in a narrative is called a kernel. It advances the plot. Kernels are nodes or hinges in the structure, branching points which force a movement into one or two (or more) possible paths. Kernels cannot be deleted without destroying the narrative logic.

In contrast, a minor plot event called a satellite can be deleted without disturbing the logic of the plot, though its omission will, of course, impoverish the narrative aesthetically. Satellites entail no choice but are solely the workings-out of the choices made at the kernels. Their function is that of filling in, elaborating the kernel. Just as an author can arrange incidents in a story in a great many ways (numerous plots can be made from one story), a person can, to some extent, arrange the elements, the dynamics, of his or her identity in many different ways.

In the shaping of our identities, much depends on the material resources available. By this I mean not only the linguistic aspects (the vocabulary, the accent), but also the place where the narrative is spoken, the medium used, and so forth. I think Foucault's remarks about discourse also apply to narratives: in any society, the production of discourse is at once controlled, selected, organised and redistributed. According to Foucault, there are a number of 'procedures of exclusion' operating, the most obvious being prohibition. We know very well that we are not free to say anything, that we cannot speak of anything when and where we like, and that just anyone, in short, cannot speak of just anything. Foucault gives an example: in ancient Greece, even as late as the sixth century BC, the truth – and power – of discourse resided not in what was said, but who said it and how it was said. I believe that it is the same with narratives.

I have stated above that narratives construct the subjectivities of men and women. I want to say that the stories we tell are often reshaped in/for the public sphere. And then, when these narratives are in the public sphere, they shape us. Narratives are, of course, sites of cultural contest, and when they become public we should ask: who is orchestrating them? This leads us to the problems of representation and power.

Sometimes these 'public' narratives become powerful myths and, even though we know how they came to be constructed, they still have a powerful force, they impel. There is also the problem of how the narratives are heard, how they are interpreted. We cannot (always) know the effects of our narratives. The self is somehow implicated in the representation of the Other, but we cannot control the effects of our narratives.

SPEAKING ABOUT THE SELF

Autobiographies usually emphasise the individual, the development of the self; but recently some 'autobiographical histories' have appeared which can be seen as trying to link the personal and the general, the individual and the social. One such work is Ronald Fraser's *In Search of a Past*, which expresses the tensions between social and psychoanalytical accounts of subjectivity.[6] It explores the autobiographical self and its place in history; it is an attempt at an autobiography which understands the self as a product of history and class, while taking up psychoanalytic concepts of subjectivity. It is a self-conscious construction of a narrative at different levels, a narrative that deals with change, both personal and social, psychoanalytical and historical.

The book interweaves Fraser's account of his sessions with an analyst, his transcriptions of interviews with the servants employed on his parents' estate between 1933 and 1945, and conversations with his brother and father. Fraser states that he was influenced by Andre Gorz's *The Traitor*, an autobiography which is, in part, an act of homage to Sartre.[7] This book has an unusual structure. Moving through the pronominal references 'we', 'they' and 'you', Gorz comes in the last section to write of himself as 'I', rhetorically and, by implication, ontologically closing the gap between the 'I' that writes and the 'I' that is written.

Let me make this clearer by quoting from Sartre's foreword to *The Traitor*. He writes:

> Today there are only two ways of speaking; the third person singular and the first person plural. We must know how to say 'we' in order to say 'I' . . . But the opposite is also true. If some tyranny, in order to establish the 'we' first, deprives individuals of the subjective image, all 'interiority' disappears and all reciprocal relations with it.[8]

The collective, thus formulated, becomes the relationship between self and other, subject and object, inner and outer. In Sartre's account, dialogue only becomes possible at the point at which an authentic self can speak itself as a first person. Fraser uses a version of Gorz's segmenting of the text, where the movement is towards some notion of authentic identity: the autobiographer/analysand moves through the analytic dialogue, towards the fullness of the autobiographical/analytic identity. Fraser finds the authentic self within a version of existentialism. The psychoanalytic dialogue is seen as Fraser's progressive movement towards the 'I' of the text. The book ends with a final reparative vision, which links to the recuperative power of writing. I will now give a short synopsis of the book and quote from it in order to give some idea of its dramatic quality and poetic style.

The book begins with a discussion between the author and his psychoanalyst (P). In this preliminary meeting, Fraser describes his childhood home, the Manor House at Amnersfield. He writes about how the servants, nanny and children lived in the old part of the house, and the way of life of his parents who lived in the new, front part. In adulthood, about ten years previously, Fraser set out to discover how the others had lived the past.

The servants at the Manor included Ilse the nanny, Bert the gardener, a groom, a butler, a cook and two housemaids. Fraser interviewed most of these people, some of whom he had not seen for thirty years. He asked them questions about their work, their wages and their perceptions of the class system and of their employers. Mr and Mrs Fraser, for example, 'were people who could do what ever they liked, who didn't need to work, who could live to ride and hunt and shoot, play tennis, bridge, entertain one another'.[9] From Fraser's interviews, we learn about the life of the servants – and the masters. The servants speak about their long, arduous work, their poor wages and meagre diet. The author arranges and rearranges selections from the recorded interviews to make an informative and poignant narrative.

The adult Fraser quarries the memories of the servants. We learn that Ronnie's father never picked him up or played with him. The nanny says: 'Even at the Manor I don't remember your mother kissing you, there was no physical contact . . . No touch. It's frightening how the English fear touching each other.'[10] Master Ronnie was a well-behaved boy; he never revealed his feelings. He spent hours in the garden or indoors on his own. He didn't have much of a family life with his parents, and he wasn't allowed to go out and have fun with the local children. Young Ronnie's life inside the Manor was like a factory running to an authoritarian discipline, in which cogs pulled him along, conveyor belts pushed him out. For the servants, Master Ronnie was a child to be pitied – a poor little rich boy.

Fraser feels a sort of emptiness, with no-one from the past inside him. Fraser discusses his thoughts and feelings about his mother and father. In analysis, at the age of 50, he realises that, in his childhood, he had two mothers: his German nanny, Ilse, was the surrogate but operative mother, while the natural mother, Janey, was the actual but the inoperative mother. As for his real father, Ronnie's first memories of him were all threatening. Ronnie found that he couldn't create something without him pulling it apart. He didn't want to be like his father, and increasingly he came to fear that he was like him . . . but Ronnie didn't like his father for another reason. He was responsible, when war broke out, for making Ronnie's beloved Ilse leave, to return to Germany. Ilse, the nanny, was the person who had really brought Ronnie up. She had done everything for him, was like a mother for him. Ronnie says:

> I can still feel the pain, the loss and the fear. My father was to blame . . . I always thought it was he who was responsible for everything that went wrong, Ilse. I've gone beyond everything now into pain. It's a laceration that's been with me since child-hood, a loss, abandonment – I don't have the words, never have had . . .[11]

Ronald suggests that the interviews with Ilse and the others served a purpose. They showed him what he was made of. What did he make of their making? – that's the part he needed to distinguish. Without it, he couldn't write about the past. He hadn't integrated the past into his life, and how could he write about his past without an 'I' as the focus?

> There's a long, almost unbearable silence. 'Psychoanalysis, you know, he says at last, doesn't set out to dispose of the past but to understand it. By understanding it one has a choice of how to deal with it.'[12]

The book contains a fascinating depiction of what (Kleinian) psychoanalytic sessions are like and, through the conversations between Ronald and the psychoanalyst, we learn some of the basic tenets of the Kleinian school.

> 'Does a child normally feel that its mother is both good and bad?'
> 'Certainly. All mothers have to be frustrating as well as loving.'

Later, the analyst continues the exposition:

> 'Well, he said, an infant had to go through a process of separation from its mother, didn't it. In a first stage, of becoming aware that the breast wasn't an extension of itself which, like magic, satisfied its desires. An original state of bliss, a Garden of Eden from which we were all banished. As it became increasingly aware of the mother as a separate and autonomous being,

of a reality in which others existed and desires weren't magically
satisfied, so its sense of self developed, ego boundaries became
drawn between the "me" and the "not-me" and the infant established a sense of autonomy. It's a long voyage of disillusionment
from a magical to a real world.'[13]

What about Fraser's identity as a writer? By the time he was seven
or eight, he knew he was going to be a writer: 'I would write about
an "I" who wasn't the "I" everyone else knew'. Fraser remembers his
decision to be a writer: 'I would be a writer, I told myself'.
Fraser remarks: 'in writing, I choose to stand outside myself'.

> Then he [the analyst] says, 'it brings to mind a child organizing
> and trying to comprehend isolated events and perceptions
> before it has an "I", while it is still a "you" . . .'
> 'Yes, you is the pronoun I most often use about myself. I
> never had a clearly defined "I".'[14]

There are discussions throughout the book about the nature of
psychoanalysis and the nature of history, and the similarities and
differences between these modes of explanation. Fraser remarks:

> 'What changes are our concerns and thus the questions we ask
> of the past. But psychoanalysis isn't history, it seems. What
> actually happened is less important than what is felt to have
> happened. Is that right?'[15]

Fraser outlined to P:

> 'The newly discovered aim of combining two different modes
> of enquiry – oral history and psychoanalysis – to uncover the
> past in as many of its layers as possible. And the two don't always
> coincide. That's my split vision. Formed by the past, a person is
> also deformed by it.' He doesn't reply at first. 'Well, it's not the
> past but what we make of the past that shapes our future and
> present, he says firmly at last. But I can see that the two voyages
> share common elements of language and memory. Perhaps you
> could contrast them in the book.' 'Well . . . Yes, they're similar
> in reconstructing a remembered past, not the past as it actually
> was. In that respect, analysis is more limiting because it recre-
> ates the past only in the forms in which it was internalised or
> repressed.'[16]

The war changed everything. For Ronnie, who was nine when it started, it was totally liberating. There were, for example, fewer class distinctions. Ronnie's sense of liberation during the war came not from a new social freedom alone but from a growing independence from his mother, who let him develop an 'I' that seemed his own. The mother seemed elusive, perhaps, because of her unauthoritative manner. Her control through the emotions was much more subtle. 'Hurt' was a word she used very often.[17] Her ability to pass on this feeling produced an emotional stress in Ronnie, a sense of guilt and depression.

Ronald and his younger brother Colin admit to each other that when their mother died they felt a sense of liberation. When she died, he never mourned her. He had got too used to losing her.

Standing by the graveside of his father, Fraser reflects that writing is a way of recuperating what has been lost; it's a way of making some reparation for the guilt he felt as a child. In one of the sessions, the analyst says:

> 'Yes . . . You want to be the subject of your history instead of the object you felt yourself to be.'
> 'The subject, yes – but also the object. It's the synthesis of the two, isn't it?'
> 'The author of your childhood; the historian of your past.'[18]

ANTI-NARRATIVES

I believe that through Fraser's story we can gain profound insights about the formation of identity. I like the way that his work shows that identity is not apprehended in the abstract; his psychoanalytic and social narrative is precisely located in space and time: his child-hood home, the Manor House at Amersfield (1933-45). Moreover, his work demonstrates that identity is both individual and collective. It is clear that the author is deeply unhappy and wants to examine his 'roots', to go back to relearn and understand something about his personal and cultural history. He discusses some of the factors that have constituted his identity: the complex relationship with his parents, the absent mother, the threatening father; the feelings of loss and abandonment and his attempts to reach his mother through writing. Writing, for him, becomes a way of recuperating what has been lost.

For me, Fraser's book raises questions about the relationship between psychoanalysis and social history, about the tension between autobiographical singularity and representativeness. However, some people have argued that appeals to psychoanalysis and theories of the social can serve to sustain dualistic oppositions between individual and history, inside and outside, psychic and social, if these categories are not questioned. It has been said that Fraser's refusal of poststructuralist thought involves a return to an earlier politics and psychoanalysis (existentialism and Laing). Laura Marcus has argued that this has produced an autobiography which follows traditional forms, and one that does not question the conventional categories of 'self' and 'society'.[19] In short, Fraser's book reproduces the dualism between individual and society; it does not account for the formation of subjectivity by and within the social and the symbolic. It is obvious that the 'I' of Fraser's text is not a Lacanian subject. His book is based on Kleinian analysis, which is a view bitterly attacked by Jacques Lacan.

Many questions come to mind. For example, people often speak of the self in terms of the narrative producing accounts of selfhood. But the problem is: does identity exist independently of the narratives which speak it? Also, what happens when a person repudiates his or her former identity? For example, in Peter Fuller's autobiography *Marches Past*, the author tries to represent the fact of two selves, a former self and new self in which the second is not a reformed earlier self but a 'transformation'.[20] A radical break between the two is posed. What is one to make of this? Third: what if the interpretative devices of a culture are also constituted by the dominant class? This would mean that there is no form of access to interpretations through which those on the outside can understand their conditions of existence in their own terms.

Drawing on contemporary French theory, I think it could be said that identity is not self-sufficient; it is necessarily accomplished by a certain absence, without which it would not exist. It seems useful to ask of every identity what it tacitly implies and what it does not say. Either all around or in its wake, the explicit requires the implicit. Just as in speech, in order to say anything, there are other things which must not be said; we could say: in order to be anything, there are other things which one cannot be.[21] What is important in identity is not only what it cannot say, but also what it cannot be.

Let me explain. There are some, not very many, moments in our lives when we have to make a choice. Later events or happenings are usually seen as consequences of earlier decisions. This happens in traditional narratives too. But now consider one kind of contemporary narrative which is an attack on this convention, the anti-story. This type of narrative regards all choices as equally valid. In all fictions when a person is faced with alternatives, s/he chooses one at the expense of the others. But in the anti-story, the agent chooses – simultaneously – all of them. All the possible solutions are taken up seriously, each one being the point of departure for other bifurcation, which are all followed.[22] These anti-narratives call into question traditional narrative logic, that one thing leads to one and only one other, the second to a third, and so on to the finale.

I think that in everyday life we are painfully aware of the few moments in our lives when we have had to make crucial decisions. In our reflections we consider what the possible paths were, and what would have happened if we had chosen them. What would have happened if I had said 'yes'? What if I hadn't done that? We still ask these questions even if nothing can be done about those decisions taken so many years ago. We still ask these questions even though we know that we can never know what the 'right' decision would have been. We often consider alternatives, but we do not continue to explore imaginatively all the bifurcating paths. We never consider all the possibilities equally seriously. It is in this sense that I can say that in order to be anything there are other things which one cannot be.

I want to argue that our freedom is always determined; our freedom is determined by the outside and the inside. But how do we conceptualise them? What is outside? And what is inside? There are many outsides and many insides. How does the external become the internal and the internal external?

Identity, in my view, may perhaps be best seen as a multi-dimensional space in which a variety of writings blend and clash. These writings consist of many quotations from the innumerable centres of culture, ideological state apparatus and practices: parents, family, schools, the workplace, the media, the political parties, the state. Human subjects have the capacity to 'work' on these differences within an individual, who is never a unified member of a single unified group. It is these very differences that create the space in which the human subject exercises a measure of interpretative freedom.

An identity is not an object which stands by itself and which offers the same face to each observer in each period. Perhaps when we are thinking about identity we should think of these 'writings' and transform aspects of them.

In this chapter, it has been suggested that listening to people's autobiographical narratives is in some way similar to the work of psychoanalysis. I gave a précis of an autobiographical history, a narrative that linked the psychoanalytic and the social, and tried to show how we construct the continually changing stories that we tell others – and ourselves.

In the next chapter, it is argued that we are not born with an identity; we begin the process of identity-construction with identification. Let us turn, therefore, to Freud's view of the unconscious and his concept of identification.

I cannot remember my mother. I think I was about five years old when she died. In fact, my first childhood memory is of her death. It was in Simla, Punjab. I remember that just inside the hospital grounds, on the right-hand side as you went in, there was a very small building. My mother had been placed there. My elder brothers, Atam and Roshan, and my sister, Sita, went in to see her, but when it was my turn I was told I was too young to go in.

NOTES

1. Vladimir Propp, 'Oedipus in the Light of Folk-Tale', in Lowell Edmunds and Alan Dundas (eds), *Oedipus, a Folk Lore Case-Book* (New York: Garland Publishing, 1984).
2. Tzvétan Todorov, 'Detective Fiction', in idem, *The Poetics of Prose* (Ithaca: Cornell University Press, 1977).
3. Laura Mulvey, *Visual and Other Pleasures* (London: Macmillan, 1989), pp. 183–6.
4. Timberlake Wertenbaker, *Sophocles: The Theban Plays*.
5. Jakobson said that all communication consists of a message initiated by an addresser, whose destination is an addressee. The 'message' does not communicate all the meaning; much of what is communicated derives from the context, the code and the means of contact. For a clear introduction, see Terence Hawkes, *Structuralism and Semiotics* (London: Methuen, 1977), p. 83. For more advanced readers: Gérard Genette, *Narrative Discourse* (Oxford: Basil Blackwell, 1986).
6. Ronald Fraser, *In Search of a Past: The Manor House, Amnersfield, 1933–1945* (London: Verso, 1984).
7. Andre Gorz, *The Traitor* (London: Verso, 1960).
8. Jean-Paul Sartre, 'Of Rats and Men', in Gorz, op. cit., p. 35.
9. Fraser, *In Search of a Past*, p. 14.
10. Ibid., p. 62.
11. Ibid., p. 123.
12. Ibid., p. 90.
13. Ibid., p. 168.
14. Ibid., p. 109.
15. Ibid., p. 95

16. Ibid., pp. 118–19.
17. Ibid., p. 165.
18. Ibid., p. 187.
19. Laura Marcus, 'Enough about you, let's talk about me': recent autobiographical writing, in *New Formations* 1 (spring 1987), 92.
20. Peter Fuller, *Marches Past* (London: Chatto & Windus, 1986).
21. Pierre Macherey, *A Theory of Literary Production* (London: Routledge & Kegan Paul, 1978), p. 85.
22. The logic of this kind of anti-story is illustrated in Jorge Luis Borges, 'The Garden of Forking Paths', in idem, *Labyrinths* (London: Penguin, 1970), p. 44.

3

·

IDENTITY AND THE UNCONSCIOUS

There are many approaches, as we have seen, to the understanding of identity. One is to find out as much as one can about it objectively, from the outside. The second choice is to describe how I and others feel about it, what I know from the inside. These two approaches, or perspectives, are the 'It is' and the 'I am', respectively the third- and first-person, positions. In the 'It is' perspective, the individual is seen from the point of view of the social; the 'I am' perspective is that of the individual in society. I want to use both approaches.

There does not seem to be a well-defined border between the individual and society. Indeed, a philosopher like Jacques Derrida would question paired words such as inside/outside, presence/absence, literal/metaphoric.[1] He would say that it is not possible to make a clear distinction between them. Identity, in my view, is a mediating concept between the external and the internal, the individual and society, theory and practice. Identity is a convenient 'tool' through which to try and understand many aspects – personal, philosophical, political – of our lives.

Is identity like a kaleidoscope where the patterns are continuously changing, or is it, rather, like the overlapping fibres of a rope where the interweaving strands make up our identity in non-essentialistic ways? Some people think of identity in terms of metaphor; others see it as a symptom. I have argued that the widespread, pervasive fascination with identity is a symptom of postmodernity. After talking to people about identity, studying it, and thinking about the interconnections between 'race', gender, class, nation and religion, it is clear that identity is not something we find, or have once and for all. Identity is a process, and that is why it is difficult to grasp it.

In the sections that follow, I will introduce Freud's concept of identification and outline Lacan's account of the subject. There is a short section on reflexivity, and the chapter concludes with some reflections on time and memory.

THE UNCONSCIOUS

Freud believed that dreams are the royal road to the unconscious, and he argued that the meaning of every dream is the fulfilment of a wish, or, to put it more accurately, a dream is a (disguised) fulfilment of a (suppressed or repressed) wish. The wish is disguised because access to consciousness is denied it.[2] In short, the subject is now conscious of all its thoughts: I have thoughts that do not appear to me; this thinking thinks without me.

This, of course, is the difference, the dissymmetry, between the views of Descartes ('I think, therefore I am') and Freud. For once it has been established that 'It' (or the id) thinks without my knowing, without the ego's knowing anything about it, then many questions arise: Who is It? Who is thinking? If the ego is not master in its own house, who represents unconscious thoughts to him, her, itself? Is the dreamer one person or two? If two subjects are involved, it is quite conceivable that one may not know what the other is thinking, or that the first may be distressed by something that pleases the second. How are we to understand that the subject knows nothing of what it desires? But what if there is an amalgamation of two separate people who are linked by some important common element? And what if they are one and the same person?

Are there some determinations that structure our identity but of which we are not aware? I believe that there are. We all know that Freud displaced the centre of the human world from consciousness to the unconscious. Freud used the image provided by the burial of the ancient world as a metaphor for the topology of the unconscious. He remarked on the fact that what was conscious was subject to the process of wearing away, while what was unconscious was relatively unchanging. He illustrated his remarks by pointing at the antiquities standing about in his room. They were objects found in a tomb, and their burial, he said, had been their preservation. The destruction of Pompeii was only beginning now that it had been dug up.

Freud pointed out that unconscious desire, once repressed, survives in displaced symbolic media that govern the subject's life and actions without his ever being aware of their meaning or of the repetitive pattern which they structure.

But what is the unconscious? The unconscious is not the simple outside of the conscious, but rather a division, *Spaltung* – a cleft within consciousness itself. According to Freud, our emotional attitudes to other people are established at an unexpectedly early stage and, secondly, relations between human beings are truly established below the level of consciousness. Freud's unprecedented discovery is the fact that the unconscious speaks⸢that the unconscious has a logic or a signifying structure, that it is structured like a language. The unconscious speaks in slips of the tongue, in dreams and in the symbolic language of symptoms.⸥

IDENTIFICATION

Men and women are not born with an identity. We have to identify to get one. Identity presupposes identification. Identification is, perhaps, the fundamental concept of psychoanalysis.⸢The word 'ident-ification' is used in many senses, but in psychoanalysis it is usually used in the sense of identification of oneself with the other.⸥It has been defined as 'a psychological process whereby the subject assimi-lates an aspect, property or attribute of the other and is transformed, wholly or partly, after the model the other provides'.[3]⸢It is by means of a series of identifications that identity is constituted.⸥Note that, for Freud, identification is not simple imitation but assimilation. He introduced the dialectic which links the narcissistic object-choice (where the object is chosen on the model of the subject's own self) with identification (where the subject or one of his/her psychical agencies, is constituted on the model of earlier objects, such as his/her parents or people around him/her). Freud also considered the effects of the Oedipus complex on the structuring of the subject in terms of identification. Of course, several different identifications can exist side by side, and a subject's identifications viewed as a whole are in no way a coherent relational system.

According to Freud, the child's most intense wish during the early years is to be like his parents. The child is always playing at being 'grown up', and in his games he imitates what he knows about the lives of his elders. When children stop playing, they fantasise. Later still, there is literary fiction. For Freud, the spectator is a person who experiences too little, who feels that nothing of importance can hap-pen; he longs to feel and to act and to arrange things. The playwright and actor enable him to identify himself with a hero.

In *The Freudian Subject*, Mikkel Borch-Jacobsen has focused on some of these questions. He suggests that desire does not aim essen-tially at acquiring, possessing or enjoying an object; it aims at a subjective identity. Its basic verb is 'to be' (to be like), not 'to have' (to enjoy).[4] Desire is not governed above all by the obtaining of pleasure but by an identificatory model. The child wants to be like grown-ups, to have what they have, only to the extent that s/he has first identified with them.

There is the story of Freud's grandson, who used to throw a wooden reel out of his cot (saying 'Fort!') then pull on the string that was attached (saying 'Da!') and so bring the reel back to him. The child repeated this game endlessly. Freud observed all this and gave many explanations; the most favoured one is that the child wants to gain mastery of the painful experience of his mother's 'disappearances'.[5] In Borch-Jacobsen's view, the child is playing at being his mother and, in so doing, is identifying with her. He loses himself in the very gesture through which he is attempting to constitute himself as a free, active and independent subject.

The desiring subject does not come first, to be followed by an identification that would allow the desire to be fulfilled. What comes first is a tendency towards identification, a primordial tendency which then gives rise to a desire. Identification brings the desiring subject into being, and not the other way around.

This brings us to the topic of love. Freud's outline of the genesis of social relations begins with the narcissistic phase: the individual takes himself as his own love-object. Then there is the first object-oriented phase, which is a homosexual phase: the other is not entirely other, but bears a likeness to the self, so one does not lose oneself entirely by the gift of self to that other, and for that reason the sacrifice is easier to make. Freud distinguishes between object-choices of the narcissistic type and object-choices of the 'attachment' (analytic) type. Narcissism is self-love, the self's desire for itself or the desire of and for the ego. It is different from object-love, by which Freud means any desire orientated towards what is not the ego itself. The example which Freud gives of object-love of the attachment type is the 'mother' – the object in relation to which all other objects will be only substitutes or copies.

It has been pointed out by Parveen Adams that Freud assumes that the child privileges one of its two parental love-objects; that is, the child makes a choice of love-object and this choice is followed by identification with the rival object. The boy's love-object is the mother, but he does not identify with her; he identifies with the father.[6]

According to Freud, there are fundamental differences between

men and women in respect of their type of object-choice. Complete
object-love of the attachment type is characteristic of the male; with
most women, there is an intensification of the original narcissism.[7]
Men and women, therefore, are not complementary. Man loves the
woman who substitutes for his mother, the mother being unique,
inimitable, irreplaceable. This is never anything but another name
for Oedipal love.

Parental love is nothing but the parents' narcissism born again;
parents see themselves in their child as they would like to be. It
seems as if no object-love escapes the 'narcissistic stigma' – each loves
him/herself in the other. Freud states that the Leader, the Führer,
too, is a narcissistic object: the group members recognise him as their
master because they recognise themselves in him, they love themselves in him.

Freud distinguishes different kinds of identification. In the first
type, identification is the earliest and original form of emotional tie
with an object. For example, a little boy will exhibit special interest
in his father. He takes his father as his ideal. He would like to grow
like him, and take his place everywhere. Identification with the
father is reinforced and takes on a hostile colouring owing to the
rivalry for possession of the mother. The child, in other words, wants
to be the father in order to have the mother. Freud writes:

> Identification, in fact, is ambivalent from the very first, it can
> turn into an expression of tenderness as easily as into a wish for
> someone's removal. It behaves like a derivative of the first, oral
> phase of the organisation of the libido, in which the object that
> we long for and prize is assimilated by eating and is in that way
> annihilated as such.[8]

How is the ego-ideal formed? Freud's answer is: by devouring,
cannibalising identification:

> Equally unable to kill his father or to submit utterly to him, the
> little boy finds an escape which approximates removal of his
> father and nevertheless avoids murder. He identifies himself
> with his father. Thereby he satisfies both his tender and hostile
> desires with respect to his father. He not only expresses his love
> and admiration for his father but also removes his father by
> incorporating his father in himself as if by an act of canniba-
> lism. Thenceforth he is himself the great admired father . . .
> This almighty, omniscient, all-virtuous father of childhood, as a

result of his incorporation in the child, becomes an internal psychic power which in psychoanalysis we call the Ego-Ideal or the Super-Ego.[9]

The ego-ideal is what one would like to be. In many forms of love-choice, the object serves as a substitute for some unattained ego-ideal of our own.

In a second type of identification, Freud writes, it becomes a substitute, in a regressive way, for a libidinal object-tie, as it were by means of, introjection of, the object into the ego. For example, when a loved person dies, the loss of the object often provokes an identification with that object in melancholia.[10]

INTROJECTION AND PROJECTION

Closely related to identification is introjection, a process in which the subject transposes objects and their inherent qualities from the outside to the inside of himself. Some writers believe that the emotional process of identification has physiological precursors in the development of infants. Thus the introjection of meanings, symbols, images or concepts of another person is based on what was once a physical process of taking in food, warmth, love.[11] Projection of oneself onto other people or concepts is also based on their physical expulsions and rejections.

Projection refers to 'the operation whereby qualities, feelings, wishes or even "objects" which the subject refuses to recognise or rejects in himself are expelled from the self and located in another person or things'.[12] Projection is a defence. Consider the person who attributes tendencies or desires to others that s/he refuses to recognise in her/himself – the racist, for example, who projects her/his own faults and unacknowledged inclinations onto the group s/he hates. In Freudian usage, projection is always a matter of throwing out what one refuses either to recognise in oneself or to be oneself.

Freud makes projection, along with introjection, play an essential part in the genesis of the opposition between subject (ego) and object (outside world).[13] There is some uncertainty about whether the operation of projection and introjection presupposes the differentiation between internal and external or whether it constitutes it. Thus Anna Freud takes the first view and opposes the view of Melanie Klein and her followers, who have brought to the fore the dialectic of the introjection/projection of 'good' and 'bad' objects, and who treat this dialectic as the actual basis of discrimination.[14]

LACAN'S ACCOUNT OF THE SUBJECT

I said earlier that the poststructuralists displaced the unitary subject. In their view, the subject is constituted, and it is composed of a set of multiple and contradictory subjectivities or subject positions. But how are such fragments held together? And if we all have many subject positions, how is it that we have an experience of continuity?

The French psychoanalyst Jacques Lacan argues that the analysand's (patient's) unconscious reveals a fragmented subject of shifting and uncertain identity. To be human is to be subjected to a law, which decentres and divides: sexuality is created in a division. The subject is split; but an ideological world conceals this from the conscious subject, who is supposed to feel whole and certain of a sexual identity.

For Lacan, then, the unitary subject is a myth; not only is the subject split, but its very production depends on the use of language. It is the entry into language which is the precondition for becoming conscious or aware of oneself as a distinct entity. This process simultaneously founds the unconscious. As language is a social system, Lacan is able to assert that the social enters into the formation of the unconscious.

Lacan is antagonistic to Anna Freud and others like her who always stress the ego and try to get their patients to model their egos on the analyst's. These ego-psychologists even believe that there can be an autonomous ego somehow protected from the unconscious. The emphasis is on being 'healthy'. In this way, psychoanalysis, particularly in the United States, turned into adjustment therapy.[15]

One contemporary example of the influence of ego-psychology in the United States is the work of Norman Holland, a literary theorist who investigates reader response with the help of psychoanalytic theory.[16] To put it briefly, the text produces turbulences in the reader which s/he has to cope with. There are gaps in the text which the reader fills in so as to negotiate the dominant unconscious fantasies which the text evokes in the reader. Holland, an adherent of ego-psychology, believes that it is the rational part of the mind which performs feats of transformation. That is to say, the reader uses a text in order to turn unacceptable private fantasies into socially approved aspirations. The responses of the reader are essentially those of a search for reassurance, a warding-off of anxiety. This security is achieved by the projection of a safe fantasy into the work. In other words, the source of pleasure we get from literature is derived from the transformation of unconscious wishes and fears into culturally acceptable meanings.

Holland believes that the infant born into the world with a 'general style' establishes an unchanging personal identity through its relation with its mother, which it will bear on all its transactions – including the reading of texts. What I want to emphasise here is not a specific theory of reading – reading as transference – but the fact that all theories are based on an implicit, often unacknowledged, view of identity. As Elizabeth Wright correctly points out, Holland, insofar as he deals with an unconscious, wants it to be under the control of the 'I' (the conscious, speaking subject), which for him is the stable ego.[17] People are continually using their life situation and experience as material for the ongoing construction of their identity, but in Holland's theory of reading, in which the reader uses a text to rework his or her fantasies, the unconscious is tamed rather than allowed to participate in the process of making new meaning.

Now to return to Lacan. I have stressed that Lacan is antagonistic to all forms of ego-psychology. In contrast, he always emphasises the importance, the positive affirmative value of the unconscious. Lacan continually asserts that the 'I' of the cogito, or the unitary rational subject, is illusory. Instead, his account prioritises the symbolic order which pre-exists the infant's birth. It is only through entering into the symbolic order as a speaking subject that full consciousness is possible at all. Language acquisition is the central process whereby subjectivity is produced.

Like Freud, Lacan assumes that immediately after birth the infant is unable to distinguish between things associated with his or her own body and the external world, and that a predominant sensation is one of fragmentation. An important change occurs, about the age of six months, with the onset of the mirror phase, when the infant catches sight of and identifies with a mirror image of a complete unified body. Marking the infant's first conscious recognition of a distinction between his or her own body and the outside world, this experience provides the infant with a first glimpse of wholeness or unity.

But, Lacan argues, this identification is based on an illusion or a misrecognition. There is a gap between the image ideal and the infant's actual state of fragmentation. It has been suggested by Catherine Clément that Lacan's mirror stage is a concept particularly useful to Marxist cultural critique because the false recognition of self at that early stage of individual development is reactivated by the ideological fix built into a variety of cultural forms (myth, drama, film) through which the subject is inserted into conservative and spectator positions.[18]

To sum up, several functions are served by the mirror (needless to say, we should not take the 'mirror' in Lacan's account literally). First, it provides a point outside the self through which the self is recognised. Second, it provides the infant with his or her first experience of corporeal unity, although an illusory one. Third, the infant is introduced to an order of imaginary relations.[19] There is a split between a glimpse of perfect unity and the infant's actual state of fragility. Though based on an ideal, the mirror episode gives the child an imaginary experience of what it must be like to be whole. It is in the mirror phase that the child begins to acquire language. And it is through the entry into language that the child is constituted as a subject.

A LINGUISTIC MODE OF REFLEXIVITY

What does it mean when people say 'learn first to know yourself'? Perhaps, in order to understand identity fully, we need a mode of reflexivity. Psychoanalysts have pointed out that the Freudian mode of reflexivity differs from the traditional humanistic mode of reflexivity, which is self-reflection. For Jacques Lacan, self-reflection is always a mirror reflection associated with 'the mirror stage'.[20] Self-reflection is said to be a symmetry that subsumes all difference within a delusion of a unified and homogeneous individual identity. In this view, self-reflection would be the illusion of a consciousness transparent to itself. The new Freudian mode of reflexivity substitutes for all traditional binary, symmetrical, conceptual oppositions a new mode of heterogeneity.

One of Lacan's main aims was to bring psychoanalysis up to date. He revised Freudian thought by importing new concepts from anthropology, linguistics and mathematics. He also went back to the German text to translate it accurately. The most famous example is *Wo Es war, soll Ich werden*. This does not mean, as Marie Bonaparte translated it, 'Ego must dislodge Id'. Lacan's translation is: 'Where It was, there ought I to become'.[21] Instead of the authoritarian jurisdiction of the Ego over everyday life, an attempt is made for 'I', the subject, to 'be'.

A salient point about Lacan's contribution to psychoanalysis is that he developed a linguistic model of reflexivity: 'It is not a question of knowing whether I speak of myself in a way that conforms to what I am, but rather of knowing whether I am the same as that of which I speak'.[22]

Lacan argues that when we call others, name them, we constitute them as subjects through our discourse: 'What I seek in speech is the response of the other. What constitutes me as subject is my question. In order to be recognized by the other, I utter what was only in view of what will be. In order to find him, I call him by a name that he must assume or refuse in order to reply to me.'[23]

Lacan goes on to make the important point that 'in order to know how to reply to the subject in analysis, the procedure is to recognise first of all the place where he is . . . in other words, to know through whom and for whom the subject poses his question'.[24]

Let me now summarise some of the key points about the unconscious from a Lacanian point of view. The unconscious is a discourse that is radically intersubjective. In language, Lacan writes, our message comes to us from the Other, in a reverse form. The unconscious is that discourse of the Other by which the subject receives, in an inverted form, his own forgotten message. But what does the Other mean? The Other refers to the position of the analyst through whom the subject hears his own unconscious discourse, and to the position of the subject's own unconscious, as other to his self, to his self-image and self-consciousness.

The Lacanian definition of a fool is somebody who believes in his immediate identity with himself, somebody who is not capable of a dialectically mediated distance towards himself. Drawing on this view, I want to argue that we often misapprehend, misrecognise our own history, our own identity. This is because the unconscious is the subject unknown to the self. It is usually misrecognised by the ego. You may remember that in Sophocles' play, Oedipus has to separate his own experience from what emerges as the social truth about it – that he has indeed killed his father and married his mother. The play shows that, far from constituting his own meaning, he has been caught as a function in a larger impersonal process utterly different to his own account of his experience. Oedipus undergoes the painful discovery that, in Lévi-Strauss's words, 'to reach reality we must first repudiate experience'.[25]

If a great deal more must be constantly going on in our minds than can be known to our consciousness, it follows that, in every case, what we think about our identity is incomplete and often not to be relied on. It is rather like Heisenberg's 'uncertainty principle': whenever we think we have located one dimension of identity, it becomes difficult to formulate the other dimensions. Human discourse can by definition never be entirely in agreement with itself, entirely identical to its knowledge of itself. It is because of the existence of the unconscious that we can never have an absolute knowledge of identity.

What, then, is the aim of Lacanian analysis? In Lacanian analysis, the aim is to bring human subjects to recognise and name their desire – the relation of a being to a lack. Lacan was convinced that the goal of analysis was the patient's recognition of incurable lack rather than any attainment of fantasised plenitude.

CONSTRUCTION OF IDENTITY: TIME AND MEMORY

Nevertheless, in spite of all the difficulties – misapprehension, misrecognition, ambiguity and uncertainty – we still carry on constructing narratives. We tell many stories to others but we also tell some of them to ourselves. These stories are often about our past. When I wrote a few autobiographical sketches recently, I was embarrassed by their brevity. I couldn't remember very much. Why did I have so little to say? I was perturbed by the sheer lack of information about my parents. Why couldn't I remember my mother's face, my father's voice? Lacan argues that what will not be memorised is tied up with repression. It is not so much a matter of a lack of information but of inner resistances.

Merleau-Ponty makes the interesting point – in writing about time, he refers to psychoanalysis and the concept of repression – that a person can have trauma which can sometimes lead to a fixation. An incident which occurred in the past can become a true present. There is a stagnation of time, a dread, a fear that chokes the subject. The traumatic experience becomes a style of being. Time stands still. The present strives to be the 'absolute present' which oppresses the person.

Gradually, the traumatic experience can become less prominent, but what is important is our memory of the past. We have a memory of a memory. Let me give two examples of this 'repression' of time. In Mozart's opera *Don Giovanni*, after seducing Donna Anna, Don Giovanni kills her father in a duel. She has an ardent fiancé who wants to marry her, but she continually puts obstacles in the way. Donna Anna always finds excuses to delay marriage. The trauma is such that she can think of nothing but her father's death. (Was she in love with him?) One incident in her past life entirely dominates her present. This is what Merleau-Ponty means when he talks of the 'absolute present'. Even after Don Giovanni has met his fate, Donna Anna says she will observe a year's mourning before marrying her lover.

The second example is from a film by Paul Cox called *Golden Braid*. A thoughtful, cultured, middle-aged man is haunted by the past. (Not surprisingly, he collects antique clocks and repairs them.) He has a lover who needs valorisation, but he often thinks of his past women friends, some of whom are dead. One day, he finds in an antique cupboard a beautiful braid of hair. Gradually, he becomes obsessed by it. He wants to take it with him wherever he goes, to a concert, to his bed. He prefers to be with his golden braid rather than with his lover. As his past comes to dominate the present completely (the 'absolute present'), she becomes jealous, and has to decide what to do to make him realise what is happening.

Shoshana Felman has suggested that 'We change many aspects of these histories of self and others as we change, for better or worse, the implied or stated questions to which they are the answers. Personal development may be characterised as change in the questions it is urgent or essential to answer.'[26]

I have often wondered why some stories are so fascinating. It is possible that stories have power over us because they are compelling us to recognise something in ourselves. When a person is telling us their story, we should be listening for its disparities and discrepancies, gaps and silences, anomalies and ambiguities, its restrictions and paradoxes. Rather than focus on what the story means, we should ask: what does the story do? This was Freud's strategy; he considered not just what the storyteller means to say but also what the storyteller is doing with, and through, the story.

Writers on identity often focus on the influence of one social dynamic at a time. Class, or 'race' or nationality, for example; this denies the multiplicity of factors that may influence human subjects in the construction of their identity. Secondly, many writers frequently adopt a highly simplified view of social structure, analysing complex issues in a one-dimensional, categorical manner. Thirdly, in their enthusiasm to explore the social dynamics, many writers deny that there are important psychoanalytical questions to be addressed as well. I think that all sociological theories about identity have within them (usually implicitly) a model of how individuals function at a psychic level.

I believe that our identities are, to some extent, constructed by social structures. To put it briefly, structures are often constraints on the way we act. These constraints can be material, or political. Political constraints mean that, in some situations, other people have the power to determine how we act and even influence how we think.

One of the main problems in this area is how and to what extent the above deterministic view relates to the voluntaristic view which insists that identities are fabricated, that is to say, they are both invented and constructed. They are never finished products. Identities are stitched together out of discontinuous forms and practices. The representation of identity is an ongoing process, undertaken on many levels, in different practices and sites of experience. Identity is articulated in multiple modalities – the moment of experience, the mode of writing or representation (for example, in fiction or film) and the theoretical modality.

An important aspect to the construction and negotiation of identity is the past–present relation and its reconciliation. The past figures importantly in people's self-representations because it is through recollections of the past that people represent themselves to themselves. We know that the past always marks the present, but often the past consists of a selectively appropriated set of memories and discourses. This may be because the stories people tell of their pasts often have much to do with the shoring-up of their self-understanding.[27] The present is by definition uncertain for everyone, since it is always in the process of emerging. It is doubly ambivalent for migrant subjects who also have to deal with racism and discrimination (or, in fashionable discourse, difference and marginality).

The past–present relation is often both contradictory and ambivalent. This can be clearly seen in the work of Keya Ganguly, who has done research in a community of postcolonial Indian immigrants to the USA on how personal memory authorises versions of migrant identity.[28] The Indians were educated, professional, married people with children, who stressed 'family values' and 'tradition'. She found that, for the men, thinking about the past was a way of affirming how much better off they were in the present. The men's rejection of their past in India as low and debased was consistent with their valorisation of the present. Though they admitted that the early years had been difficult to negotiate, immigration had provided them with the ticket to financial security and higher social status. Most of the men, then, downplayed their experiences of marginality and emphasised their present material 'freedom'. How narratives of the past inflect the construction of identity in the present can be clearly seen here. For these men, remembering the past served to make them realise exactly how rewarding the immigrant experience had been. The attempt to consolidate respectability in the bourgeois, diasporic context requires constructing the past as something unpleasant. However, the devaluation of the past indicates and itself produces the present hybrid identity of immigrant men.

The women thought of their past very differently. In contrast to the men, the women emphasised the comforts and privileges of their pre-immigrant past. The researcher remarks that there seemed to bé a consistent inconsistency between the men's and women's narratives of personal history. There was a tacit assumption among the women that the past was a sensitive subject, not to be discussed with the men. For the women, life in India had been more relaxed, even for families without a lot of money. The past may be recollected as a time for better living because, at some level, they refuse the ideology that immigration is a rewarding experience. Though these women, mainly housewives, enjoy material comforts, they cannot replace the losses incurred by leaving home. They know there is no going back and, moreover, they cannot undermine their husbands' positions by criticising their present life in the USA. Their management of these competing and disturbing realities takes the form of romanticising the past. Remaking the past, then, serves at least a dual purpose. It is a way of coming to terms with the present without being seen to criticise the status quo; it also helps to recuperate a sense of the self not dependent on criteria handed down by others. The past is what the women can claim as their own.

In short, it was found that both men and women reinvented the past and themselves, but in contrasting ways. It was in the interests of men to downplay their pre-immigrant circumstances. As stated earlier, men seemed to be more concerned with representing the constraints of their pasts and with privileging the present. Materially, at least, people are better off in the USA, so recollecting the hardships of the past is one way of justifying immigration as the right option. The women look back to a happier time when their family and kinship ties were still intact. In the USA, they find themselves alone and without the support systems they were brought up to believe in and rely on. Now they find themselves confined to being isolated wives and mothers. Moreover, when they step out of the house, they experience acute alienation. Outside the house, these women signify their difference and otherness by their appearance, dress and accents. Mixing with white people is difficult. Most Indians believe that their affluence should guarantee acceptance into mainstream society, but of course it does not. These women cannot criticise the present. The presence of the past offers a way for these women to say what otherwise cannot be said: that emigration has brought with it a betrayal of the promise of equality. The certainty and security of their identity has been disrupted in the immigrant context; consequently, individuals remember their personal histories as a way of reconciling disjunctions in their notions of themselves.

CONCLUDING REMARKS

There is a lot of insecurity and uncertainty about who we are. Many thinkers are wondering whether there will be new forms of identity. Perhaps because many of us are uncertain of our identities and boundaries, some writers stress that we must work with ambivalence. Homi Bhabha, for example, is very concerned with the concept of cultural difference. He is very aware that cultural incommensurability has to be negotiated, and is interested in exploring the interstices in and between cultures.[29] Will these new subjectivities reflect the new social conditions? Of course, these anxieties about the subject are not new – there have always been writers deploring the lack of coherent identity, 'the crisis of identity', and so on.

Mikkel Borch-Jacobsen suggests that the extraordinary epidemic of Multiple Personality Disorder (MPD) may be a new form of subjectivity. It occurs in the USA, predominantly among women, where, apparently, it has been known for some of them to switch from one personality to nine or ten other personalities. Therapists see MPD as arising from child abuse and, increasingly, from satanic ritual abuse. While it may be argued that MPD reveals the underlying nature of the subject, critics, like Borch-Jacobsen, claim that it is a product of therapy itself.

Groups have a similar structure to 'community': they like to define themselves as homogeneous. All groups draw a boundary; on the inside are 'us', on the outside are the other, 'them'. Identities, however, are fragile and unstable, and so what political agencies try to do is to institutionalise group identity. The 'political' is interested in the representation of the group as a unity. In this type of discussion, there is often a conflation between the personal, the social and the political. I want to underline the fact that, though representation works in all these areas, the personal, the social and the political are three distinct levels.

Some idealists have talked of going beyond political identification; this sounds very attractive, but it seems highly unlikely in a world where there is so much fragmentation, a characteristic, many believe, of postmodernity.

To conclude this chapter, let me tell you the story that Catherine Clément narrates about a transformation of identity. One fine day, Mme Victoire turned up at a clinic in a working-class district in the outskirts of Paris. Mme Victoire had come with her daughter Janine for psychotherapy; led by her daughter, she had really come for herself, as do all parents who unconsciously use the child as a go-between to express their malaise. The analysis of Mme Victoire, a cleaning lady, went on in secret since the clinic dealt only with children. After four years, she reached the end of her analysis. Mme Victoire remarked on what had happened to her:

> Before, nobody talked to me; now, everywhere I go, they talk to me, everywhere I go to clean, they used to treat me like a bird-brain; now it seems like people are always asking me for advice. You can't believe what people can say without realizing it, it's really embarrassing. Just like in here . . . but I can't say any of it, they'd think I'm crazy . . . I'm no analyst . . . Maybe I help them after all because I listen to them, and no one else really does. It makes me laugh sometimes, I feel like telling them, 'I'm only your cleaning lady, you know'. But sometimes, I don't feel too good. Not like before when nobody would talk to me, in fact it's much worse. They talk to me and I can't answer. So I'm even more lonely than I was before.[30]

NOTES

1. In Derridian deconstruction, the first move of reversing and displacing the hierarchies of dominant binary oppositions is usually successfully transgressive. The second move, of dissemination, is much more difficult.
2. Sartre objected to the concept of the unconscious. The agency which has to censor the material does not belong to the unconscious. The agency must then belong to the conscious – but how can the conscious know what it has to censor from itself? According to Sartre, this made the unconscious a modality of 'bad faith': Jean-Paul Sartre, *Being and Nothingness* (London: Routledge & Kegan Paul. 1969), pp. 50–7.

3. J. Laplanche and J. B. Pontalis, *The Language of Psycho-Analysis* (London: The Hogarth Press, 1973), p. 205.

4. Mikkel Borch-Jacobsen, *The Freudian Subject* (Stanford: Stanford University Press, 1988), p. 28. This section owes a great deal to the above author.

5. The 'fort-da' game is described in Sigmund Freud, 'Beyond the Pleasure Principle', in idem, *On Metapsychology* (London: Penguin, 1984), p. 284. For Lacan's comments on the game, see Jacques Lacan, *Ecrits: A Selection* (London: Tavistock, 1977), p. 103.

6. On identification and object-choice in Freud's work, see Parveen Adams, 'Per Os(cillation)', in James Donald (ed.), *Psychoanalysis and Cultural Theory: Thresholds* (London: Macmillan, 1991).

7. Sigmund Freud, 'On Narcissism', in *On Metapsychology*, op .cit., p. 82.

8. Sigmund Freud, 'Group Psychology and the Analysis of the Ego', quoted in Borch-Jacobsen, p. 179.

9. Sigmund Freud, 'Thomas Woodrow Wilson', quoted in Borch-Jacobsen, p. 221.

10. Sigmund Freud, 'Mourning and Melancholia', in *On Metapsychology*, op. cit.

11. Claire Pajaczkowska and Lola Young, 'Racism, Representation, Psychoanalysis', in James Donald and Ali Rattansi (eds), *'Race', Culture and Difference* (London: OU/ Sage, 1992), p. 200. They explain clearly how film and literature employ the viewer/ reader's identification, providing characters and situations which are introjected and become part of the reader's imaginative world. Similarly, the reader projects onto the text, either its characters or its scenario, aspects of his or her experience, fantasy or memory which bring the texts 'to life' or endow them with meaning.

12. Laplanche and Pontalis, op. cit., p. 349.

13. Lacan argues that too often the strong ego is taken as the criterion for reality, normality or health. In Kleinian psychoanalysis, for example, the ego of the analyst serves as a model for the development of the ego in the patient. For Lacan, the ego is not the subject; it is the outcome of a series of narcissistic identifications.

14. Juliet Mitchell (ed.), *The Selected Melanie Klein* (Harmondsworth: Penguin Books, 1986).

15. Madan Sarup, *Jacques Lacan* (London: Harvester Wheatsheaf, 1992), p. 72.

16. Norman Holland, *The Dynamics of Literary Response* (Oxford: Oxford University Press, 1968).

17. Elizabeth Wright, 'The Reader in Analysis', in James Donald (ed.), *Psychoanalysis and Cultural Theory*, op. cit., p. 166.

18. Catherine Clément, *Miroirs du sujet* (Paris: UGE, 10/18, 1975).

19. Cathy Urwin, 'Power Relations and the Emergence of Language', in Julian Henriques et al., *Changing the Subject: Psychology, Social Regulation and Subjectivity* (London: Methuen, 1984), p. 285.

20. Jacques Lacan, 'The Mirror Stage as Formative of the Function of the I', *Ecrits: A Selection* (London: Tavistock, 1977). The mirror phase is fully explained in Madan Sarup, *Jacques Lacan*, op. cit.

21. Jacques Lacan, *Ecrits: A Selection*, p. 128.

22. *Ecrits*, op. cit., p. 165.

23. *Ecrits*, op. cit., p. 86. The Marxist theory of ideology incorporated some psychoanalytic concepts from Lacan. From these quotations, one can see how Althusser came to argue that the subject is interpolated, how social practices address and so interpolate us as subjects for their discourse. See Slavoj Zizek, *The Sublime Object of Ideology* (London: Verso, 1989), p. 43.

24. *Ecrits*, op. cit., p. 89. Some readers may find the following criticisms of Lacan useful. He argues that the unconscious, produced through entering the symbolic order as a speaking subject, is 'structured like a language'. But quite how far the workings of the unconscious can be understood through language has been questioned. Secondly, as in all structuralist accounts, there is a tendency towards a universalist mode of explanation. The universal, contradictory subject is not situated historically, is bound by language and is incapable of change because of it. Lacanian theory

has also been criticised for its idealism and phallocentrism. Catherine Clément has argued that Lacan turned psychoanalysis away from psychology, in which it was getting mired, and introduced the need for cultural knowledge. In her view, the psychoanalyst is no longer a therapist: he is a cultural agent; his mission is to transform culture.

25. Claude Lévi-Strauss, *Tristes Tropiques* (London: Cape, 1973), quoted by Robert Young, 'Psychoanalysis and Political Literary Theories', in James Donald (ed.), *Psychoanalysis and Cultural Theory*, op. cit., p. 141.

26. Shoshana Felman, *Jacques Lacan and the Adventure of Insight: Psychoanalysis in Contemporary Culture* (Cambridge, MA: Harvard University Press, 1987), p. 99.

27. 'Men plug the dikes of their most needed beliefs with whatever mud they can find.' See Clifford Geertz, *Local Knowledge: Further Essays in Interpretive Anthropology* (New York: Basic Books, 1983), p. 80.

28. Keya Ganguly, 'Migrant Identities: Personal Memory and the Construction of Selfhood', *Cultural Studies*, 6:1 (January 1992).

29. See Homi Bhabha (ed.), *Nation and Narration* (London: Routledge, 1990), p. 4.

30. Catherine Clément, *The Weary Sons of Freud* (London: Verso, 1987), p. 87. She attacks psychoanalysis for neglecting treatment and cure and serving the interests of a new intelligentsia, the 'nouveaux riches' of a narcissistic literary culture and publishing industry.

4

———— • ————

IDENTITY AND DIFFERENCE

INTRODUCTION: DECENTRING IDENTITY

I suggested in an earlier chapter that it is in the construction of a narrative, the making and telling of a story, that we produce the self. The past does not exist except in the sense that we have to interpret past events and, in so doing, create history, identity and ourselves.

The Cartesian subject ('I think, therefore I am') was considered unitary, but we now live in a post-Cartesian world. Copernicus, Darwin, Marx and Freud have all, in their different ways, decentred the human subject. By 'decentring', I mean that individual consciousness can no longer be seen as the origin of meaning, knowledge and action. Psychoanalysis has been very influential in our thinking about the self by its stress on the unconscious. Now, after Freud, we must accept the fact that the conscious is not all that there is; the unconscious is expressing itself all the time and in everything we do. The subject is no longer unitary but split.[1] Unknown to our conscious selves, we can think and feel very differently from what we believe or say.

Ferdinand de Saussure also contributed to the break-up of the Cartesian system by stressing the idea that language speaks us, rather than we speak it. There are now many thinkers who understand the need to substitute language for the person who had been supposed to be its author. It is language that speaks, not the author's identity. Structuralists would want to stress the importance of language in the ongoing construction of identity. It is through the acquisition of language that we become human and social beings: the words we speak situate us in our gender and our class. Through language, we come to 'know' who we are. In the previous chapter, we saw how Lacan, in elaborating and extending Freud's work, emphasised the crucial importance of language as the signifying practice in and through which the subject is made into a social being.[2]

Identity is contradictory and fractured. Identity in postmodern thought is not a thing; the self is necessarily incomplete, unfinished – it is 'the subject in process'. I mentioned earlier that identity is constructed in and through language. I want to add the point that it is always within representation that we recognise ourselves. Moreover, identity is always related to what one is not – the Other. We should remember that identity is only conceivable in and through difference.

Because identification forges a unity with the Other, it also poses an imaginary threat. To maintain a separate identity, one has to define oneself against the Other: this is the origin, for Lacan, of that aggression towards the Other who threatens separateness, and thereby identity. That one is not what the Other is, is critical in defining who one is. Thus the truism that an individual is most likely to define her/himself against who or what s/he is most like.[3] Though it is hard, we should perhaps try and think of identity and difference together, dialectically.

Though people can share cultural features (art, language, religion) and have many similarities with each other, nevertheless there are also differences to consider. In certain situations or contexts, politicians and others stress identity, in the sense of sameness. This may lead to homogeneity, a feeling of togetherness, unity or solidarity. Social welfare is supposed to treat everybody the same; but, in practice, this often means that the specific needs of particular groups are denied. At other times, a group may stress (or be forced to stress) difference. A sense of difference can strengthen the solidarity of a minority group, especially if it is facing threats from the dominant group.

THE PROLIFERATION OF IDENTITIES

In the past, it was commonly held that the 'self' persisted throughout political change. It was taken for granted that, while the self remained the same, it was the world that changed. Some writers have argued that, during the events of 1968, it became clear that the traditional view of class was inadequate. New groups fractured the old collectivities. A new politics of identity arose, each group valorising its own experience which had previously been ignored or silenced.[4]

Of course, looking back, we can say that class was never really a simple, unitary concept. It was always difficult to define. In the nine-teenth century, most workers spent many hours in a factory and so, possibly, they had a unified identity. But now that people spend a lot of their time doing many things in different places, there is a decline in unified identities. There is an increase, a proliferation of identities, and this implies that there is a plurality of democratic struggles. People have now begun to channel their politics by working in groups based on ethnicity, 'race', gender, religion and nation.

If identity is the unique conjuncture of certain elements, what are the elements of which identity is composed? In my view, the identity of the human subject is, in some ways, an effect of (what I shall call) dynamics such as class, ethnicity, 'race', religion and nation, but the subject is not entirely determined by them. Our identities are not completely determined by socialising institutions, the ideological state apparatuses. Through 'free will' – the processes of choice in interpretation, selection – we can, to some extent, limit or adapt the external determinations. And so we have always to ask: what is the role of chance, randomness and contingency in decision-making?

I want to argue, dialectically, that identity is, in some ways, an effect of socialising institutions – mother, father, the family, school-ing, the factory/office, friends, media – but, at the same time, we can choose to stress some elements in certain circumstances and historical conditions. All identities, whether based on class, ethnicity, religion or nation, are social constructions.

Poststructuralism argues that the human subject has been decentred and fragmented. Indeed, we may feel that the concept of identity has been destabilised. I think that if we look at identity in isolation, we lose something of value. We need, therefore, to place questions of identity in the context of history, language and power. Many con-temporary thinkers have drawn attention to the fact that though identity may be constructed in many different ways, it is always constructed in the symbolic, that is to say, in language. As politics is about the production of identities – politics produces the subject of its actions – we should study more seriously processes of identifica-tion; how identity is constructed with 'components' such as class, gender, ethnicity, 'race', nation and religion.

The traditional Marxist perspective has always stressed that we are class agents; everything is subsumed under class. The orthodox model is rather simplistic because dynamics such as 'race' and gender are marginalised. The current (poststructuralist) model of self stresses that the human subject is decentred, contradictory and fragmented. The emphasis is on the subject in process. We are now beginning to understand some of the ways in which identity is criss-crossed by many social dynamics.

It has been suggested by Ernesto Laclau that we are now living in a more subjective society. In a peasant society, for example, the space for the development of subjectivity was limited; in 'disorganised capitalism' (another term for postmodernity), however, subjectivity has come to the fore. We know that capitalism can only exist by a continual subversion of previously existing social relations. Disorganised capitalism leads to dislocation. Laclau argues that there is now more fragmentation in society but, at the same time, there may be more possibilities for human emancipation.[5]

Some historians believe that the period from the 1880s onwards was the period of the new mass worker. Everything was on a mass scale: there were mass organisations, mass media, mass identities. But, since then, there have been vast changes as heavy industry has declined. 'Post-Fordism' is one term given to the new conditions. It is said that we now live in a diversity of social worlds. We live in a variety of social realities and occupy a series of positionalities. According to philosophers like Jean-François Lyotard, there is such a vast pluralisation of experience that there is no unitary idea that holds society together any longer. An enormous relativisation has occurred. This brings us to the subject of modernity and postmodernity.

UNDERSTANDING MODERNITY

I want now to put the above introductory discussion about identity and difference in a social and political context. I will do this by focusing on modernity and its links with 'reason' and the state. The sections that follow will deal with the relationship between modernity and socialism and the emergence of an influential post-Marxist theory. There is then an outline of the main features of postmodernism and a discussion of some of the controversial debates taking place in the area.

To understand postmodernity fully, we must know something about modernity. Zygmunt Bauman's book *Modernity and Ambivalence* is most useful in this respect.[6] His Foucauldian argument emphasises that modern mastery is the power to divide, classify and allocate in thought and in practice.

He begins by making a distinction between modernity and modernism. Modernity is a historical period that began in Western Europe with a series of profound social-structural and intellectual transformations in the seventeenth century and achieved its maturity as a cultural project with the growth of the Enlightenment and, later, with the development of industrial society. Modernity is associated with order, certainty, harmony, humanity, pure art, absolute truth. It is often said that existence is modern insofar as it is sustained by design, manipulation, management and engineering. Modernism is very different; it is an intellectual and artistic trend. Modernism is a comprehensive term for an international tendency in the arts of the West in the last years of the nineteenth century and subsequently affecting the character of most twentieth-century art. As a stylistic term, modernism contains and conceals a wide variety of different movements. In modernism, modernity turned its gaze upon itself.

Bauman argues that in the eighteenth century there arose an affinity between the legislating ambitions of philosophy and the designing intentions of the rising modern state. Modern rulers and philosophers were first and foremost legislators; they found chaos, and set out to tame it and replace it with order. For example, Kant, in the *Critique of Pure Reason*, insisted that the philosopher is not merely an artist but a law-giver legislating for human reason.[7] The rulers and the philosophers tried to secure supremacy for a designed, artificial order. Keeping order means making friends and fighting enemies. This demands unity of the realm and security of its borders. The boundary has to be sharp and clearly marked. The vital distinction between inside and outside has to be kept. Inevitably, this means the suppression of ambivalence.

Ambivalence is the possibility of assigning an object or event to more than one category. Most of us experience ambivalence as a discomfort and a threat. We should not blame language for lack of precision or ourselves for linguistic misuse. Ambivalence is a normal aspect of linguistic practice. The typical modern practice is the attempt to abolish ambivalence. Bauman points out that, as long as the urge to put paid to ambivalence guides collective and individual action, intolerance will follow. Intolerance is the natural inclination of modern practice.

At the threshold of the modern era, rulers such as Frederick the Great set the tone for the social engineering ambitions of the state. Unprecedented technological resources and managerial capacities were offered by the modern state. The state split the population into the useful and the useless. Gardening metaphors were often used: useful plants were to be encouraged and tenderly propagated, and the weeds were to be removed or rooted out.[8]

According to this viewpoint, both Hitler's Germany and Stalin's Russia were offspring of the modern spirit, of that urge to assist and speed up the progress of mankind towards perfection, of that optimistic view that scientific and industrial progress, in principle, removed all restrictions on the possible application of planning, education and social reform in everyday life.

As one example of scientific planning, Bauman considers eugenics, which was pioneered simultaneously in several Western countries. Nazi eugenics (the classification and selection of people on the basis of supposed genetic 'value') was not confined only to sterilisation and euthanasia; it laid down criteria of assessment, categories of classification and forms of efficiency that were applicable to the population as a whole. Bauman has argued that modern genocide is not an uncontrolled outburst of passions, and hardly ever a purposeless, totally irrational act. It is, on the contrary, an exercise in rational social engineering, in bringing about, by artificial means, that ambivalence-free homogeneity that messy and opaque social reality failed to produce.[9]

The distinctive features of modernity can now be summarised: the ability to coordinate human actions on a massive scale; a technology that allows one to act effectively at a large distance from the object of action; a minute division of labour which allows for spectacular progress in expertise on the one hand and the floating of responsibility on the other; the accumulation of knowledge incomprehensible to the lay person and the authority of science which grows with it; and the science-sponsored mental climate of instrumental rationality that allows social-engineering designs to be argued and justified.[10]

Bauman's critique (based on Weber and Foucault) of the Enlightenment project raises several questions. Are the above-listed features the distinctive features of modernity? Are we still in this historical period, or are we moving towards postmodernity? Are there new forms of subjectivity, and, if so, what are the effects on personal and social identity?

THE NEW FORMS OF SUBJECTIVITY

During the last few years, we have all come across a new expression: identity politics. What does it mean, and in what way is it different from traditional party politics? The term is used to refer to a commitment to one of the new social movements which emphasises one element in the construction of our identity: gender, sexual orientation, 'race', ethnicity or nation. We have to decide whether identity politics represents a narrowing of political thinking – or an opening-out and enlargement of one of the spaces that capitalism, so far, has not been able to bloc. Certainly, a concept such as identity politics could only develop in a postmodern society where people have become used to a high standard of living and introversion.

I want now to consider briefly three interrelated questions about the subject and subject-positions; the emergence of the new 'communities of interest' and identification; and political agency in relation to new forms of subjectivity. I want to suggest that whenever we are reading or listening we should always ask: what theory of the subject is being used? And what are the implications of this for understanding human agency?

I agree with Michèle Barrett that the term 'subjectivity' is popular because it includes both conscious aspects of private experience – reflection upon experiences, memories, etc. – and also the unconscious and its effects.[11] This broad term allows us to speak of private experience, emotionality and affect. There is no doubt in my mind that psychoanalytic concepts have now become rooted in the culture. People are now making use of psychoanalytic knowledge in their everyday lives.[12]

Why, then, has Marxism tended to exclude discussion of subjectivity?[13] Perhaps Marxism has ignored Freudian psychoanalysis because it stresses the limitations of reason, rationality and consciousness? Psychoanalysis questions the traditional concept of a subject as a conscious, centred, fully capable agent – the Cartesian model. In contrast, psychoanalysis emphasises the powerful role of the unconscious. Now, there was a theorist who stressed that consciousness is constructed and that we are not the free centres of consciousness that humanism supposes; a Marxist who tried to incorporate Lacanian psychoanalysis: Louis Althusser.

ALTHUSSER: THE CONSTRUCTION OF CONSCIOUSNESS THROUGH IDEOLOGY

Louis Althusser is well known for his attack on humanist Marxism, the Marxism that draws on Hegel's phenomenology and was exemplified in the existential Marxism of Jean-Paul Sartre. Althusser maintained that the notion of 'man' that Sartre used was derived from a particular ideological definition of the human subject which repressed Marx's insight that the human subject is not the centre of history, together with Freud's view that the subject is not centred in consciousness. For Althusser, both history and the subject are equally decentred: his attack on Sartre's claims for a unitary history was (therefore) accompanied by a critique of the notion of the unitary human subject that constitutes it.

Althusser's 1970 essay on 'Ideology and Ideological State Apparatuses' brought about a radical breakthrough in the theory of ideology.[14] This essay reorientated the study of ideology by emphasising that ideologies have, first of all, a material existence. He gives an approximate list of institutions in capitalist societies whose operations are largely ideological: the apparatuses of religion, education, the family, the law, the system of party politics, the trade unions, communications and culture.

Althusser holds that consciousness is constructed through ideologies. Ideologies, the beliefs, meanings and practices in which we think and act, exist in apparatuses forming part of the state. Ideologies, formed as means of domination and resistance, are never simply free to set their own terms but are always marked by what they are opposing; no ideology takes shape outside a struggle with some opposing ideology.

This essay, which became very influential in the 1970s, is in two parts. Some sociologists took up the social reproduction part and used it for theorising about the family. Other theorists used the second part to theorise about subjectivity. Althusser's central thesis is that 'ideology interpolates individuals as subjects'. Every ideology, through the mechanism of recognition, calls individuals into place and confers on them 'their' identity. Ideology is addressed to individuals so that – answering, turning round, converted – they become 'freely' subjected to it. Althusser writes:

> interpolation . . . can be imagined along the lines of the most common place everyday police (or other hailing: 'Hey, you there!' . . .). The hailed individual will turn round. By this mere one-hundred-and-eighty-degree physical conversion, he becomes a subject. Why? Because he has recognised that the hail was 'really' addressed to him, and that 'it was really him who was hailed' (and not someone else).[15]

I would agree with Althusser that our consciousness is not free-floating but constructed. In his view, beliefs and meanings come to us through ideologies operating in ideological state apparatuses (ISAs). Our consciousness is constructed under the form of an imaginary subjection. In the apparatuses of ideology, in their day-to-day practices, we become particular individuals acting in the beliefs given to us to think. Althusser cites Pascal: 'Kneel down, move your lips in prayer, and you will believe'. Althusser, in short, provides a theory of how the 'obviousness' that you and I are subjects (and that does not cause any problems) is an ideological effect. His argument is that we exist as subjects only in ideology, constituted there as subjects in a double sense: held to be responsible, centres of initiative, through being subjected and tied to an imaginary identity.

Althusser correctly identified a major lacuna in Marxist thinking about ideology: the inadequate theorisation of the subject. Althusser's work is important in that he suggested that modern psychoanalytical ideas have a role to play in thinking about ideology and subjectivity. He believed that ideology is the process by which individuals are constituted as subjects, and he wanted to integrate Marx and Freud in his theory. It could be said that psychoanalysis is based on some version of the subject in that the analysand is presupposed as having capacities of gathering and reflecting upon meaning. In the second part of his famous essay, 'Ideology and Ideological State Apparatuses', Althusser attempted to understand subjectivity through the use of Jacques Lacan's rereading of Freud.[16] He used some of Lacan's concepts, such as the mirror phase, but the reconciliation of Marxism and psychoanalysis proved very difficult. He did not manage to theorise a convincing account of the constitution of subjectivity. Though Althusser failed, the attempt to synthesise the two theories was very important. It led to influential work in film.[17]

LACLAU AND MOUFFE: THE CONSTRUCTION OF NEW IDENTITIES

The present political crisis of socialism is expressed in the wide-ranging poststructuralist critiques of Marxism.[18] Consider, for example, the new theory of subjectivity being developed by Ernesto Laclau and colleagues. Drawing on the work of Derrida, Foucault and Lacan, he attacks all forms of essentialism. Rejecting the model of society as a totality, he believes that society should be thought of in terms of aggregates rather than totality. Laclau argues that classical Marxism stresses social management; there is an agent which incarnates the community as a whole. For Marx, the pure human essence is incarnated in the proletariat – it represents the totality. He believed that history would produce a homogeneous society. Laclau argues that a homogeneous society would be one that is not free. He does not argue against power; he asserts that power is a condition of freedom. The total elimination of power would also mean the elimination of freedom.

One could say that Ernesto Laclau and Chantal Mouffe are engaged in a rereading of the Marxist tradition through the lens of poststructuralism. The concepts and arguments that they use against Marxism are often drawn from the work of Foucault and others. While classical Marxists always stress class ideology, Laclau draws attention to non-class elements of ideology. It is suggested, for example, that fascist ideology addressed, and therefore constituted, its subjects as 'the people' rather than as the working class.[19] Their argument, in other words, is a challenge to 'class primacy'. Even Gramsci is seen as an essentialist because he places the working class in a privileged position. In short, Laclau and Mouffe argue against the privileging of class in Marxist analysis and reject the 'class essentialist logic' of Marxism.

Post-Marxists like Laclau and Mouffe are critical of Marxists because the latter assume that class is the primary form of collective agency, and that other oppressed groups such as women and blacks must, in the last instance, be subsumed to class. Post-Marxists challenge Marxists to explain the existence of national, racial, ethnic and gender oppression. Laclau and others argue that the straightforward oppositional structure of capital and class does not work any more. If we think in terms of Hegel's master–slave dialectic, then rather than the working class being the obvious universal subject-victim, many others are also oppressed: women, particularly black women, gays, ethnic minorities. Now, any single individual may belong to several of these, but the forms of oppression, as of resistance or change, may not only overlap but may also differ or even conflict. As soon as there is no longer a single master and no single slave, then the classic Hegelian reversal model, on which Marxism depends and on which it bases its theory of revolution, is no longer adequate.

Laclau and Mouffe argue that class essentialism must give way to the pluralist demands of the new social movements, the new communities of interest; these include groups concerned with anti-racism, environmentalism, feminism, gay rights, lesbianism, peace and so forth. They are called the 'new' social movements in that they are not class movements.

Drawing on Foucault's work, Laclau and Mouffe suggest that the bureaucratisation of postwar, Western capitalist society has led to the imposition of multiple forms of regulation which previously had been part of the private domain. They note that another development in the postwar period is the expansion of mass communications. They write of the resistance to the commodification and the increasing homogenisation of social life. Laclau and Mouffe believe that there is a proliferation of particularisms, a tendency towards the valorisation of 'differences' and the creation of new identities which tend to privilege cultural criteria (such as clothes, music, language, etc.).[20]

Laclau states that he is using the Marxist concept of ideology less and less, and that he finds the psychoanalytic model very useful, particularly the Lacanian concept of lack. Identity is now less fixed. Compared with the eighteenth century, there are now a plurality of centres of power. This may seem more dangerous, but, on the other hand, there are also more possibilities.[21]

Let me reiterate that post-Marxist thinkers like Ernesto Laclau and Chantal Mouffe are against the universalist values of the Enlightenment. They and many other intellectuals are beginning to doubt the master narratives. They no longer have the confidence in the totalising universal truth-claims and beliefs of Marxism.

Laclau and Mouffe believe that modern societies have no centre, no single articulating or organising principle, and do not develop according to the unfolding of a single 'cause' or 'law'. Contemporary societies, they argue, are characterised by 'difference'; they are cut through by different social divisions and antagonisms which produce a variety of different identities or 'subject-positions'. Under certain circumstances, the different elements can be articulated together. But this articulation is always partial, and the structure of identity remains open.

Laclau and Mouffe have emphasised the partial and incomplete character of identities. In their view, social identities are structured 'like a language' in that they can be articulated into a range of contradictory positions from one discursive context to the next, since each element in ideology and consciousness has no necessary belonging in any one political code or system of representation. Individuals occupy diverse, heterogeneous and contradictory positions in their actual lives. This reminds me of a riddle: 'What do a trade unionist, a Tory, a Christian, a wife-beater and a consumer have in common? They can all be the same person.'[22]

Our identities are multiple and mobile. Though the process of change dissolves the fixed, stable, homogeneous identities of the past, it also opens the possibility of new articulations – the construction of new identities, the production of new subjects.

Laclau and Mouffe argue that people no longer identify their social interests exclusively in class terms. There are new, emerging identities associated with the new social movements: feminism, black struggles, national liberation, ecological and green movements. It is said that identity shifts according to how the subject is addressed or represented. In short, there has been a shift from a politics of class identity to a politics of difference. Laclau and Mouffe take a positive view about this. They emphasise social and cultural pluralism and believe that postmodernism opens up many political possibilities.

There is no doubt that, within and between the various new social movements, more and more people are asserting their difference, their particularism. This proliferation of differences is highly ambivalent, as it raises the issue of relativism. Is the difference of cultures something that cannot be accommodated within a universalist framework? Is there an incommensurability between the cultures of different groups? Some thinkers are now beginning to theorise about these issues in terms of universalism and particularism. But, before I give an outline of the debate, I need to provide a short introduction to binary oppositions.

BINARY OPPOSITIONS

Binary oppositions reduce the potential of difference into polar opposites: Self/Other; rational/emotional; metropolis/periphery. In binarism, one term represents the dominant centre, the other term represents the subordinate margin. (I should add that, in Derrida's thinking, the supplement marks what the centre lacks, but also what it needs in order to define fully and to confirm its identity.)[23] The important thing about binarism is that it operates in the same way as splitting and projection: the centre expels its anxieties and contradictions onto the subordinate term. The Other often mirrors and represents what is deeply familiar to the centre, but projected out of itself.

I find thought-provoking the idea that, if one considers the opposition Self and Other, the Other is always to some extent within. That is to say, what is considered marginal and peripheral is actually central. This view is, of course, beautifully illustrated in Hegel's 'Master and Slave' story. Much of what we think is socially marginal is symbolically central.

Consider, for a moment, the rational/emotional opposition. Raymond Williams described the emerging identities of new social groups being confronted by a dominant culture whose discourses do not allow them to articulate fully their experience. He wrote of this struggle for a voice as being at the very edge of semantic availability – those necessary words that will represent us both to ourselves and others are not quite in our grasp. Now, most people think of emotion as being subordinate to rationality. Williams confronts this polarity by insisting that emotions are cognitive: 'we are talking about . . . not feeling against thought, but thought as felt and feeling as thought'. This is what Williams meant by the 'structure of feeling'.[24]

THE RIGHT TO DIFFERENCE

I remarked just now that more and more people are asserting their difference. There has been an astonishing explosion of ethnic and national identities all over the world. Many problems have arisen from the struggle of these contending groups. Let us consider one of these: the relationship between universalism and particularism.

The struggles of ethnic, national and other groups represent a proliferation of particularisms, while universality is increasingly put aside as something old-fashioned to do with the Enlightenment project, invalidated by Foucault and other poststructuralists. In a difficult, sometimes opaque but worthwhile paper, Ernesto Laclau tries to think through some of the problems of group identity.[25] He begins by explaining how European imperialist expansion had to be presented in terms of a universal civilising function. Europe, we were told, represented universal human interests. The resistances of other countries were presented not as struggles between particular cultures and identities, but as part of a struggle between universality and particularisms. It was said that the colonised peoples had no history, which was another way of saying that they were incapable of representing the universal.[26]

Something similar, Laclau suggests, occurred within Marxism.

The universal class, the proletariat, was conceived as the cancellation of all differences. Between the universal character of the tasks of the working class and the particularity of its concrete demands, an increasing gap opened which was filled by the Party as representative of the historical interests of the proletariat.

I think Laclau's main argument is that an appeal to pure particularism is no solution to present-day problems. The assertion of pure particularism (independent of any content and of the appeal to a universality transcending it) is a self-defeating enterprise. If particularism is the only accepted principle, there is an unsolvable paradox:

> I can defend the right of sexual, racial and national minorities in the name of particularism; but if particularism is the only valid principle, I have to accept also the rights to self-determination of all kinds of reactionary groups involved in anti-social practices . . . As the demands of various groups will necessarily clash with each other, we have to appeal . . . to some more general principles.

Laclau notes that the relations between groups are constituted as relations of power; each group insists on its difference on the basis of the exclusion and subordination of other groups. An example is apartheid, 'separate development', in South Africa, where only the differential aspect was stressed while the relations of power on which apartheid was based were systematically ignored. In his view, one cannot assert a differential identity without distinguishing it from a context; and in the process of making the distinction, one is asserting the context at the same time.

It is argued by Laclau that an oppositionist force whose identity is constructed within a certain system of power is ambiguous vis-à-vis that system, because it is the latter (the system) that prevents the constitution of the identity and it is, at the same time, its condition of existence.[27] Moreover, any victory against the system destabilises also the identity of the victorious force.

Laclau then considers the constitution of the identity of an ethnic minority. He says that if this differential identity is fully achieved, it can only be so within a context such as nation-state, and the price to be paid for total victory within that context is total integration to it. If total integration does not take place, it is because that identity is not fully achieved; there are unsatisfied demands such as access to higher education, etc. Now, these demands cannot be made in terms of difference, but of some universal principles that the ethnic minority shares with the rest of society: the right of everybody, for example, to have access to good schools, etc.

Laclau insists that the construction of differential identities on the basis of total closure to what is outside them (the context) is not a viable political alternative. He reminds us that the logic of apartheid is not only a discourse of the oppressor. At its very limit, understood as mere difference, the discourse of the oppressor and the discourse of the oppressed cannot be distinguished. Why is this? If the oppressed is defined by its difference from the oppressor, such a difference is an essential component of the identity of the oppressed. But in that case, the latter cannot assert its identity without asserting that of the oppressor as well.

Ambiguity, in other words, is inherent in all forms of radical opposition. The opposition, in order to be radical, has to put in a common ground both what it asserts and what it excludes, so that the exclusion becomes a particular form of assertion. In his view, there is no clear-cut solution to the paradox of negating a system of power while remaining implicitly dependent on it. It is well known how opposition to certain forms of power requires identification with the very places from which the power emanates.

Laclau reminds us that if we invert the relation of oppression, the other (the former oppressor) is maintained as what is now oppressed, but the inversion of the contents leaves the forms of oppression unchanged. And, as the identity of the newly-emancipated groups has been constituted through the rejection of the old dominated ones, the latter continue shaping the identity of the emergent groups. The operation of inversion takes place within the old formal system of power.[28]

What, then, are the courses of action that could be followed? One possible way is to affirm the right of cultural ethnic groups to assert their differences and their separate developments. Laclau calls this the route to self-apartheid, a total segregationism, the opposition of one particularism to another. The problem is that the separation, the right to difference, has to be asserted within a global community. But how can that coexistence be possible, Laclau asks, without some shared values, without a sense of belonging to a community larger than each of the particular groups?[29]

TOWARDS A POLITICS OF DIFFERENCE

Let us continue the debate further by focusing on the discourse of ethnicity: the recent history of the category 'black'. In the past, one ethnicity, Englishness, was dominant, hegemonic; it marginalised all other ethnicities. And then, in the late 1960s and 1970s, the term 'black' began to be used as an organising category of a politics of resistance. It was used among groups and communities which had, in fact, very different histories, traditions and ethnic identities. The term 'black' was used to unify people who came from Africa, India and the Caribbean. It drew attention to the fact that black experience was marginalised, but the category also had a negative effect – black people were stereotyped and their experience simplified.

In contrast, there is now an increasing recognition of the extraordinary diversity of subjective positions, social experiences and cultural identities which compose the category 'black'. This new awareness, argues Stuart Hall, marks the end of the essential black subject. In other words, some fictions – that all black people are good, or indeed that all black people are the same – are not now necessary. The aim now is to construct a politics which works with and through difference, a politics which does not suppress the real heterogeneity of interests and identities. Moreover, there is a growing realisation too that the black subject cannot be represented without reference to the dimensions of class, gender, sexuality and ethnicity.

Stuart Hall believes that we are beginning to see a new conception of ethnicity: a new cultural politics which engages rather than suppresses difference and which depends, in part, on the cultural construction of new ethnic identities.[30] This more diverse conception of ethnicity, what he calls a 'positive conception of the ethnicity of the margins', would be neither homogeneous nor normative, but always negotiated and in a state of becoming.

To conclude the chapter, I would just like to signal some of the issues that are being currently debated. Is a society based on difference possible? And, what is the relationship between freedom, justice and difference? It is often said that a positive feature of postmodernist thinkers is that they want to stress diversity. They have drawn attention to difference. But, as we all know, there are differences which exist and which should not exist; and there are also differences which do not exist which should exist. What are the procedures to get agreement on these questions? How are disagreements going to be resolved?

In my view, communities of interests are not new forms of identification: there have been people in the past who have seen themselves as 'black', feminist, homosexual; but, with the decline of 'class interest', a new emphasis is being placed on these social movements. Moreover, it is clear that even within these communities of interest there are many divisive groupings. For example, within feminism there are liberal, radical, socialist, black and other identifications. I think that, behind the insistence to respect difference nowadays, there may be lurking the traditional individualism in a new guise. On the other hand, one of the positive features of the new social movements is that they attach considerable importance to issues to do with subjectivity and identity politics.

People are asking whether the so-called 'lapse' of the subject leaves us only with subject-positions. I believe that with the very rapid changes in Western society (in terms of technology, work, communications, space–time compression, etc.) there is an increasing complexity and fragmentation; but it is not a 'lapse' of the subject. This fragmentation is felt by people as uncertainty and self-doubt, but is experienced by some people as a positive experience.

I would say that if we strongly identify with the new social movements and if we have a sense of belonging through them, then we are what I shall term 'processual' subjects. If, however, we act differently at different times, as daughter, mother, consumer, voter, lover, without one predominant identification, then we take up different and, sometimes, contradictory subject positions.

With the fragmentation of the human subject, increasing pressure from different subject-positions, and the growth of heterogeneous social movements with their new, varied interests, how does one rethink political agency in relation to new forms of subjectivity? And how does all this relate to social justice? Postmodernists assert that modernists try to seek or enforce consensus, while they show tolerance of dissent. Survival in the world of contingency and diversity is possible only if each difference recognises another difference as the necessary condition of the preservation of its own. But is tolerance enough? If tolerance is ego-centred and contemplative, perhaps there should be a stress on solidarity? Solidarity implies readiness to fight and joining the battle for the sake of the other's difference, not one's own.[31]

Many commentators have suggested that postmodernists associate modernity with uniformity and universalism. They argue that modernism is connected with an urge to overcome ambivalence and promote monosemic clarity. Postmodernity is first and foremost an acceptance of ineradicable plurality of the world. The question of difference is linked with political pluralism. However desirable, pluralism must have limits. What are these limits to be, and how are these limits to be decided?

An American postmodernist philosopher, Richard Rorty, has argued that if we take care of political freedom, truth and goodness will take care of themselves. All too often in the past, taking care of truth and goodness resulted in the loss of political freedom. Unlike science and political ideology, freedom promises no certainty and no guarantee of anything. In practice, it means constant exposure to ambivalence; that is, to a situation with no decidable solution.

Even if we agree with Rorty that providing we take care of freedom then truth and goodness will take care of themselves, the idea that social justice will equally take care of itself is less easy to agree with. Bauman thinks that this is because leaving the case of justice alone means refusing assistance to those who need it.[32]

Though I feel ambivalent about many aspects of these issues, there is one point that I would like to stress: in discussion of diversity, difference and heterogeneity, the question that must be addressed is that of inequality. The crucial problem is this: remaking society may only make it worse than it was, but, on the other hand, to abandon social engineering as a valid means of political practice means to discard all visions of a different society.

I find myself in full agreement with Terry Eagleton, who has argued that

> the final purpose of our universality, of our equal rights to participate in the public definition of meanings and values, is that the unique particularities of individuals may be respected and fulfilled. Particularity returns again at a 'higher' level; difference must pass through identity if it is to come into its own . . . The universal, then, is not some realm of abstract duty set sternly against the particular; it is just every individual's equal right to have his or her difference respected, and to participate in the common process whereby that can be achieved. Identity is to this extent in the service of non-identity; but without such identity no real non-identity can be attained.[33]

As a small child in India, I remember being admitted to hospital. I do not know what my illness was, but I remember the ward as being long, dark and 'high up'. Bubi came to take me home, and it was a delightful occasion. This is my first memory of Bubi, the first sign of my attachment to her.

Who was Bubi? When my oldest brother Atam studied and worked in England, he had an affair with the wife of a famous English film director. My brother, who called himself Ronnie at the time, returned to India to work with Imperial Airways in Karachi. Bubi followed him there. I don't know if he was surprised, but it must have caused consternation at the time: an English woman leaving her husband, coming to India on her own, and openly living with an Indian.

Ronnie rented a large house in Karachi, and I lived there for a while. I remember the large rooms, the stray donkey that was domesticated and fitted up with a saddle for me to ride. I have a treasured photograph of myself on the donkey between two women. My sister Sita, in a sari, is on one side, and Bubi on the other. I have been told that it was Bubi who taught me table manners and English customs. She introduced me to 'Englishness'.

After a while, I returned to Simla to live with my father. He was in the Indian Civil Service, and when he had six months' leave I came with him to England. We went to Ronnie's house in Isleworth, and Bubi was there. It was September 1939. I was astonished to see searchlights sweeping the night sky, the barrage balloons; I didn't understand what they were or what they were for. I didn't know what was happening in the world, and nobody explained anything to me. I certainly didn't have a concept of war.

A few months later, we all moved to Bristol where Ronnie had got a new job. He rented a typical suburban house, and my father returned to India. My next memory of Bubi is that one day she gave me some money to have lunch at a local café and then go to the pictures. I returned home three hours later and found the house completely empty. She had left and taken everything. There was nothing in the house – not a cup, not a teaspoon.

Years later, I overheard vague stories about her: that she had joined one of the women's forces and worked as a driver during the Second World War. And so Bubi passed out of my life. Years later, perhaps, I could have asked Ronnie about her, but by that time he had become Rashid. He had adopted another identity. He seemed to move in an adult world which I, a schoolboy, did not understand. I feel very positive about Bubi because she looked after me. It seems strange to me that, though she was my second 'mother', I know so little about her. I don't know her beginnings or her end. Her abrupt and complete disappearance was never discussed or explained. And I never asked.

NOTES

1. For a discussion of the above points, see Madan Sarup, *An Introductory Guide to Post-structuralism and Postmodernism* (London: Harvester Wheatsheaf, 1993).
2. Jacques Lacan, *Ecrits: A Selection* (London: Tavistock, 1977). See, for example, the essays 'The Function and Field of Speech and Language in Psychoanalysis' and 'The Agency of the Letter in the Unconscious or Reason since Freud'.
3. Teresa Brennan (ed.), *Between Feminism and Psychoanalysis* (London: Routledge, 1989), p. 11.
4. Sherry Turkle, *Psychoanalytic Politics: Freud's French Revolution* (London: Burnett Books, 1979).
5. Ernesto Laclau, *New Reflections on the Revolution of our Time* (London: Verso, 1990).
6. Zygmunt Bauman, *Modernity and Ambivalence* (Cambridge: Polity Press, 1991). I am indebted to Bauman's book for much of what follows in this section.
7. Immanuel Kant, *Critique of Pure Reason* (London: Dent, 1969).
8. Metaphors are not merely poetical or rhetorical embellishments but are a part of everyday speech that affects the way we perceive, think and act. Reality itself is defined by metaphor. See George Lakoff and Mark Johnson, *Metaphors We Live By* (Chicago: University of Chicago Press, 1980).
9. Zygmunt Bauman, *Modernity and the Holocaust* (Cambridge: Polity Press, 1989).
10. Bauman has been influenced by many European thinkers concerned with modernity. His view about instrumental rationality stems from the work of Max Weber, and his concern about science is drawn from the theorists Adorno and Horkheimer, critical theorists of the Frankfurt school. A pervasive influence is the work of Michel Foucault, particularly the stress on ordering and classifying. (Several writers have remarked on the similarities between the projects of Weber and Foucault.) Other influences on Bauman include Ivan Illich (the critique of experts and our increasing dependence on them), and Braverman (on how Taylorism and Fordisation lead to de-skilling). Bauman has synthesised these concerns into a postmodernist argument which insists that the Enlightenment project has failed.
11. Michèle Barrett, *The Politics of Truth: From Marx to Foucault* (Cambridge: Polity Press, 1991), p. 91.
12. James Donald (ed.), *Psychoanalysis and Cultural Theory: Thresholds* (London: Macmillan, 1991).
13. There are, of course, notable exceptions: Wilhelm Reich, Erich Fromm, Herbert Marcuse. See Russell Jacoby, *Social Amnesia* (Hassocks: Harvester, 1975).
14. Louis Althusser, 'Ideology and Ideological State Apparatuses', in idem, *Lenin and Philosophy and Other Essays* (London: New Left Books, 1971), p. 137.
15. Ibid., p. 163.
16. Louis Althusser, 'Freud and Lacan', in idem, *Lenin and Philosophy*, op. cit., p. 181.
17. Sprinkler and Kaplan, *The Althusserian Legacy* (London: Verso, 1993).
18. Poststructuralist critiques of Marxism include: Barry Smart, *Foucault, Marxism and Critique* (London: Routledge, 1983); Robert Young, *White Mythologies: Writing History and the West* (London: Routledge, 1990).
19. Ernesto Laclau, *Politics and Ideology in Marxist Theory: Capitalism, Fascism, Populism* (London: New Left Books, 1977), p. 111.
20. Ernesto Laclau and Chantal Mouffe, *Hegemony and Socialist Strategy, Towards a Radical Democratic Politics* (London: Verso, 1985), p. 164.
21. Laclau argues that there has been a decline in class politics and makes a distinction between 'acting as a class' and 'acting as a people'. One implication of his stress on the new social movements is a greater awareness of the importance of coalitions. See Ernesto Laclau, *New Reflections*, op. cit.
22. The 'riddle' is quoted in Kobena Mercer, 'Welcome to the Jungle', in Jonathan Rutherford (ed.), *Identity: Community, Culture, Difference* (London: Lawrence and Wishart, 1990), p. 57.

23. The notion of supplement floats between its two senses of that which is added on and that which substitutes for and supplants. This addition and/or replacement is an example of the undecidability on which Derrida's deconstructive readings are often made to turn. Jacques Derrida, 'That Dangerous Supplement', in idem, *Of Grammatology* (Baltimore: John Hopkins Press, 1976), p. 141.

24. Raymond Williams, 'Structures of Feeling', in idem, *Marxism and Literature* (Oxford: Oxford University Press, 1977), p. 128.

25. Ernesto Laclau, 'Universalism, Particularism and the Question of Identity', in *October* (New York: Routledge, 1992), pp. 83–90.

26. 'In the nature of things the work of a Western writer is automatically informed by universality. It is only others who must strain to achieve it.' Chinua Achebe, *Hopes and Impediments: Selected Essays* (New York: Doubleday/Anchor, 1989), p. 76.

27. Said has noticed this too: when supposedly neutral departments of culture like literature and critical theory converge upon the subordinate culture and interpret it, 'the striking consequence has been to disguise the power situation and to conceal how much the experience of the stronger party overlaps with and, strangely, depends on the weaker'. Edward Said, *Culture and Imperialism* (London: Chatto and Windus, 1993), p. 231.

28. Again, a similar thought is in Said: 'We know that the national bourgeoisies and their specialized elites tended to replace the colonial force with a new class-based and ultimately exploitative one, which replicated the old colonial structures' (ibid., p. 269).

29. Some readers may find the following brief comments on Laclau's paper useful: I detect an idealist element; perhaps it would be better to say a non-materialist, aspect to his work. An example of this is the way he seems to think of countries as 'cultures'. Secondly, I note that parts of Laclau's arguments are rather like those of Hegel on the master–slave relationship. I find this intriguing because most postmodernist thinkers are drawn not to Hegel but to Nietzsche's philosophy. Thirdly, I am glad that Laclau realises that 'pure particularism' among, say, ethnic groups, would entail relativism, and he therefore argues for some universal principle. I think that this is a move away from a Foucauldian position which emphasises the specific rather than the universal. Finally, about South Africa, the paper contains a philosophical analysis of apartheid when the political struggle has destroyed it. Apartheid, in my dictionary, is defined as racial segregation; but in the paper it is euphemistically called 'separate development'. Why is this? The political reality, as usual, is far ahead of the philosophical analysis.

30. Stuart Hall, 'New Ethnicities', in James Donald and Ali Rattansi (eds), *'Race', Culture and Difference* (London: OU/Sage, 1992), p. 258.

31. Zygmunt Bauman, *Modernity and Ambivalence*, op. cit., p. 256.

32. Ibid., p. 270.

33. Terry Eagleton, *The Ideology of the Aesthetic* (Oxford: Basil Blackwell, 1990), pp.414–15.

5

---•---

FOUCAULT: DISCIPLINE AND THE SELF

THE POSTSTRUCTURALIST CRITIQUE OF MARXISM

I begin this section by a brief outline of the main themes in the post-structuralist critique of Marxism. Common criticisms of Marxism are that it is historicist (in other words, rather like a 'grand narrative') and totalising. It stresses universality rather than singularity, similarity rather than difference. Many 'post-Marxist' ideas can be seen in the work of Michel Foucault.

Poststructuralists, like Derrida, Foucault and Lyotard, have a distrust of simple historicism, the notion that history is an emancipatory process of self-realisation. Lyotard, for example, is best known for his scepticism towards historicist universal narratives, advocating instead the possibility of heterogeneous, conflicting and incommensurable histories. Many poststructuralists believe that Marxists invoke history rather like 'the political', as if it were concrete, exterior to theory, unaffected by it. Rejecting the Marxist theory of history as the progress of a single narrative of class struggle, the grand narrative of History, poststructuralists stress the heterogeneous and the discontinuous.

Recently, a British poststructuralist critic, Robert Young, has argued that Marxism, insofar as it inherits the system of the Hegelian dialectic, is implicated in the link between structures of knowledge and the forms of oppression of the last 200 years – a phenomenon that has become known as Eurocentrism.[1] In his view, Marxism's universalising narrative of the unfolding of a rational system of world history is simply a negative form of the history of European imperialism. Marx, though critical of British imperialism, concluded that the British colonisation of India was ultimately for the best because it brought India into the evolutionary narrative of Western history, thus creating the conditions for future class struggle there. This, Young writes, is an arrogant and arrogating narrative.

Poststructuralists are highly critical of writers (such as Sartre) who believe that there is only one 'History' with one meaning. In this view, this is only achieved through the exclusion of all other histories with other meanings; totalisation can only totalise if everything which remains other to it is excluded.

There is a counter-argument to this view. Terry Eagleton has made a scathing attack on Foucault's views on totality. He believes that it is ironic that at the present time, when the system which radicals oppose has never shown itself quite as total, these theorists want to discredit the concept of totality. Though they have valuably challenged various idealist and essentialist versions, there is a serious problem: how far should this process of dismantling totalisation be taken?[2]

Poststructuralists, such as Foucault and Lyotard, are mainly concerned with the attempt to isolate and emphasise singularity as opposed to universality. This quest for the singular is clearly related to the project of constructing a form of knowledge that respects the other without absorbing it into the same.

Some poststructuralists draw on the work of Emmanuel Levinas, who believes that totality has dominated Western philosophy in its long history of desire for Unity and the One. He observes that through the totality, the individual takes on meaning; the present is sacrificed to a future which will bring forth an ultimate, objective meaning when the totality of history is realised. He is against this view.

Levinas argues that in Western philosophy, when knowledge or theory tries to understand the Other, then the alterity of the Other vanishes as it becomes part of the same. In all cases, it involves violence towards the Other. This 'ontological imperialism' has political implications; it amounts to a philosophy of power: the relation with the Other is only possible through assimilation into the self. In his view, language's function in conceptualising thought is to suppress the Other and bring it within the aegis of the same. Levinas proposes not the ontological subject but an ethical subject defined in relation to the Other. It follows from this argument that there must be respect for the Other's heterogeneity. This is why poststructuralists are antagonistic to similarity and stress the importance of difference.

THE NORMALISATION OF INDIVIDUALS

Most of the themes I have mentioned above can be found in the work of Michel Foucault. Foucault is sceptical of numerous concepts

– the subject, ideology, class, the state; in fact, any general theory of society – and he emphasises that his work does not lay claim to universal or general categories.[3] He objects to historicism and Western humanism to the extent that they assume a continuous development, progress and global totalisation. This is why he is critical of Marxism, which assumes a rational, progressive and teleological historical development, and has a desire to discover a meaning in history. Foucault stresses the move away from vast unities towards phenomena of rupture, discontinuity, displacement and transformation.

In his work, Foucault has focused on the question: how is subjectivity constituted by the marginal? He has done considerable work on psychiatric institutions and has drawn attention to what could be called 'normalisation'. He has studied the origin and development of discipline techniques for altering individual behaviour. He states that, besides crimes and offences, judgements are now being made on drives and desires. Schools, for example, largely determine not only what people do but also what they are, will be, may be.

Foucault believes that the production of the subject by the human sciences as an object of knowledge enabled a new form of political control. He thinks that the individual is not a pre-given entity which is seized on by the exercise of power; the individual with his or her identity and characteristics is the product of a relation of powers exercised over bodies. In Foucault's work, the absence of the category of consciousness inevitably plays down the role of individual subjects and thus of human agency and resistance. Dispensing with the subject necessarily also means the end of the use of the category 'ideology'. Marxist theories of ideology also have another problem – they imply that Marxists know the truth, that they are 'scientific'. It was because of the problems with the ideology/truth opposition that Foucault started using the term 'discourse'. In short, the term short-circuits epistemological problems. Foucault also argues that, just as there can be no general theory but only particular answers to particular questions, so the intellectual can best hope to be specific rather than universal (universal in the sense of proposing transcendental values, systems, totalities, narratives or teleologies).

The most important debates about ideology include the following: Is ideology pejorative or neutral? Is ideology some sort of group consciousness or is it partial knowledge, distortion, counterposed to truth? If ideology is a form of mystification that serves class interest, the question arises: how do you use the concept to deal with gender and/or racial oppression? This may be an appropriate place to make a few brief remarks about the current debate about the usefulness of the concept ideology. Influenced by Foucault and other poststructuralists, Ernesto Laclau and Chantal Mouffe are criticising the Marxist theory of ideology. They have broken the link between ideology and class and argue that there is no connection between them. There are some theorists who are now saying that ideology is a word to which many people have attached different meanings at different times. Michèle Barrett, for example, argues that ideology is too amorphous a concept and that it has too many incompatible meanings. The word 'ideology' should be replaced by the word 'mystification'.[4] Against such a (post-Marxist?) view, some, like Terry Eagleton, argue that we have got to say that some things are false. The concept of ideology is useful and necessary because it helps identify the struggles that are central.

Michel Foucault has said that his objective has been to create a history of the different modes by which, in our culture, human beings are made subjects. Foucault's work has been examining the so-called human sciences, their history and their consequences. That work challenged the 'truth' of the human sciences, by posing questions about the historical conditions in which their discourses emerged. He has developed an 'archaeology' that questioned some of the shifts in Western thought over the last 400 years. Looking at some of the transformations that have taken place, he has asked: what has made possible different knowledges?

Foucault has written of 'the full range of hidden mechanisms through which a society conveys its knowledge and ensures its survival under the mask of knowledge: newspapers, television, technical schools and the lycée (even more than the university)'.[5] His project is to dismantle the idealist notions that all knowledge has a continuous form expressing human thought and reflecting the truth of things.

Foucault's *Madness and Civilization* (1961) is a study of the history of madness.[6] His account is interesting because he does not start from the nature of mental illness and ask how well this was reflected in classical thought. It starts from institutions which shut up the mad. What is most positive in Foucault's work is the focus on the connections between knowledges and institutions. He examines practices within the asylum and focuses on two instances – the reforming of Bicêtre by Pinel into an asylum for the insane, and the setting-up by Tuke of an English Quaker asylum, the Retreat – and describes, in both, asylum life modelled on forms of bourgeois ideology. For example, in Tuke's Retreat, the mad were treated as children.[7] They were placed under 'family tutelage' in a model of family relations that was both bourgeois and patriarchal. The mad 'child' in the Retreat was submitted to the authority of the Father and to the care of the rational adult. Foucault's study, in short, suggests that institutional practices have a primacy over forms of knowledge.

It was claimed by Foucault that in *Madness and Civilization* he was writing a history of the Other. Another French poststructuralist, Jacques Derrida, has criticised this. Derrida contends that if madness is constituted as madness, as other, by reason, then this means that reason is itself defined through it and therefore already contains and depends upon it.[8] After Derrida's criticism, Foucault rethought the distinction between the Same and the Other; he came to the conclusion that the histories of the Other and of the Same are necessarily implicated within each other. The Other is always inside.

From the idea that institutional practices influence or determine identity, Foucault shifts in *The Archaeology of Knowledge* (1969) to the idea of discourse and of what he calls 'discursive practices'. A discourse may be identified by the institutions to which it relates and by the position from which it comes and which it marks out for the speaker. A discourse takes effect indirectly or directly through its relation to, its address to, another discourse.

Foucault remarks that a discourse may be identified by a set of rules. One of his examples of rules which form modes of speaking or 'enunciations' is clinical medicine. Rules dictate who 'is accorded the right' and the 'status' to make medical statements, and from what 'institutional sites', such as the hospital and the laboratory, statements may come. But Foucault is also aware of the controls which act upon discourse from outside or inside it. Some of the controls which act on discourse from the outside include prohibitions. There are also ways to control and distribute who may speak or come within what discourse.[10]

As Michèle Barrett has pointed out, the most important general point to grasp about Foucault's concept of a discourse – the production of 'things' by 'words' – is that it enables us to understand how what is said fits into a network that has its own history and conditions of existence.[1] Discourses are composed of signs but they do more than designate things, for they are practices that systematically form the objects of which they speak.

One of the many questions discussed in discourse theory is whether discourses can have reference to an outside. Some theorists deny that they can. Barry Hindess and Paul Hirst, two well-known sociologists in Britain, deny that they can; whatever things a discourse refers to 'are constituted in it and by it'.[12] Ideas set up things. They suppose that objects of discourse exist only in discourse.

In contrast to Althusser's structural Marxism, Foucault's thought is heavily indebted to Nietzsche. The uniqueness of Foucault's work is that it develops and applies Nietzsche's method of genealogy. A central hypothesis of this view is that knowledge is power. Nietzsche identifies the will-to-knowledge with the will-to-power, and Foucault accordingly labels what he is studying 'power/knowledge'. The solidus suggests that for his purposes power and knowledge are not to be studied separately. Power/knowledge is a device for studying the social and scientific practices that underlie and condition the formation of beliefs.[13]

Nietzsche's concept of genealogy is very different from the traditional historian's search for origins; it is rather more like a search for descent:

> recasting origins as descent enables one to think of difference rather than resemblance, of beginnings rather than a beginning, of exterior accident rather than internal truth. For Foucault searching for descent is the opposite of erecting foundations; it is to disturb the immobile, fragment the unified and show the heterogeneity of what was thought to be consistent.[14]

There was a change of emphasis in Foucault's work yet again with the publication of *Discipline and Punish* (1975).[15] It examines the spread of disciplinary mechanisms since the seventeenth century: techniques through which modern societies train and regulate individuals. Foucault's research focuses on discipline which, beginning in the seventeenth and eighteenth centuries, has been introduced in the school, the hospital, the factory and the army. Foucault demonstrates how, in the day-to-day running of institutions, discipline trains, individualises, regiments, makes docile and obedient subjects. Whether in the school, factory or hospital, many people become caught within all the regulations, timetabling and examinations by which discipline is imposed.

Foucault shows how it is through the body that discipline takes effect. The main principles of discipline were the control of movement and of the timing and space of activities. There was a minute control of gesture, behaviour and activity so that the body could be conditioned to become 'more obedient as it becomes more useful'.

Besides movement, the timing and succession of activities and the space that they might occupy were regulated in detail.

Discipline was more than a coercion of bodies. In the factory, for example, the place to which each worker was allotted was also an operation, a job, that could characterise her or him. The ranking of pupils in school or their passage through graded tasks was joined to an assessment that could decide what abilities they might have and how good they are. According to Foucault, characterisations, assessments and hierarchies decide who people are. [Discipline is something that at the same time 'makes' individuals and 'normalises' them.] QUOTE

Foucault's studies suggest that discipline, as a procedure of subjection, does indeed tie each individual to an identity. [He remarks that it is not that the individual is amputated, repressed, altered by our social order; it is rather that the individual is carefully fabricated in it.] Foucault argues that the techniques of discipline distribute bodies to various places and activities. [They prescribe the body's movements, impose norms on its activity, watch out for any deviation, and exclude the non-conforming. In these ways, the body is connected with processes of meaning: it is tied to an identity.] QUOTE QUOTE

CONCLUSION OF THE EARLY WORK

I have said that the central part of Foucault's work is an analysis of the social and human sciences. He argues that in Western culture these sciences have increasingly constituted discourses which have provided reasons, principles and justifications for objectifying and subjectifying practices through which people have been classified, examined, trained, divided from others, and formed as subjects.

I am sympathetic to Foucault's view that the subject should be thought of as constituted rather than given *a priori*. This is Lacan's view as well, but Foucault rejects the Lacanian thesis that the subject is constituted in language; what Foucault is interested in are the practices that constitute the subject.

Drawing on Foucault, it could be argued that there is no such thing as a universal identity. [It would seem to me that every person's identity is a site of struggle between conflicting discourses.] Discourses emerge and function as a means of struggle, and, at the same time, a series of controls master and constrain discourses. And in the struggle of discourses, not only words change their meanings, but identities also. QUOTE

In the previous chapter, I outlined, briefly, the contribution of Althusser to an understanding of the construction of identity. Althusser stressed that consciousness is constructed through ideologies which exist in the state apparatuses. For him, identity is something conferred on people; we become subjects acting in the beliefs given to us to think. He argued that we exist as subjects only in ideology. Many theorists, finding Althusser's thesis too functionalist and deterministic, turned against his work.

I think that I ought to add that an important theoretical advance has been made by Michel Pêcheux. He has added to Althusser's account by sketching three mechanisms through which subjects may be constructed: identification, counter-identification and disidentification. Identification is the mode of 'good subjects', those who 'freely consent' to the image held out to them, while 'bad subjects', trouble-makers, refuse it. Counter-identification is the mode of the trouble-maker who turns back those meanings lived by the good subjects who are only stating the obvious. The main features of counter-discourses is that they are held in a kind of symmetry, which consists in resisting only within and on the terrain of the prevailing ideologies which they would challenge. Disidentification can be described as an effect of working 'on and against' prevailing practices of ideological subjection. A disidentification can be brought about by political and ideological practices which work on and against what prevails.[16]

In this chapter, I underlined the fact that Foucault's work changed emphasis several times. At first, it appears that identity is formed through institutions, through institutional practices. There then seems to be a period when he stressed discourses or discursive practices. Then Foucault changed tack again and began to emphasise the role of discipline and how it takes effect through the body.

One of the problems with Foucault's theory (as with Althusser) is its determinism. In his work, there is no reference to the interpretation of events or the construction of a plausible, ever-changing narrative by a human subject of his or her identity. Foucault is rather weak and inadequate on the question of agency and the subject and finds it impossible to deal with identity as experienced. Moreover, his history tends to have no active subjects at all. And though it is true that he was not interested in social class, he was very interested in sexual identity.

In summary: Foucault, in his main works, tried to show how we have indirectly constituted ourselves through the exclusion of some others: criminals, mad people – and, I would add, women and black people, categories which are absent in his works. Exclusion, of course, depends on power.

One of the problems of Foucault's concept of power is that it is not located in agencies such as individuals, economic forces or the state. He focuses not on determining social structures but on 'micro' operations of power. Power is not attached to agents and interests but is incorporated in numerous practices. Foucault argues that power can be heterogeneous rather than simply adversarial.

And so instead of the unity of the working class (the agent of universal emancipation) we have heterogeneous social movements, the new communities of interest. But how can these fragmented movements work collectively? How does one rethink political agency in relation to new forms of subjectivity?

I think that it is too often assumed that we know what a person is. Anthropology is important in this context because it reminds us that there are many ways of conceiving the self. Like anthropological research, the purpose of Foucault's comparisons between past and present is to problematise our culture. As he moves from one topic to another, his views of the human subject seem to change. The structuralist doxa was that there was no subject. In his early work, Foucault denied the subject and the concept of agency. Then, in his later work, the human subject became the central element again. He became interested in subjectification. For Foucault, the construction of subjects was to do with the development, the invention of certain practices and techniques. It is generally believed that he is not interested in who has power; he is interested in the processes by which subjects are constructed as effects of power. In 1981, Foucault surprised everyone by saying that the goal of his work during the previous twenty years had not been power at all but experience. This interest in the constitution of subjectivity can be most clearly seen in his last work, *The History of Sexuality*, where he begins to discuss 'the technologies of the self'.[17]

NOTES

1. Robert Young, *White Mythologies: Writing History and the West* (London: Routledge, 1990), p. 2.
2. Terry Eagleton, *The Ideology of the Aesthetic* (Oxford: Basil Blackwell, 1990), p. 381.
3. Michel Foucault, *Language, Counter-Memory, Practice* (Oxford: Blackwell, 1977), p. 225.
4. See Michèle Barrett, *The Politics of Truth: From Marx to Foucault* (Cambridge: Polity Press, 1991).

5. Quoted in Diane Macdonell, *Theories of Discourse* (Oxford: Basil Blackwell, 1986), p. 14.
6. Michel Foucault, *Madness and Civilization: A History of Insanity in the Age of Reason* (London: Tavistock, 1967).
7. Ibid., p. 252.
8. Jacques Derrida, 'Cogito and the History of Madness', in idem, *Writing and Difference* (Hemel Hempstead: Routledge and Kegan Paul, 1978), p. 34.
9. Foucault's concept of discourse, or more precisely a discursive formation, is formally explained in his major methodological work, *The Archaeology of Knowledge* (London: Tavistock, 1972). For a clear exposition, see Michèle Barrett, *The Politics of Truth* op. cit., pp. 126–31.
10. Michel Foucault, 'The Order of Discourse', in Robert Young (ed.), *Untying the Text: A Post-Structuralist Reader* (London: Routledge, 1981), p. 56.
11. Michèle Barrett, *The Politics of Truth*, op. cit., p. 126.
12. Barry Hindess and Paul Hirst, *Mode of Production and Social Formation* (London: Macmillan, 1977), p. 20.
13. Michel Foucault, *Discipline and Punish: The Birth of the Prison* (London: Penguin Books, 1977).
14. Some thinkers have found Foucault's innovative work very useful. Edward Said's *Orientalism* is based on Foucauldian assumptions. Jeffrey Weekes, in his books on sexuality, has made use of Foucault's approach. Some feminists, too, have found him useful because of the attention he gives to the body, to bio-politics. On the other hand, it has to be conceded that Foucault discusses the body cerebrally. He refuses to discuss the affective, the emotional aspects of identity, and in his theoretical work there is little sense of political agency. Moreover, Foucault tends to ignore areas of experience, such as alienation, art and religion, which humanism considers seriously. And what about his notion of power – is it so broad as to be indeterminate and empty? Commenting on Foucault's belief that power is all-pervasive, Eagleton remarks: 'Foucault's whole attitude to power thus carries with it a profound ambivalence, which reflects his attempt to combine Nietzsche with radical or revolutionary politics'. See Terry Eagleton, *The Ideology of the Aesthetic*, op. cit., p. 390.
15. Michel Foucault, *Discipline and Punish*, op. cit.
16. See Michel Pêcheux, *Language, Semantics and Ideology: Stating the Obvious* (London: Macmillan, 1982).
17. See, particularly, Michel Foucault, *The History of Sexuality*, vol. 3, *The Care of the Self* (London: Penguin, 1990). Foucault's understanding of his own sexuality is an important aspect of his work. In his youth, homosexuality could not be publicly admitted. He died of an AIDS-related illness in 1984 at the age of 57. For an excellent biography, see Didier Eribon, *Michel Foucault* (London: Faber, 1992). For the argument that Foucault's entire work is about the self, and his in particular, see James Miller, *The Passion of Michel Foucault* (New York: Simon and Schuster, 1993).

6

---•---

FOUCAULT: SEX AND THE TECHNOLOGIES OF THE SELF

THE ROLE OF SEX

Most people think of Foucault's writings as always being about how the human subject is created by forces of repression. This is not true. In the last years of his life, Foucault became very interested in how we constitute ourselves as subjects. In many ways, Foucault's project on the self was the logical conclusion to his historical inquiry over twenty-five years into insanity, deviancy, criminality and sexuality. Throughout his works, Foucault had concerned himself largely with the technologies of power and domination, whereby the self has been objectified through what he termed 'dividing practices'. By 1981, he had become increasingly interested in the genealogy of how the self constituted itself as a subject. He began to study what he termed 'technologies of the self'. He returned to the traditional concerns of French philosophy: human subjectivity and selfhood. Like Nietzsche, who attacked the idea of a fixed human nature or essence, Foucault studied features of human beings that individuals generally take to be fixed but that historical study shows to be malleable. He pays attention to the practices by which individuals train themselves to become a certain sort of person. Unlike the prison book, *Discipline and Punish*, which studies how people constrain others, *The History of Sexuality* studies how people constrain themselves.[1] In the volumes of the latter, Foucault begins to focus on the ethics of the self. He shows the increasing moralisation and anxiety around sex that develops within antiquity and is carried forward in the Christian epoch. Foucault asks: what is the role of sex in the constitution of the self? Today we assume that sex is central to our identity. Foucault asks: why is it, and how have its forms of being changed?

In volume 1, Foucault wants us to start thinking differently about sexuality by suggesting that only recently has it seemed necessary to think of human beings as if their possession of certain organs

determined their gender and behaviour, or as if sexuality and personality were totally conditioned by particular orientations towards how
these organs are used.

[Foucault believed that the notion that we have of sexual nature is
itself a product of those modes of knowledge designed to make us
objects of control. Our acceptance that we have such a nature makes
us an object of such control.]For now we have to find it, and this
requires the 'help' of experts. We have to put ourselves in the care of
priests, or psychoanalysts and social workers. Our self-understanding
in terms of an enigmatic nature requiring expression has made us
into modern sexual beings, where a key element of the good life is
some kind of sexual fulfilment. We are, then, objects of control in all
sorts of ways which we barely understand. We are not controlled on
the old model, through certain prohibitions being imposed on us.
[We may think we are gaining some freedom, when we throw off
sexual prohibitions, but in fact we are dominated by certain images
of what it is to be a full, healthy, fulfilled sexual being.]These images
are in fact very powerful instruments of control.[2]

In volumes 2 and 3 of *The History of Sexuality*, Foucault studies
how sexual self-understanding has been different in the past, and
offers evidence that sexuality is a specific historical concept. One of
the salient features of Foucault's work has been that he begins at a
point of difference. What he does in examining a time so different
from our own is to throw our own needs and aspirations into relief.

THE GRECO–ROMAN TRADITION:
TAKING CARE OF THE SELF

Foucault began with the Greeks; in their sexual practice, the love
between free, adult males and boys was the central question. He
suggests that sexual desire was not the problem for the Greeks;
rather, it was that of individual freedom or ethics. In Greek society,
anyone could became a love-object for a Greek master: wife, mis-
tress, slave, boy. The ruling class valued the active posture because it
alone was commensurate with their freedom. The moral issue for
them concerned the question of placing boys from the ruling class in
a passive position during sexual relations with free adult males. They
were troubled by the fact that the boys were supposed to be passive
and pleasureless, and this was inconsistent with the fact that the
same boy was supposed to grow up to be an active citizen. Numerous
discourses were developed by the masters of the period because they

feared that the practice might accustom the boys to patterns of passivity, hence undermining their freedom and the freedom of the polis. In short, sex became a moral problem for the Greeks (of the fourth to the second centuries BC) because the passive positioning of free males contradicted the ethics of freedom.

Foucault insists that the Greeks found sexual conduct as problematic as moderns do, but in different ways. For them, it was not how or with whom one had sex that was crucial, but whether one was master or slave of one's passions. So the Greeks could not have been opposed to what came to be called perversion or deviancy, but only to the aesthetic of any degree of physical excess.

During the first two centuries AD, important changes occurred in the place of sex in the constitution of the self. In the passage from Ancient Greece to Hellenistic Rome, the major change concerning sexuality was a shift of emphasis from the love of boys to the marriage tie. In place of the elaborate subculture surrounding the love of boys, the wife became the centre of the man's sexuality, and accordingly the locus in which he constituted his subjectivity. During the Early Roman Empire, sex, while not intrinsically evil or bad, was seen as the source of many serious dangers for the self. The focus on the marital tie implied that intercourse with boys or servants was increasingly avoided. While extramarital relations were not strictly speaking prohibited, they became an area of question for the culture of the self. In short, Hellenistic Rome witnessed a shift in sexual objects, an intensification of prohibitions concerning sexuality and a deepening subjectification of the self.

Foucault located the roots of the modern concept of the self in first- and second-century Greco–Roman philosophy. In the Hellenistic and Greco–Roman periods, the emphasis was not on the knowledge of the self but on the concern with oneself. This Socratic notion became a common, universal philosophical theme. In *Alcibiades*, attributed to Plato, Alcibiades inquires how he might achieve self-knowledge. Socrates responds that he would come to know himself if he takes care of himself. Self-knowledge is the function of certain obligations associated with taking care of the self. In *Alcibiades*, one can see that concern for self always refers to an active political and erotic state. It is always a real activity and not just an attitude; taking care of oneself was not only a principle but also a constant practice. Pliny, for example, advises a friend to study, to read, to prepare for misfortune or death. It was a meditation and a preparation.

Foucault also discusses the three Stoic techniques of self: letters to friends and disclosure of self; examination of self and conscience, including a review of what was done, of what should have been done, and the comparison of the two. The third technique involved remembering. In Stoicism, it's not the deciphering of the self which is important, it is the memory of what you've done and what you've had to do.[3] The Stoic ideal was not self-denial, as it would be for later Christians, but rather self-care. Stoic techniques were designed to enable one to cope with the realities of this world more effectively, not to prepare for a spiritual world beyond. The Platonic and later Stoic traditions emphasise the activity of self-disclosure always in terms of another; this dialogical activity is social. Self-knowledge is the result of a 'caring for the self', characterised by a network of external obligations and practices.

Let me now summarise what Foucault says in the third volume on the care of the self. He writes that there was a growth in the Hellenistic and Roman world of an 'individualism' that began to stress the private aspects of existence. He focuses on the development of what he calls 'cultivation of the self', wherein the relations of oneself to oneself were intensified and valorised.[4] Care of the self implies labour; it takes time. One can set aside a few moments in the evening or the morning for introspection, for examining what needs to be done, for memorising certain useful principles, for reflecting on the day that has gone by. There were also retreats which enabled one to commune with oneself, to recollect one's bygone days, to place the whole of one's past life before one's eyes, to get to know oneself.

Time is filled with different sorts of exercises. Besides the care of the body, there are the meditations, the readings, the notes that one takes on books or on the conversations one has heard: 'Around the care of the self, there developed an entire activity of speaking and writing in which the work of oneself on oneself and communication with others were linked together'.[5]

It was considered important to subject oneself to self-examination. The morning examination served mainly as an occasion to consider the tasks and obligations of the day, so as to be sufficiently prepared for it. The evening examination, for its part, was devoted much more specifically to reviewing the day that had gone by. There was an evaluation of one's progress at the end of the day: 'when he had retired for the night, Sextius would question his soul: "what bad habit have you cured today? What fault have you resisted? In what respect are you better?"'[6]

The whole art of self-knowledge developed with precise recipes, specific forms of examination and codified exercises. There were even testing procedures to enable one to do without unnecessary things. Foucault notes that in the examination to which Seneca subjects himself, there are phrases such as 'appear before the judge', 'give report of my own character', 'plead my cause'. These elements seem to indicate the division of the subject into a judging authority and an accused individual. But the process also calls to mind a kind of administrative review where it is a matter of evaluating a performed activity in order to reactivate its principles and ensure their correct application in the future.

This cultivation of the self was concerned with the manner in which the individual needed to form himself as an ethical subject: 'The task of testing oneself, examining oneself, monitoring oneself in a series of clearly defined exercises, makes the question of truth – the truth concerning what one is, what one does, and what one is capable of doing – central to the formation of the ethical subject'.[7]

What, then, were the main differences between Greek and modern forms of sexuality? For the Greeks, the codes and restrictions that governed sex were minimal, a contrast with the Christian period where regulations over sex were detailed and comprehensive. Then, too, for the Greeks sex was good, for the Christians it was bad or evil. Marriage for the Greeks was more a social and political arrangement than a joining of two souls in a sacred relationship, as it would later become. For the Greeks, there was no preoccupation with the self as a desiring subject. They did not characterise individuals by their sexual practices or desires, and the distinction between heterosexual and homosexual did not exist. For the Greeks, the question of sexuality was placed in the register of the free activity of the individual to constitute oneself. In short, sex was an aesthetic question, a matter of life-style.

THE CHRISTIAN TRADITION: KNOWING ONESELF

The change outlined by Foucault from the Greek constitution of the self, through discourses on the sexual practice of the love of boys, to the Christian constitution of the self through elaborate restrictive codes against the pleasures of the flesh, is a fascinating story. Like Nietzsche, Foucault sees the main historic rupture occurring with Christianity. For Foucault, the basic technique of the self of the last 1,800 years was developed by the Christians. They instituted an elaborate code, universally applicable, to regulate sexual conduct and thoughts. They based the code on the principle of the sinful nature of the self. They established a practice of confession through which their discourses on sex governed social action and thought. And, above all, they established sex as the truth about the self. This is what Foucault is interested in; he wants to trace the path through which individuals become, in the modern period, subjects whose truth is their sexuality. In the past two centuries, there has been a proliferation of discourses on sex, the writings of doctors, psychoanalysts, therapists, researchers and many others, all sharing the premise that some deep truth about individuals was bound up with their sexuality.

The Christian tradition, in contrast to the Greco–Roman tradition, emphasised 'know thyself'. Each person has the duty to know who he is, that is, to try to know what is happening inside one, to acknowledge faults, to recognise temptations, to locate desires; and everyone is obliged to disclose these things either to God or to others in the community. We must remember that Christianity is not only a salvation religion, it's also a confessional religion.

Monastic Christianity stressed obedience and contemplation. There is not a single moment when the monk can be autonomous. This technology of self-examination is much more concerned with thought than with action. The Christian model of the self, with its deciphering of inner thoughts, implies that there is something hidden in ourselves and that we are always in a state of self-illusion which is hiding something. There is an analytical and continual verbalisation of thoughts carried on in complete obedience to a master. This relation is modelled on the renunciation of one's own will and of one's own self. Discourse of self is the renunciation of one's own self.[8]

There are two well-known techniques of asceticism in Christianity: monasticism and Puritanism. Monasticism is associated with renouncing the world, with developing a rigorous programme of training in humility – the condition of entrance to the next world. This technique can be called world-rejecting.

The Puritans adopted quite a different paradigm, one based on suspicion of self. The Puritans replaced Catholic confession to a priest with the confessional diary, an account-book of one's state of sin. Every night symbolised death, so that at the end of every day Puritans might go over their 'accounts' accordingly. This technique can be called 'innerworldly'.[9]

In the monastic model, subjectivisation has not taken place. The monk renounces any possibility of self, in favour of soul, at the out-set of his career. But in the Puritan model the centre of gravity shifts, the enemy is now a more formidable competitor and threat to God: man's own self. Because the Puritans had not renounced their worldly selves totally, as the monks had, it is not surprising that the Puritans' self became freighted with ambiguity.

Puritan journals are fascinating because they show the Protestant self as both accuser and accused. With the absence of a Catholic confessor, or superior, confessing and examining becomes an entirely internalised dialogue between two facets of self, the observer and the observed. Is this like the contemporary suspicious and cognitive self that indefinitely looks over its own shoulder and observes its own observing, its own fabrications? Puritan writing, in short, not only presupposed the importance of self, 'the seeing I', but also prefigured the modern division of self into opposing parts.

According to Foucault, there are several reasons why the Christian 'know thyself' model has obscured the 'take care of yourself' model. It is partly because our morality, a morality of asceticism, insists that the self is that which one can reject. The second reason is that, in traditional philosophy from Descartes to Husserl, knowledge of the self (the thinking subject) takes on an ever-increasing importance as the first step in the theory of knowledge.

ROUSSEAU: THE CELEBRATION OF THE AUTONOMOUS SELF

It has been suggested that, in the story of the constitution of our-selves as subjects of knowledge, Jean-Jacques Rousseau (1712–78) played an important part.[10] He was one of the first authors to insist upon his own singularity, to stress his emotional life ('I felt before I thought', he wrote) as the basis for individuality. The emergence of an individuality (a clearly-defined self) and the valorisation of the emotive life was connected to, and dependent on, the activity of writing.

Motivated by guilt and shame, Rousseau discovered a secular form of the religious practice of confession. If one examines the Confes-sions, one sees that the modern secular confessional, as invented by Rousseau, involves not merely the recital of sins but the enumeration of each and every experience that has made one what and who one is. In order for a man or woman to be constituted as a subject, he or she must first be divided from the totality of the world. For a 'me' to emerge, a distinction must be made between the 'me' and the 'not-me'. The first, and essential, move in the constitution of self is division. In dividing ourselves from the world, we constitute ourselves as subjects of knowledge and examination.

The Confessions, then, is the recounting of the history of the self so that the self can concurrently create itself in writing and affirm that self it has created. Rousseau constitutes the self as subject by objectivising the speaking subject in language, by presenting him to the gaze of the knowledgeable reader. He objectivises the subject by division. And he refines a technique (the written confession) by means of which the self comes to recognise itself as subject, and object. In short, Rousseau helped to invest, to justify and to circulate those techniques which constitute the modern subject.[11]

What are the techniques that Foucault says agents practise on themselves to make themselves into the persons they want to be? There are four major types:

1. technologies of production, which permit us to produce, transform or manipulate things;
2. technologies of power, which determine the conduct of individuals;
3. technologies of sign systems, which permit us to use symbols or signification;
4. 'technologies of the self, which permit individuals to effect by their own means a number of operations on their own bodies and souls, thoughts, conduct, and way of being so as to transform themselves in order to attain a certain state of happiness, purity, wisdom, perfection or immortality'.[12]

Of course, these four types of technologies hardly ever function separately, although each of them is associated with a certain type of domination. Each implies certain modes of training and the modification of individuals, their skills and their attitudes.

I ought to mention here that there is some ambiguity in Foucault's use of the terms 'self' and 'subject'. He does not define them. The 'self' is a neutral term, almost a synonym for individual. 'Subject' seems to be an active, historical term that refers to the process of interiorisation. The subject takes shape through historically experienced discourses – practices. But the problem is this: since Foucault rejects the notion of absolute truth, he also rejects the concept of the subject as source or foundation of truth. His notion of the subject is both decentred and relativist.

FREUD AND FOUCAULT: THE PROBLEM OF THE PSYCHE

Having given an exposition of Foucault's thesis of how the conception of the self changed from the Greco–Roman idea of taking care of the self to the Christian goal of self-renunciation, I want now to look at some differences between Freud and Foucault about the psyche.

One common depiction of Freud's theory of psychoanalysis is that it is based on a model of a tripartite psyche in which the self (ego) wrestles with the conflicts between the drives of unconscious impulses (id) for free expression and the demands of conscience (superego) for their renunciation.[13] In his view, one's sense of self is shaped by powerful precedents out of the past. To know oneself, therefore, is to retrieve from the oblivion of the unconscious mind lost memories of painful experiences or unresolved conflicts.

Foucault approaches the problem of the psyche from the opposite direction. All of his early work was concerned with the ways in which external authority shapes the structure of the mind.[14] He demonstrates how the 'classical age' (the eighteenth century) was committed to the disciplining of human affairs by public and quasi-public agencies. It is through the policing process that the modern frame of mind has been formed. This process fosters a mentality that requires ever more explicit definitions of what is appropriate to human behaviour. The policing process involves the construction of modes of discourse and of action through which we shape our conception of human nature.

Let's take, as an example, the discourse about sexuality. Foucault shows how the inculcation of a discipline of self-control in sexual matters has generated an imperative to seek knowledge of the self. Beginning in seventeenth-century Catholic confessional practices and continuing in twentieth-century psychoanalysis, the task of scrutinising our sexual behaviour came to be understood as a means for understanding ourselves better. Making sense of our sexuality is perceived in the modern age to be a method for discovering the truth about who we are.

Foucault contends that Freud appropriated the techniques of aural confession of the Catholic Church and thereby clothed the examination of conscience, a religious practice, in medical covering. Foucault then retraces the lineage of seventeenth-century confessional practices to the Christian Roman Empire, specifically to the prescribed routines of monastic life. But even these rituals for self-examination,

Foucault continues, are derived from still earlier practices. Many of these techniques predate Christian practice. As we have seen, some were borrowed from the Stoics who had developed an elaborate regimen of discipline in the first and second centuries AD to further a different, purely humanistic notion of self-analysis. Practices such as spiritual retreat, meditation, ritual purification and deference to a mentor, all subsequently employed by Christian spiritual directors, had been used by Stoic teachers for quite different purposes.

There are many far-reaching differences between Freud and Foucault, and I will mention just a few of the important ones. Freud believed that our task is to refine our theory so that we may approach the truth about the psyche's nature more closely. Foucault, on the other hand, argues that the self is not an objective reality to be described by our theories but a subjective notion that is actually constituted by them. Foucault, then, inverts Freud's proposition about the relationship between knowledge and power. Whereas Freud sought to explain how knowledge gives us power over the self, Foucault seeks to demonstrate how power shapes our knowledge of the self.[15]

Freud's main concern is self-knowledge. To know oneself is to discover the forgotten influences that have made us what we are. In reaching back to origins to recollect fragments of our experiences, memory makes us whole once more by reaffirming our connection with the past. Whereas Freud asks how our past experience shapes our lives in the present, Foucault asks why we seek to discover truth in the formal rules that we have designed to discipline life's experiences. And while Freud stresses the power of the past to determine our present behaviour, Foucault emphasises the random, the fortuitous, the discontinuous. Freud provides a method for investigating the internal workings of the psyche; Foucault, however, seeks to show how the method itself is an ancient technique of self-fashioning that has, over the centuries, shaped the mind externally.

One of Foucault's achievements is that he has sketched out a history of the different ways in our culture that humans develop knowledge about themselves. To reiterate: in Greco–Roman culture, knowledge of oneself appeared as the consequence of taking care of oneself; in the modern world, knowledge of oneself constitutes the fundamental principle. As we are continually being reconstituted by the forms that we create along the way, perhaps, in the end, the meaning of the self, for Foucault, is less important than the methods we employ to understand it.

FOUCAULT'S ETHICS OF THE SELF

It is in the second and third volumes of *The History of Sexuality* that Foucault writes about ethics. What Foucault means by ethics is a study of the self's relation to itself. He took ethics to be one part of the study of morals. In addition to ethics, morals consist of people's actual behaviour, that is, their morally relevant actions, and of the moral code which is imposed on them. By the moral code, Foucault understood, for example, the rules that determine which actions are forbidden, permitted or required.

The relationship to oneself has four major aspects: ethical substance, mode of subjection, self-forming activity, and telos. (There is, of course, some independence between them.) The first aspect, the ethical substance, is that part of ourselves or our behaviour which is taken to be the relevant domain for ethical judgement. Are ethical judgements to be applied to feelings, intentions or desire? What part of ourselves is to be the substance or matter of ethics? Foucault believed that the ethical substance of Greco–Roman ethics was quite different from both Christian and modern categories of ethical substance.

The second aspect of ethics is the mode of subjection. This aspect concerns the way in which people are invited or incited to recognise their moral obligations – whatever it is that we use to recognise and internalise moral obligations as being revealed by divine law, imposed by the demands of reason, political conviction, personal obsession, or as resting on convention, or as deriving from the attempt to give one's existence the most beautiful form possible. It could be political conviction or personal obsession – anything that we take as authority. Foucault wanted to show that different people and distinct historical periods may be subjected to the same rules in different ways. The mode of subjection provides the linkage between the moral code and the self, determining how this code is to get a hold on our selves.[16]

The third aspect of ethics concerns the means by which we change or elaborate ourselves in order to become ethical subjects, our self-forming activity. This aspect of ethics is about how we get it to work. What are we to do to moderate our acts, or to decipher what we are, or to eradicate our desires, or to use our sexual desire in order to obtain certain aims like having children, and so on? This self-forming activity, Foucault says, is a form of asceticism, because it is cutting off some possible ways to be or to behave, in order to serve some immediate end. One source of self-helping activity is ascetic manuals and self-help books.

The fourth aspect of ethics, telos (a teleology), is the kind of being to which we aspire when we behave morally. Should we become pure or immortal, or free, or masters of ourselves? What is the goal to which our self-forming activity should be directed?

Two features of Foucault's ethics of the self need underlining. More than anyone, Foucault has taught us the dangers of essentialism.[17] He wants to stress the specific character of an ethics of the self because he wants to avoid lapsing into a reverse essentialism. Secondly, he insists that an ethics of the self is primarily a practical rather than a reflective activity. His insistence on the practical nature of an ethics of the self derives, in part, from his rejection of notions of ideology and signification as idealist categories, and his corresponding insistence on the positive effects of power/knowledge complexes.

Just before Foucault's sudden and unexpected death from an AIDS-related illness at the age of 57 in 1984, there were signs of further intellectual developments. It is said that he was going to elaborate his own conception of a good life. This would seem to be based on a rejection of the idea that we have a deep self or nature which we have to decipher. Foucault believed that Christianity introduced this false turn into Western culture. As we have seen, the Greco–Roman tradition of 'care of the self' was concerned with self-making and self-mastery; Christian spirituality was preoccupied rather with purity and self-renunciation. 'From that moment on the self was no longer something to be made but something to be renounced and deciphered.'[18]

It is possible that, finally, Foucault committed himself to a conception of the good life as a kind of self-making. He argued that an ethics of the self was the only way in which an individual could resist the normalising effects of disciplinary power. In this later work, Foucault conceives of the self as constituted through certain 'practices' or techniques which are determined by the social context but are mediated through an active process of self-fashioning by the individual. This reinvention of the self is primarily an aesthetic experience, an 'aesthetics of existence', the principal aim of which is to make of one's life 'a work of art'. This, of course, raises the question: What is (for Foucault) 'a work of art'?[19]

Now, there are some contemporary writers who have dismissed aesthetics as an irredeemable bourgeois category and have criticised Foucault's ethics of the self for its amoral aestheticism and elitism.

For example, the stress on experimental self-stylisation has been criticised as a 'project for privileged minorities, liberated from all functions in the material reproduction of society'.[20] It could be argued that Foucault is not retreating into an amoral, elitist ethics; he is more concerned with rethinking the notions of creativity and aesthetics by removing them from their high cultural niche. He does not want to dismiss aesthetics but to radicalise it by drawing upon its critical and Utopian function.

It has been reported that Foucault told the American writers Dreyfus and Rabinow: 'What strikes me is the fact that in our society, art has become something which is related only to objects and not to individuals or to life . . . But couldn't everyone's life become a work of art?'[21]

As a modern example of work on oneself, Foucault refers to Baudelaire's advocacy of the asceticism of the dandy who makes of his body, his behaviour, his feelings and passions, his very existence, a work of art. Baudelaire was, in a sense, the first modernist.

Foucault derived his ethics from the notion of a Baudelairean dandy, and some of the problems with an ethics of the self arise from the way in which it is elaborated through Baudelaire, a writer associated with the heroic transfiguration of the ephemeral and fleeting moment. For Foucault, Baudelaire is very important; he is the paradigmatic modern individual and exemplar for the mode of relationship that has to be established with oneself:

> Modern man, for Baudelaire, is not the man who goes off to discover himself, his secrets and his hidden truth; he is the man who tries to invent himself. This modernity does not 'liberate man in his own being'; it compels him to face the task of producing himself.[22]

This is actually one of the limitations of Foucault's ethics of the self. The notion of self and agency that Foucault proposes relies upon an unexamined identification with a Baudelairean notion of the heroisation of the self. What is problematic is the way in which Foucault deflects his discussion of a contemporary ethics of the self onto Baudelaire: 'a lyric poet in the era of high capitalism'. According to Walter Benjamin, Baudelaire's construction of the artist as dandy, as *flâneur*, represents an attempt to capture the 'last shimmer of the heroic in times of decadence' which rested on anomie. 'Baudelaire found nothing to like about his time . . . Because he did not have any convictions he assumed ever new forms himself.'[23] For one feminist writer, Lois McNay, Foucault locates the frontiers of identity in an established canon of male avant-garde literature. Moreover, Foucault has a nostalgic fantasy of masculine agency.[24]

The second criticism of Foucault's ethics of the self concerns reflexivity. Reflexivity is central to Foucault's theory, providing it with its ethical dimension. In his view, the autonomy of the individual can only be affirmed through the reflexive examination of the construction of oneself – a critical hermeutics of the self which can 'grasp the points where change is possible and desirable, and to determine the precise form this change should take'.[25] Foucault writes that there must be a process of self-monitoring, but then goes on to argue that the analytical links between the self and the social context (the economic, political and social structures) must be rejected. This injunction arises from his concern to escape the 'regimes of truth' imposed on the body and its pleasures by the juridical–moral codification of Christianity, psychoanalysis and science.

In the stress on self-making, one cannot help noticing Foucault's affinity with Nietzsche. We are left with many important unanswered questions. Can we repudiate all that comes to us from the Christian tradition of inwardness? And, even if we can set this aside, is the alternative aesthetic of existence really much better? I realise that if Foucault does not want ethics of the self to become a form of reverse essentialism, he must insist on its contingent, local, specific and experimental nature. But the important point is this: as Foucault does not make the link between practices of the self and the way in which they are mediated through social and symbolic structures, it is unclear how individuals can acquire any insight into the implications of their actions.

We know that the process of reflexivity may never be fixed and complete but, nevertheless, there must be a systematic interrogation of how the self is imbricated in wider cultural dynamics. If one cannot consider the relationships between an ethics of the self and social structures, the individual can only obtain knowledge of the self from some kind of unmediated aesthetic experience that speaks directly to the self. If the individual is unable to assess the normative implications of his or her action via reference to overarching social dynamics, then it is the process of aesthetic self-fashioning itself that provides the criteria for evaluation. In short, as Foucault does not have a theory of mediation, it is unclear how the individual is to know whether the creation of the self is a radical move or whether it is another example of 'pseudo-individuality'.[26] One of the criticisms that has often been made of Foucault is that he sounds as though he believed that, as a historian, he could stand nowhere, identifying with none of the 'regimes of truth' or structures of power whose coming and going he impartially surveys.

Some of the most trenchant criticisms of Foucault's work, his views on the human subject and the Enlightenment, have been made by Terry Eagleton:

> Foucault evinces a well-nigh pathological aversion to the whole category of the subject, one considerably more negative than that manifested by Nietzsche himself. In his drastically undialectical attitude to the Enlightenment, he eradicates at a stroke almost all of its vital civilizing achievements, in which he can see nothing but insidious techniques of subjection.[27]

Towards the end of his life, however, he denied that he was a counter-Enlightenment thinker in the sense of one who denied that we did not still in large part depend on it.

Commenting on *The Use of Pleasure*, Eagleton writes:

> Foucault is finally able to fill one of the gaping voids in his work – the question of ethics – with an aesthetic alternative to humanist morality. The theme of aestheticization explicitly emerges in this book. To live well is to transfigure oneself into a work of art by an intensive process of self-discipline.[28]

The autonomous individual that emerges in Foucault's book is a matter of surface, art, technique or sensation. Finally, what are we to make of Foucault's position on the question of the subject and subjectivity? We have the body and its pleasures instead of the subject and its desires; love is a technique without reference to tenderness, affection and emotion.

At the beginning of the Second World War, my brother Rashid had to join the Army; he became an officer and was posted to India. My family (which had moved in the other direction and was living in Bristol) moved to a smaller house near to the one we had left. There was Sita my sister, my elder brother Roshan, and me. Both Sita and Roshan were studying at university. Roshan was away in London most of the time, and so it was Sita who, besides studying and doing the housework, looked after me.

I didn't appreciate her difficulties, nor was I helpful. I was getting interested in girls, and I spent a lot of time hanging around waiting, trying to pick up girls and not knowing how. My sister was worried about this and other things I did. For example, one night during an air raid in Bristol, I went out to the local park. I remember it being lit up, like fairy lights, with incendiary bombs. Sita must have been very worried, as she didn't know where I was. This was one of many thoughtless, selfish acts that I committed. It cannot have been easy for her, providing me with a comfortable home and clean clothes, and giving me my meals, while studying herself.

After finishing her studies, Sita wanted to get married, and so she returned to India. I went out into 'digs' (a room plus meals) in the house of a schoolfriend. I was sixteen at the time. During this time, I had no contact with anyone who could advise me or give me guidance. Here is a typical example of the sort of thing that used to happen. For a long time, I couldn't see the blackboard even when I sat at the front of the class. It took me a long time to realise that I needed glasses. One day I went to the Old Market, found a barrow with twenty or thirty pairs of spectacles on it, tried on a few, and bought my first pair. I was delighted that I could see.

I have always felt lonely, and, even when I married, ten years later, I continued to have feelings of loss — feelings that I have never understood. And now that I think I am beginning to understand, the people that I want to talk to have died. Perhaps it doesn't matter now. But then, why am I writing? Is my writing an attempt to put it all together? Does one have to rewrite the past in order to understand it?

NOTES

1. Michel Foucault, *The History of Sexuality*: vol. 1, *An Introduction* (Harmondsworth: Penguin, 1981); vol 2, *The Use of Pleasure* (Harmondsworth: Penguin, 1987; vol 3, *The Care of the Self* (Harmondsworth: Penguin, 1990); vol 4, *Les Aveux de la chair* (Harmondsworth: Penguin).
2. Charles Taylor, 'Foucault on Freedom and Truth', in David Hoy (ed.), *Foucault: A Critical Reader* (Oxford: Basil Blackwell, 1986), pp. 78–9.
3. Luther H. Martin, Huck Gutman and Patrick H. Hutton (eds), *Technologies of the Self: A Seminar with Michel Foucault* (London: Tavistock, 1988), p. 35.
4. Michel Foucault, *The History of Sexuality*, vol. 3, *The Care of the Self* (London: Penguin, 1990), p. 43.
5. Ibid., p. 51.
6. Ibid., p. 61.
7. Ibid., p. 68.
8. Martin, Gutman and Hutton (eds), *Technologies of the Self*, op. cit., p. 48.
9. This section is based on an essay by a Foucauldian scholar, William Paden, 'Theatres of Humility and Suspicion: Desert Saints and New England Puritans', in *Technologies of the Self*, op. cit., pp. 69–78 (p. 71).
10. This section draws on Huck Gutman, 'Rousseau's Confessions', in *Technologies of the Self*, op. cit., pp. 101–9.
11. Ibid., p. 117.
12. *Technologies of the Self*, p. 18.
13. I think that this is a vulgar view of Freud's constantly changing theory which he himself popularised in *An Outline of Psychoanalysis*. The self is not the ego; it is

much more. The French psychoanalyst Jacques Lacan emphasised the view of the psyche which Freud expressed in *The Interpretation of Dreams, Psychopathology of Everyday Life*, and *Jokes and the Unconscious*. Lacan argued that ego-psychologists stressed the adaptation of the individual to the social environment and that they have watered down and sweetened Freud's ideas about the unconscious and sexuality. Jacques Lacan, *Ecrits: A Selection* (London: Tavistock, 1977), p. 135.

14. Patrick Hutton, 'Foucault, Freud and the Technologies of the Self', in *Technologies of the Self*, op. cit., p. 125.

15. Ibid., p. 135.

16. Moral codes change very slowly. By codes, Foucault means quite specific general instructions (like the Ten Commandments, for example). We have long had manuals giving techniques for self-improvement. Most techniques of the self – meditation, confession, exercise, diet, exemplary role models – are as old as the old codes, but the ways in which they are employed may differ from generation to generation. And so, for Foucault, a genealogy of ethics would be a study of what these techniques really are and how we use them upon ourselves.

17. Foucault has, in fact, been accused of essentialism. There is a tendency to essentialise certain forms of knowledge in his earlier work. He assumes that disqualified or subjugated knowledges have some sort of cognitive privilege. Such a view uncritically valorises the concrete experience of the oppressed. See Jürgen Habermas, *The Philosophical Discourse of Modernity* (Cambridge: Polity Press, 1987), p. 21.

18. Charles Taylor, 'Foucault on Freedom and Truth', in David Hoy (ed.), *Foucault: A Critical Reader* (Oxford: Blackwell, 1986), p. 98.

19. Michel Foucault, 'On the Genealogy of Ethics: An Overview of Work in Progress', in Paul Rabinow (ed.), *The Foucault Reader* (Harmondsworth: Peregrine, 1984), p. 351.

20. Rainer Rochlitz, 'The Aesthetics of Existence: Post-conventional Morality and the Theory of Power in Michel Foucault', in T. Armstrong (ed.), *Michel Foucault Philosopher* (Hemel Hempstead: Harvester Wheatsheaf, 1992), p. 225.

21. Hubert Dreyfus and Paul Rabinow, *Michel Foucault: Beyond Structuralism and Hermeneutics* (Chicago: University of Chicago Press, 1982), quoted in Didier Eribon, *Michel Foucault* (London: Faber and Faber, 1993), p. 331.

22. Michel Foucault, 'What is Enlightenment?', in Paul Rabinow (ed.),*The Foucault Reader*, op. cit., p. 41.

23. Walter Benjamin, *Charles Baudelaire: A Lyric Poet in the Era of High Capitalism* (London: New Left Books, 1973), p. 97.

24. Lois McNay, 'The Problems of the Self in Foucault's Ethics of the Self', *Third Text*, 19 (summer 1992), 5. See also Lois McNay, *Foucault and Feminism: Power, Gender and the Self* (Cambridge: Polity Press, 1992).

25. Michel Foucault, 'What is Enlightenment?, in Paul Rabinow (ed.), *The Foucault Reader*, op. cit., p. 46.

26. Charles Taylor, 'Foucault on Freedom & Truth' in David Hoy (ed.), *Foucault: A Critical Reader*, op. cit., p 99.

27. Terry Eagleton, *The Ideology of the Aesthetic* (Oxford: Basil Blackwell, 1990), p. 385.

28. Ibid., p. 389.

7

.

THE CONDITION OF POSTMODERNITY

MODERNISM AND POSTMODERNISM

There have been enormous and astonishing social changes in the
world since the 1970s. This change is bound up with the emergence
of new ways in which we experience space and time. There is some
kind of necessary relation between the rise of postmodernist cultural
forms, the emergence of more flexible modes of capital accumulation,
and a new round of 'time–space compression' in the organisation of
capitalism. These changes are not signs of the emergence of some
entirely new postindustrial or postcapitalist society; they are merely
shifts in surface appearance. This is the view of David Harvey in
his book, *The Condition of Postmodernity*.[1] He begins by discussing
modernity because, after all, it is modernity that is being rejected by
postmodernity. Modernity is usually perceived as positivistic, tech-
nocratic and rationalistic. It has identified with the belief in linear
progress, absolute truths, the rational planning of ideal social orders,
and the standardisation of knowledge and production. The project
of modernity came into focus during the eighteenth century. That
project was an extraordinary intellectual effort on the part of Enlightenment thinkers to develop objective science, universal morality
and autonomous art. Enlightenment thinkers embraced the idea of
progress; they believed in justice and in the possibility of happiness
of human beings. In the twentieth century, these hopes have been
cruelly shattered.

For Max Weber, the legacy of the Enlightenment was the triumph
of purposive–instrumental rationality. He held that the growth of
purposive–instrumental rationality led not to the realisation of universal freedom but to the creation of an 'iron cage' of bureaucratic
rationality from which there is no escape. Some thinkers, like
Adorno and Horkheimer, believed that the Enlightenment project
had turned against itself and transformed the quest for human

emancipation into a system of universal oppression in the name of human liberation.[2]

Modernity, after 1848, was very much an urban phenomenon. Modern life exposed us to an incredible diversity of experiences and stimuli. (This has, perhaps, been achieved at the expense of treating others in instrumental terms.) At the beginning of the twentieth century, modernity took on multiple perspectivism and relativism as its epistemology for revealing what it still took to be the true nature of a unified, though complex, underlying reality. One wing of modernity appealed to the image of rationality incorporated in the machine, the factory, the power of contemporary technology, or the city as a 'living machine'. There is, then, a keen awareness of flux and change, a fascination with language and technique, with speed and motion, with the machine and the factory system. The telephone, wireless telegraph, X-ray, cinema, automobile and aeroplane established the material foundation for new modes of thinking about and experiencing time and space. Indeed, modernity may be interpreted as a response to a crisis in the experience of time and space.

Over the last two decades, there has been another vast cultural transformation in Western societies. This shift in sensibility and practice, the nature of society, is generally called postmodernism. Here are some of the key features that are usually associated with postmodernism. First, there is an acceptance of ephemerality, fragmentation, discontinuity. Writers like Michel Foucault and Jean-François Lyotard explicitly attack any notion that there might be a metalanguage, or metatheory through which all things can be connected or represented. There is an intense distrust of all global or 'totalising' discourses, a rejection of metanarratives, of large-scale theoretical interpretations, of universal application. Condemning the metanarratives of Hegel, Marx and Freud as totalising, they insist upon the plurality of 'power-discourse', or of language games. Postmodernists reject the Hegelian view of history and the idea of progress; in philosophy there is a tendency, associated with poststructuralism and postmodernism, to be suspicious of any project that seeks universal human emancipation.

I think I can perhaps begin to describe postmodernism by listing the following features: One, a new depthlessness. Depth models (like those of appearance/essence in Marxism) are replaced by a conception of practices, discourses, textual play, surfaces and textuality. Two, history not as the real but as representation, as pastiche. This foregrounds the 'historicity' of history. Three, a new form of private temporality whose schizophrenic structure Fredric Jameson links to textuality, *écriture*, or schizophrenic writing. Four, the sublime. This is the way in which postmodernism involves the unrepresentable. The enormous force, or power, of the Kantian sublime is now no longer nature but the forces of global capitalism. Five, a new form of 'postmodern hyperspace' which has managed to transcend the capacities of the individual body to locate itself. Jameson refers to the incapacity of our minds, at least at present, to map the great global multinational and decentred communicational network in which we find ourselves caught as individual subjects.

These features have been drawn from Fredric Jameson, who has distinguished postmodernism from modernism and identified it with poststructuralism.[3] He argues that a radical break occurred between modernism and postmodernism; in his view, the latter is not a style or fashion but what he calls the 'culture in dominance' of late capitalism. Jameson contends that the final effect of the postmodern condition is the abolition of critical distance. At the same time, the prodigious new expansion of multinational capital has penetrated the pre-capitalist enclaves, Nature (the 'Third' World) and the Unconscious.

What does postmodernism mean on the cultural and political levels? On the cultural level, postmodernism implies the repudiation of the modern movement: abstract expressionism in painting, the international style in architecture, existentialism in philosophy. On the political level, it is a sharp attack on Marxism. Postmodernists actually reject the following models: the model of authenticity and inauthenticity; the semiotic opposition between signifier and signified; the Freudian model of latent and manifest; and the Marxist one of appearance and essence (the view that the empirical world 'appearance' is casually connected to deeper levels, the structures and processes of the real, 'the essence'). These 'depth' models have been replaced by a conception of practices, discourses and textual play.

THE PREOCCUPATION WITH IDENTITY

Another problematic facet of postmodernism is its view of the self. Jameson has used Lacan's description of schizophrenia as a linguistic disorder, as a breakdown in the signifying chain of meaning that creates a simple sentence. When the signifying chain snaps, then 'we have schizophrenia in the form of a rubble of distinct and unrelated signifiers'. If a person's identity is forged through 'a certain temporal unification of the past and future with the present before me', and if sentences move through the same trajectory, then an inability to unify past, present and future in the sentence betokens a similar inability to unify the past, present and future of our own biographical experience or psychic life. This fits with postmodernism's preoccupation with the signifier rather than the signified, with participation, performance and happening, rather than with an authoritative and finished art object, with surface appearance rather than underlying essence.

One of the consequences of the postmodernist view is that we can no longer conceive of the individual as alienated in the classical Marxist sense, because to be alienated presupposes a coherent rather than a fragmented sense of self from which to be alienated. It is only in terms of such a centred sense of personal identity that individuals can pursue projects over time, or think cogently about the production of a future significantly better than time present and time past. There is good reason, then, to believe that alienation of the subject is being displaced by fragmentation of the subject.

The reduction of experience to a series of pure and unrelated presents further implies that the experience of the present becomes powerfully, overwhelmingly vivid; the world comes before the schizophrenic with heightened intensity. The image, the appearance, the spectacle can all be experienced with an intensity, joy or terror, made possible only by their appreciation as pure and unrelated presents in time. The immediacy of events, the sensationalism of the spectacle become the stuff of which consciousness is constituted.

As David Harvey and others have pointed out, preoccupation with identity, with personal and collective roots, has become far more pervasive since the early 1970s. It could be said that the impulse to preserve the past is part of the impulse to preserve the self. Perhaps people try and retain their sense of identity by maintaining their links with the past? Without knowing where they have been, it is difficult to know where they are going. The past is the foundation of individual and collective identity; objects from the past are the source of significance as cultural symbols. The nostalgic impulse is an important agency in adjustment to crisis; it is a social emollient and reinforces (national) identity when confidence is weakened or threatened.

In the late nineteenth century, Britain's industrial supremacy was being challenged by Germany. Capital was going through periods of slumps and booms. Imperialism was a useful ideology because class interest could be subordinated to the British nation, the British Empire. Recently I visited the exhibition 'The Raj: India and the British 1600–1947' to learn something about the history of the country of my birth. I believe that, for many English people, the exhibition expressed nostalgia for a time when Britain was secure and strong. The Raj represented British glory. There have been so many traumatic changes during the last twenty years that many people have a longing for the past. Consider for a moment the prevalent metaphors of the present. We hear and read of fracture, crack, fault-line, gap, fissure. Why are these metaphors so prevalent? Perhaps the problem is how to live with uncertainty? In a period of rapid change, there seems to be a demand for fixed certainties.

I believe that Britain's obsession with its past is entropic (a measure of increasing disorganisation/disorder). When one sees the popularity of the 'heritage industry', which has suddenly become big business in Britain (it has even been suggested that Britain is rapidly turning from the manufacture of goods to the manufacturing of heritage!), one can believe that for many people the past seems more attractive than the present. The search for historical roots is a sign of a search for more secure moorings and longer-lasting values in a shifting world.[4] Images of the past influence the present – and the future. And there are many conflicting pasts.

One postmodernist writer, Charles Jenks, has suggested that all of us carry around with us a *musée imaginaire* in our minds drawn from experience of other places and knowledge culled from films, television, exhibitions and popular magazines.[5] It is inevitable, he says, that all of these get run together. Why, if one can afford to live in different ages and cultures, restrict oneself to the present locale? Eclecticism is the natural evolution of a culture with choice.

TIME–SPACE COMPRESSION

David Harvey's basic argument is this: the postwar boom from 1945 to 1973 was based on a Fordist–Keynesian system, but there has been a shift from Fordism to what might be called a 'flexible' regime of accumulation. There have been accelerations in turnover times in production, exchange and consumption. Capitalism is necessarily technologically dynamic because of the coercive laws of competition. There is the creation of new wants and needs. The result is to exacerbate insecurity and instability as masses of capital and workers shift from one line of production to another, leaving whole sectors devastated, while the perpetual flux in consumer wants, tastes and needs becomes a permanent locus of uncertainty and struggle.

In other words, the relatively stable aesthetic of Fordist modernism has given way to all the ferment, instability and fleeting qualities of a postmodernist aesthetic that celebrates difference, ephemerality, fashion and the commodification of cultural forms. There has been a shift in emphasis from the production of goods to the production of 'events' and spectacles. Postmodernism is concerned with the signifier rather than the signified, the medium (money) rather than the message (social labour). The emphasis is on fiction rather than function, on signs rather than things, on aesthetics rather than ethics.

Many commentators have attributed the postmodern shift to a crisis in our experience of space and time, a crisis in which spatial categories come to dominate those of time, while themselves undergoing such a mutation that we cannot keep pace. Beneath the veneer of common sense and seemingly natural ideas about space and time, there lie hidden terrains of ambiguity, contradiction and struggle. How we represent space and time in theory is important because it affects how we and others interpret and then act with respect to the world. Symbolic orderings of space and time provide a framework for experience through which we learn who or what we are in society.

According to Harvey, the relations between money, space and time are interlocking sources of social power. He makes frequent reference to the concept of 'time–space compression', the processes that so revolutionise the objective qualities of space and time that we are forced to alter how we represent the world to ourselves. The word 'compression' is used to convey the point that the history of capitalism has been characterised by a speed-up in the pace of life.

Consider the effects on our lives of the innovations in transport: between 1500 and 1850, the best average speed of horse-drawn coaches and sailing ships was 10 mph; between 1850 and 1930, steam locomotives averaged 65 mph. In the 1950s, propeller aircraft flew at 400 mph. In the 1960s, jet passenger aircraft flew at 500–700 mph. In the 1980s, supersonic aircraft attained speeds greater than sound – 800 mph.[6]

Harvey then considers the development of maps and their functions; how, for example, the totalising vision of the map allowed strong senses of national, local and personal identities to be constructed in the midst of geographical differences.

The world is changing so rapidly that the result has been the production of fragmentation, insecurity, an ephemeral, uneven development within a highly unified global economy of capital flows. In the realm of commodity production, the primary effect has been to emphasise the values and virtues of instantaneity and disposability. But what profound changes are taking place in human psychology? Alvin Toffler has suggested that these changes create temporariness in the structure of both public and personal value systems which in turn provide a context for the 'crack-up of consensus' and the diversification of values within a fragmenting society.

In such a society, images have, in a sense, become commodities. This phenomenon has led the French sociologist Jean Baudrillard to argue that Marx's analysis of commodity production is outdated because capitalism is now predominantly concerned with the production of signs, images and sign systems rather than with commodities themselves.[7]

I will be discussing Baudrillard's work fully in the next chapter, but I would like to introduce here the concept of 'simulacrum' which he has done much to popularise. By 'simulacrum' is meant a state of perfect replication where there is no 'original' and the copy becomes almost impossible to differentiate. The production of simulacra is relatively easy, given modern techniques. Insofar as identity is increasingly dependent upon images, this means that the replication of identities, individual, corporate, institutional and political, becomes a very real possibility and problem. (We know that image-makers and the media are assuming a very powerful role in the shaping of political identities.) This raises the question: what happens to cultural forms when the imitations become real, and the real takes on many of the qualities of an imitation?

This general implication is that through the experience of everything from food to culinary habits, music, television, entertainment and cinema, it is now possible to experience the world's geography vicariously, as a simulacrum. The interweaving of simulacra in daily life brings together different worlds of commodities in the same space and time. But it does so in such a way as to conceal almost perfectly any trace of origin, of the labour processes that produce them, or of the social relations implicated in their production.

What Harvey's book does very well is to draw attention to the intensity of time–space compression in Western capitalism since the 1960s with all its congruent features of excessive ephemerality and fragmentation in the political and private as well as in the social realm. He sees postmodernism as part of a history of successive waves of time–space compression generated out of the pressures of capital accumulation, with its perpetual quest to annihilate space through time and reduce turnover time. Harvey thinks that the emphasis, in postmodernism, upon ephemerality, collage, fragmentation and dispersal in philosophical and social thought mimics the conditions of flexible accumulation. In such a situation, there is a search for personal and collective identity.

Most people agree that a massive cultural shift has occurred, but few agree about what it means. Does postmodernism represent a radical break with modernism, or is it simply a revolt within modernism against a certain form of it? What is the effect of its opposition to all forms of metanarratives ('the big stories')? Some writers depict postmodernism as the exhaustion of modernism. Others, like Jameson, see postmodernism as nothing more than 'the cultural logic of late capitalism'.

I think that Harvey and Jameson are in broad agreement: they both see postmodernism as a cultural expression of the economic changes taking place within capitalism. While Jameson draws on the economic theory of Ernest Mandel, Harvey refers to the work of Michel Aglietta.[8] (It should be noted that other theorists, such as Scott Lash and John Urry, also refer to the same economic changes but use the term 'disorganised capitalism'.)

Harvey, being a geographer, emphasises the effects of time–space compression, and sees postmodernism as a historical–geographical condition of a certain sort. Clearly wishing to influence geographers, he gives a geographical reading of postmodernism. His book is a brilliant attempt to redefine the field so that it incorporates recent debates.

I have few criticisms of Harvey's compressed account. He refers to Foucault, Derrida, Lyotard, Baudrillard and others in passing, but there is no systematic discussion of any of these influential thinkers. Of course, I know that his book is not meant to be a philosophical work. But, on the other hand, it could be argued that these are the theorists who have intellectually created and popularised many of the ideas associated with postmodernism.

Harvey concedes that the metanarratives, the 'big stories' of modernism, tended to neglect important differences. As postmodernism privileges heterogeneity and difference, there is a re-emergence of concern for the validity and dignity of 'the other'. Postmodernism has been particularly important in acknowledging the multiple forms of otherness as they emerge from differences in subjectivity, gender, sexuality, class and 'race'.

However, many thinkers believe that the rhetoric of postmodernism is dangerous, for it avoids the reality of political economy and the circumstances of global power. Metatheory cannot be dispensed with. In Jameson's view, postmodernists simply push it underground where it continues to function as a 'now unconscious effectivity'.[9]

What I find valuable in Harvey's text is his concern with difference and otherness, not as something to be added on to more fundamental Marxist categories (like class, and productive forces), but as something that should be omnipresent from the very beginning in any attempt to grasp the dialectics of social change. Secondly, his work is useful in that, besides drawing our attention to the dimensions of space and time, he recognises that the production of images and discourses are important activities that have to be analysed. Thirdly, he draws attention to what is valuable in historical materialism; he wishes to emphasise narrative against the image, of ethics against aesthetics, of the project of Becoming rather than Being, and the search for Unity within Difference.

There are many problems in this area. What is the nature of the present? Are we still in a stage of modernity? Or, are we living in a completely new stage, which some call postmodernity? Very briefly, one current debate within this area runs as follows: when postmodernism is being discussed, whose condition is being talked about?

Is postmodernism a generalised experience? There is, however, the argument that people are actually placed in very different positions. Consider a woman trying to collect water for five hours a day in the Sahel, an old pensioner in a cold bedsit in London, and a young person, who loves music and football, living a life of poverty in a Brazilian *fevala*. There are, it seems to me, a huge number of people who do not experience the time–space compression that is supposed to be characteristic of postmodernism.[10]

I would like to present a counter-example. Though the developing countries do not have the same economic conditions as the West, they are all being penetrated by capitalist culture and technology – particularly in the cities. Someone was telling me the other day about television-viewing in a Nigerian village. On the day 'Dallas' is being shown, everyone gathers together, and the young people explain what is happening on the screen to the old people. The young people, it could be argued, are learning some of the subtle complexities of human relationships in rapidly-changing societies. You may think that 'Dallas' is an example of American cultural imperialism. Are these programmes wishful dreams of the poor? But, after all, is this not similar to what the popular Indian cinema provides? One of the ironies of postmodernism is that, philosophically, it rejects universalism and espouses relativism. And yet it is postmodernism in the Developing World that is universalising sensibilities and transforming identities.

I may have given a false impression of the current debate as if it was between two polarised, bitterly divided, camps: neo-Marxists and pro-Enlightenment thinkers versus post-Marxists and postmodernists. This is too simple a picture. There are social theorists who are critical of some aspects of Marxism and postmodernism and have developed a range of quite complex positions.

To conclude this chapter, I want to mention briefly some criticisms that have been made of postmodernism. While postmodernism seems to celebrate intellectual and social indeterminacy, its own self-definition inevitably confers a degree of unity and coherence upon social evolution; and yet unity, coherence and evolution are just the sort of values which postmodernism wants to abandon. To put it simply, postmodernism is against big intellectual stories (metanarratives), but postmodernism is itself such a story.

Postmodernism cannot be said to be new; after all, most of what it advocates was already present in Nietzsche's work. We have to admit either that postmodernism has been around for a very long time, or that modernism has contained within itself, for quite a long time, a postmodern dimension.[11]

From the fact that there exist a great many different discourses or 'language games', Lyotard states that there can be no possible common standards which cut across all discourses. It has been argued that this is a wrong inference and that there must be some overarching notions of validity which govern all mini-discourses. A relativist position is invalid because, like all relativism, it is self-contradictory. To say that values are incommensurable is, in a way, an absolute claim to validity, and this is something which relativists hold to be impossible. Furthermore, relativism encourages intellectual and human indifference. If all values are relative to specific cultures, discourses or languages, then why make any claims at all about what is right, just or true? Why bother to hold any views about anything?[12]

Anthony Giddens, who has made some of the above criticisms, argues against two ideas: first, that there are indubitable foundations, truths or methods; and, second, that history has a hidden, essential meaning and direction. Antagonistic to both these ideas, he believes in a form of critical reason that involves questioning all beliefs. This critical 'voice', which exists within modern thought, is suspicious of reason and progress. Giddens calls this inherently self-critical aspect of the Enlightenment project 'reflexivity'.[13]

In his view, postmodernism is best understood as 'radicalised modernity', modernity coming to terms with its own intrinsic reflexivity. Giddens connects the rise and fall of Enlightenment reason with the rise and decline of Western civilisation more generally. He states that the Enlightenment project, with its intellectual tools of reason and progress, was in a way an industrial, capitalist, Western project which dominated other cultures.

NOTES

1. David Harvey, *The Condition of Postmodernity* (Oxford: Basil Blackwell, 1989).
2. Max Horkheimer and Theodor Adorno, *The Dialectic of Enlightenment* (New York: The Seabury Press, 1972).
3. See Fredric Jameson, 'Postmodernism, or the Cultural Logic of Late Capitalism', *New Left Review*, 146 (1984): 53–92. A version of this article is in Hal Foster (ed.), *Postmodern Culture* (London: Pluto, 1985), p. 118.
4. R. Hewison, *The Heritage Industry: Britain in a Climate of Decline* (London: Methuen, 1987). A thoughtful book on these themes is Patrick Wright, *On Living in an Old Country: The National Past in Contemporary Britain* (London: Verso, 1985).
5. Charles Jenks, *The Language of Postmodern Architecture* (London: Academy Editions, 1984).
6. Harvey, op. cit., p. 241.
7. Jean Baudrillard, *For a Critique of the Political Economy of the Sign* (St Louis: Telos Press, 1981).
8. Ernest Mandel, *Late Capitalism* (London: Verso, 1978); Michel Aglietta, *A Theory of Capitalist Regulation* (London: Verso, 1979); Scott Lash and John Urry, *The End of Organized Capitalism* (Oxford: Oxford University Press, 1987).
9. Jameson, op. cit.
10. I underline experience because, at the present time, different accounts of postmodernity are being advanced by different authors. There is much confusion and conceptual slippage. Postmodernity, according to Wayne Hudson, is characterised as a myth, a periodisation, a condition or situation, an experience, a historical consciousness, a sensibility, a climate, a crisis, an episteme, a discourse, a poetics, a retreat, a topos, a task or project. These diverse characterisations of postmodernity may represent different entry points into the discussion. See Wayne Hudson, 'Postmodernity and Contemporary Social Thought', in Peter Lassman (ed.), *Politics and Social Thought* (London: Routledge, 1989).
11. For useful discussions of the 'founding propositions' of postmodernism, see the articles by Lyotard, Habermas, Jameson and others in Thomas Docherty (ed.), *Postmodernism: A Reader* (London: Harvester Wheatsheaf, 1993).
12. Peter Dews (ed.), *'Introduction' to Habermas: Autonomy and Solidarity* (London: Verso, 1986).
13. Anthony Giddens, *The Consequences of Modernity* (Cambridge: Polity Press, 1990).

8

•

BAUDRILLARD: IMAGES AND IDENTITY
IN CONSUMER SOCIETY

Dogs sexuality against norms marginalization

Our identities are influenced, among other things, by what we consume, what we wear, the commodities we buy, what we see and read, how we conceive our sexuality, what we think of society and the changes we believe it is undergoing. Our identities are formed, partly, by what we think of ourselves, and how we relate to everyday life. Of course, the role of language and culture is crucial in all this. Advertising, fashion, popular culture and the mass media are also powerful institutions to be considered.

identity as social rejection of consumer myths create own identities

The ways in which we relate to, use, dominate or are dominated by objects is an important area of study. Consumption is a mode of being, a way of gaining identity, meaning and prestige in contemporary society. How does consumption constitute us? How does possession of objects and display of signs of affluence affect us and our view of others? Why do we want prestige only in certain areas and not in others?

There are many topics to be examined. To what extent is the new postmodern era constituted by simulations, new forms of technology, culture and experience? Are the new technologies altering our sense of ourselves? Some people believe that television, for example, privatises individuals, trapping them in a universe of simulacra in which it is impossible to distinguish between the spectacle and the real. One of the elements in our sense of identity is the body and its experiences. Moreover, sexuality can no longer be a private, individualised affair; it is socially defined and normalised. And what is the modern individual's attitude to death, and how does this influence identity? Some of these topics will be raised and discussed in this chapter. I will do this by looking at the work of the French philosopher, Jean Baudrillard. I have selected Baudrillard for two reasons: first, he is typical of many continental theorists who have shifted from neo-Marxism to the political right. Second, his work is valuable in that he draws attention to the increasingly fundamental role of signs and images in a postmodernist world.

IDENTITY IN THE CONSUMER SOCIETY

Jean Baudrillard was trained as a sociologist, and in his early work during the 1960s and 1970s, he merged the Marxian critique of capitalism with studies of consumption, fashion, media, sexuality and the consumer society. These texts can be read as a reconstruction of Marxian theory in the light of the new social conditions then appearing in France.

France (like other advanced nations) was qualitatively different in the 1960s from the France of the 1950s. There were different analyses of this change, and thinkers had different names for these changes. Baudrillard called the new social formation 'the consumer society', while others referred to it as 'the technological society' (Ellul), 'the post-industrial society' (Aron and Touraine), 'the society of the spectacle' (Debord), or 'the bureaucratic society of controlled consumption' (Lefebvre).[1]

The young Baudrillard was deeply influenced by the work of Henri Lefebvre, his teacher, and Roland Barthes. Lefebvre believed in taking seriously phenomena from everyday life where they had been neglected previously and which tended to remain separated from the domain of 'high culture'. A Marxist, he was interested in the possibilities of change within everyday life, and wrote influential studies on consumption, architecture, urbanisation, the role of language and culture.

Roland Barthes is well known for his analyses of the way in which the mythologies of advertising, fashion, popular culture and the mass media attempt to transform petit-bourgeois culture into a universal 'nature'. He saw these mythologies/ideologies as naturalising contemporary bourgeois society, making it appear that a historically-produced society was an expression of nature by erasing and covering over contradictions or making them appear 'normal'. At its best, Baudrillard's early work provides the sort of critical theory and concrete analysis of everyday life and the social world produced by Lefebvre and Barthes.[2]

Baudrillard's first three books focus on the ways in which culture, ideology and signs function in everyday life.[3] They are written, broadly, from a neo-Marxist point of view. The first book, *Le système des objets*, begins with a description of the ways in which we relate to, use, dominate or are dominated by the system of objects and signs which constitute our everyday life. The analyses given presuppose the theory of the commodification of everyday life under capitalism advanced by Marxists like Georg Lukács, semiological theories in which objects are interpreted as signs which are organised into systems of signification.[4]

The second book, *La société de consommation*, states that in the new world of consumption there are affluent individuals who are no longer surrounded by other human beings, as they were in the past, but by objects. Just as the wolf-child becomes a wolf by living among them, so we are ourselves becoming functional objects. He suggests that consumption constitutes a total homogenisation and organisation of everyday life. The consumer believes that possession and display of the signs of affluence will bring happiness and prestige.

Baudrillard argues that the entire system of production produces a system of needs that are rationalised, homogenised, systematised and hierarchised. Individuals are induced to buy not a single commodity but an entire system of objects and needs through which one differentiates oneself socially, yet integrates oneself into the consumer society.

Consumerism requires a vast labour to learn about the products, to master their use and to earn the money and leisure to purchase and use them. Consumption is thus a productive activity which requires education and effort; it is normative behaviour which signifies that one is a member of this society. The consumer cannot avoid the obligation to consume, because it is consumption that is the primary mode of social integration and the primary ethic and activity within the consumer society.

Just as rural populations were indoctrinated in the nineteenth century into industrial labour, the production sector, the masses are socialised in the twentieth century into the consumption sector. In the consumer society, consumption has replaced production as the central mode of social behaviour. Consumption is a mode of being, a way of gaining identity, meaning and prestige in the contemporary society. In this early work, Baudrillard was much influenced by Thorstein Veblen's *Theory of the Leisure Class*. Whereas in Veblen's book display is confined to the upper classes, Baudrillard sees the entire society as organised around consumption and display of commodities through which individuals gain identity and prestige.

Influenced by the structural linguistics of Saussure, Baudrillard argues that commodities are structured into a system of sign values governed by rules, codes and a social logic. What are sign values? Marx analysed the commodity in terms of 'use value' and 'exchange value'. Use value was defined by the use and enjoyment of a commodity in everyday life, whereas exchange value was defined by its worth in the marketplace. To Marx's concepts, use and exchange value, Baudrillard has added the concept 'sign value'. Sign values are socially-constructed prestige values which are appropriated and displayed in consumption. Commodities are not the locus of the satisfaction of needs, as classical political economy claims, but confer social meaning and prestige, which serve as indices of social standing in the consumer society.

This theory implies that certain objects or brands are chosen over others because of their sign value – that is, their relative prestige over other brands or types of commodities. Consumer societies are constituted by hierarchies of sign values in which one's social standing and prestige are determined by where one stands within the semiological system of consumption and sign values.

Against classical Marxism, Baudrillard argues that the object of political economy must be conceptualised as a sign as well as a commodity, at the same time suggesting to semiologists that objects be regarded as commodities as well as signs. I think that Baudrillard's analysis of consumption provides a useful supplement to classical Marxism: through objects, a stratified society speaks.

THE PROLIFERATION OF SIGNS

In his first three books, Baudrillard assumed that the logics of production and signification were intertwined in contemporary societies. From *The Mirror of Production* (1975), Baudrillard gradually erased political economy and capital from his theory.[5] Baudrillard repudiates Marxism altogether in this book. He rejects Marxism both as a 'mirror' or reflection of a 'productivist' capitalism and as a 'classical' mode of representation that purports to mirror 'the real'. Using Jacques Lacan's concepts of 'the mirror stage' and 'the imaginary', he argues that, in Marxism, individuals come to an 'imaginary' understanding of production, labour and value.[6] This Marxian imaginary speaks to what is wrong with life under capitalism, alienated labour, exploitation and so on, and provides a fantasy of a non-alienated life. Yet the Marxian imaginary, Baudrillard maintains, simply reproduces the primacy of production. Marx's productivist logic is reductive because it reduces everything to labour and the mode of production and so cannot account for many social phenomena like communication.

In place of the domination of all human activity in capitalist society by exchange value or use value (that is, the idea that what is valuable is that which is useful or has monetary worth), Baudrillard proposes valorisation of what has no value in capitalist terms, but only symbolic value. Thus he proposes a new term, that of symbolic exchange.

Baudrillard sharply contrasts symbolic exchange to production and consumption. The term derives from George Bataille's notion of a 'general economy', in which expenditure, waste, sacrifice and destruction were claimed to be more fundamental than economies of production and utility. Bataille took as his model the sun, which freely expends its energy without asking anything in return. The sun bestows its energy and warmth on the earth, thereby providing a model of unilateral gift-giving and free bestowing of excess. Both Bataille and Baudrillard presuppose here a contradiction between human nature and capitalism. They assume that humans 'by nature' gain pleasure from such things as expenditure, waste, festivities and sacrifices, in which they are sovereign, and are free to expend their energy excess and thus follow their 'real nature'.

Baudrillard also presupposes a fundamental dividing line in history between symbolic societies – that is, societies organised around symbolic exchange – and productivist societies; that is, societies organised around production. He thus rejects the Marxian philosophy of history which posits the primacy of production in all societies, and the concept of socialism, arguing that it does not break radically enough with capitalist productivism. It offers itself merely as more efficient and equitable organisation of production rather than a completely different sort of society with a different logic, with different activities and values.

To recapitulate, Baudrillard contrasts his ideal of symbolic exchange to the logic of production, utility and instrumental rationality which governs capitalist societies. Baudrillard celebrates symbolic exchange. This includes activities like gratuitous gift-giving, festivities, destruction, sacrifice and waste.[7] In other words, it involves the giving of gifts or goods for no particular reason, the expenditure of time and energy for no particular purpose, and engagement in activities – festive, destructive, or whatever – from which one gains no benefits or profits and which have no discernible uses.

One of Baudrillard's main theses is that the era of production is over and that we have now entered a new era in which the production of objects has been replaced by the production and proliferation of signs. In *L'échange symbolique et la mort* (1976), Baudrillard writes that we live in an era in which the new technologies – media, computers, information processes, entertainment and knowledge industries – replace industrial production and political economy as the organising principle of society.[8] Labour is no longer a force of production, but is itself a sign among signs. Signs and codes have become the primary constituents of social life.

THE BODY AND ITS DEATH

Another topic on which Baudrillard has written provocatively is the body. Both modern and postmodern French theory have focused a lot of attention on the body. In the 1940s, Maurice Merleau-Ponty and Jean-Paul Sartre discussed the body and its experiences as a reaction against the previous mentalist tradition in philosophy. Later, French writers like Roland Barthes, Michel Foucault, Jacques Derrida and others rejected the tradition of Cartesian mind–body dualism, and focused attention on bodily experiences, modes of dressing, fashion, pleasure, desire and suffering.

Baudrillard noted the ways in which design was transforming the body: 'Everything belongs to design, everything springs from it, whether it says or not: the body is designed, sexuality is designed, political, social, human relations are designed . . .'.[9] There is a spiralling expansion of fashion, and it is penetrating into ever more domains of experience. Since the late 1920s, there has been a convergence of propaganda and advertising; thus advertising today tends to be propaganda for itself and for whatever product, politician, idea or life-style it is trying to sell.

Baudrillard has written perceptively on what he sees as the repression of death in Western thought since the sixteenth century. Psychologically, people in modern societies want to repress death, not to think or talk about it. He notes that the dead were placed in cemeteries which were gradually moved further and further away from the centre of towns. All value is placed on life and on the living, and thus 'it is not normal to be dead'. Yet this exclusion of death from 'normality' means that it haunts us all the more powerfully.[10]

In so-called primitive societies, there was no real division between life and death. One lived with the dead, their spirits, their memories and their achievements. In these societies, symbolic exchange between life and death continuously took place. There was no fear of death or obsession with death, for it was an integral part of everyday life. This was also true of the West during the Middle Ages. It is only during the beginning of the sixteenth century that death becomes individualised, repressed and excluded from social life. Deprived of the intimate relation with death, the modern individual lives haunted by the fear of death and readily submits to social authorities, the Church and/or the State, which promise immortality or protection from death.

Baudrillard asserts that the division between life and death serves as foundation for social exclusion; the dead are the paradigm of social exclusion and discrimination. Life and death, society and nature, the real and the unreal – all divisions contain the projection of an imaginary of its opposite by the privileged term. Baudrillard argues against binary oppositions in general.

THE ROLE OF THE MEDIA

It has already been stated that whereas modernity centred on the production of things, commodities and products, postmodernity is characterised by a proliferation of signs. Following Marshall McLuhan, Baudrillard interprets modernity as a process of explosion of commodification, mechanisation, technology and market relations, in contrast to postmodern society, which is the site of an implosion of all boundaries, distinctions between high and low culture, appearance and reality.[11] Baudrillard argues that we live in a 'hyperreality' of simulations in which images, spectacles and the play of signs have replaced the logic of production and class conflict.

In the new, postmodern era, the model structures social reality. There is an erosion of the distinction between the model and the real. Using McLuhan's cybernetic concept of implosion, Baudrillard claims that in the contemporary world the boundary between representation and reality implodes, and that, as a result, the experience and ground of 'the real' disappear. In this new social order, it is signs and codes that constitute the 'real'.

Baudrillard believes that contemporary theories refer (intertextually) primarily to other theories rather than to a 'real' outside. He suggests that individuals are so caught up in a world of commodity signs, media spectacles, representations and simulations that there is no longer any access to a real which is itself presented as an effect of the code or system. In such a world, everything becomes undecidable.

It becomes increasingly difficult to distinguish true from false, or good from bad, for in the society of simulations it is impossible to gain access to a real, or to perceive what is determining or constituting various events and processes.

Previously, the media were believed to mirror, reflect or refer to reality, whereas now they are coming to constitute a 'hyperreality'. Baudrillard sees the function of television and mass media as prevention of response, by isolating and privatising individuals, trapping them in a universe of simulacra in which it is impossible to distinguish between the spectacle and the real.[12] In such a situation, individuals come to prefer spectacle to reality. Through the media, we enter a new form of subjectivity, in which we become saturated with information, images and events. The media now provide a simulacra of actual events which themselves become more real than 'the real' which they supposedly represent. We internalise the media and thus become merely terminals within media systems. There are many references in Baudrillard's writings to the masses, the silent majorities, who passively consume commodities, television, sports, politics and information to such an extent that traditional politics and class struggle have become obsolete.

FROM THE ERA OF PRODUCTION TO THE ERA OF SIMULATION

As mentioned in the previous chapter, Baudrillard has developed a theory of simulacra. Simulacra are reproductions of objects or events. The 'orders of simulacra' form various stages in the relationships between simulacra and the 'real'. I will now outline Baudrillard's historical sketch of the orders of simulacra. In the feudal era, there was a fixed social order which established a hierarchy of signs of class, rank and social position. Signs at this stage were fixed, restricted, perfectly clear and transparent. During this period, one could readily read from an individual's clothes and appearance his or her social rank and status. From the Renaissance to the beginning of the Industrial Revolution, the unmediated real was replaced by the 'counterfeit'. In the first order of simulacra, stucco, theatre, fashion and baroque art, for example, are valorised over 'natural' signs. Instead of the fixed, feudal hierarchy of signs, there was an artificial, democratised world of signs which valorised artifice.[13]

The second order of simulacra (modernism) appeared during the Industrial Revolution, when infinite reproducibility was introduced into the world in the form of the industrial simulacrum or series. Production then became mechanised, and turned out series of mass objects, exact replicas, infinitely produced and reproduced by assembly-line processes and eventually automation. Baudrillard illustrates the difference between the first and second order of simulacra by a comparison between an automaton, mechanical imitations of humans, and a robot. As Walter Benjamin pointed out, with the introduction of photography and then film, even art was taken over by mechanical reproduction and lost its aura.[14]

The third order of simulacra: this is the stage in which we live now, no longer that of the counterfeit of an original as in the first order, nor that of the pure series as in the second. In the third order or simulacrum (postmodernity) which is our current system formed after the Second World War, production is replaced by the simulation model. The functioning of social logic passes from commodity to sign. In this order, there is binarism. Two parties, two superpowers, centre/periphery (youth, women, gays, blacks), capitalism/communism guarantee the stability of simulacrum. What Marx considered as the 'non-essential' part of capital, such as advertising, media, information and communication networks, becomes the essential sphere. This is the stage in which simulation models come to constitute the world, and overtake and finally 'devour' representation. Models take precedence over things.

market
area
vs
capitalism

Media practices have rearranged our senses of space and time. What is real is no longer our direct contact with the world, but what we are given on the TV screen. Television is the world: TV is dissolved into life, and life is dissolved into TV. No longer is there any space between subject and object, seeing and seen, cause and effect. Nothing separates one pole from the other; there is a sort of contraction in each other, a fantastic telescoping, a collapsing of the two traditional poles into one another: an implosion.

A SOCIETY OF SIMULATIONS

Baudrillard believes that everything is reduced to a binary system whose two supposedly dominant poles – political parties, world superpowers, seemingly opposing forces or principles – cancel out their differences, and serve to maintain a self-regulating, selfsame, self-reproducing system. What appear to be oppositional, outside, or threatening to the system are really functional parts of a society of simulations, mere 'alibis' which only enhance social control.

Baudrillard gives a few examples. In his view, the Watergate affair exhibited the political scandals and illegal acts of the Nixon administration so as to create the illusion that the system in fact respected and embodied law and order.[15] The scandal thus served to mask the perception that the system itself is fundamentally a scandal, being immoral and cruel. In a similar manner, Baudrillard claims that Disneyland presents itself as an imaginary space so as to conceal the fact that it is the 'real' country. In fact, all of 'real' America is Disneyland. Disneyland is meant to be an infantile world, in order to make us believe that adults are elsewhere in the 'real' world, and to conceal the fact that real childishness is everywhere.

The era of modernity was dominated by production and industrial capitalism. The new postmodern era is constituted by 'simulations', new forms of technology, culture and experience. Modernity was the era of Marx and Freud, the era in which politics, culture and social life were interpreted as epiphenomena of the economy, or everything was interpreted in terms of desire or the unconscious. These 'hermeneutics of suspicion' used depth models to demystify reality and show the underlying realities behind (or underlying) appearance, the factors that constituted the facts. Modernity is grounded in the dialectics of history, the economy or desire, and it is assumed that there is a hidden dimension, an unseen yet stable and fixed substratum or foundation. In contrast, in postmodern society everything is visible, explicit, transparent, unstable, temporary.

Though having much in common with Michel Foucault, Baudrillard attacked his work in the book *Forget Foucault* (1977). Foucault conceptualised power as if it was dispersed in/through a multiplicity of sites, discourses, practices and strategies, but he failed (argues Baudrillard) to analyse simulations of power, the ways in which power is feigned, masqueraded and simulated, and the ways in which signs of power often displace and replace actual relations of force and discipline.[16]

Like Foucault, Baudrillard has written on sexuality. Baudrillard believes that, in a society in which sexuality speaks in advertising, fashion, the media and other popular discourses, it is manifest and open throughout social life. With sexuality no longer private and hidden or repressed, its discourses take on new meanings. Sexuality has lost its mystery: it is no longer a private, individualised, personal affair, but is socially defined and normalised. Sexuality is henceforth something that is encouraged, organised and colonised by social discourses. Everything is sexuality. And if everything is sexuality, then nothing is really sexuality any more.

Baudrillard contrasts the logic of production which governs Freudian–Marxian theories of sexual liberation with his own theory of seduction. In Baudrillard's work, the term 'seduction' replaces symbolic exchange as the privileged oppositional term to the world of production. Seduction is that which is everywhere and always opposed to production. Ever since Plato, seduction has been a polemical target of the philosophers who have worried about misguided souls being seduced by appearances and missing out on the reality behind the seductive veil of perceptual illusion. In the philosophical tradition, seduction is traditionally taken as the realm of artifice and appearance, versus that of nature and reality.

Baudrillard does not interpret seduction in the sense of enticing someone to have sexual intercourse, but as a ritual, a game, with its own rules, charms, snares and lures. It takes place on the level of appearance, surface and signs, and is thus fundamentally artificial, unlike the 'natural' pursuit of sexual power.

In his later work, one of Baudrillard's themes is the triumph of objects over subjects within the proliferation of an object world so completely out of control that it surpasses all attempts to understand, conceptualise and control it. For example, in his book *Les stratégies fatales* (1983), Baudrillard describes the 'fatal strategies' whereby objects come to fascinate, challenge, seduce and ultimately overpower the subject. One of Baudrillard's constant themes, from the beginning, has been the growing power of the world of objects over the subject. I have already referred to Baudrillard's early work in which he explored the ways in which commodities fascinate individuals in consumer society.

Fascination with the object has accelerated rapidly, and the subject has found him or herself more and more immersed, plugged in, networked, and seduced by the world of things. The defeat of the subject by the object renders dreams of liberation a mirage and an illusion. It seems that Baudrillard has forgotten that it is impossible to envisage a world of objects without human subjectivity. Surely we need to adopt a dialectical view? The subject is in some ways an effect of objects, but at the same time the object is in some ways an effect of subjects.

Jacques Derrida and others have argued that metaphysics is simply a form of binary thinking which takes one term of a series of binary oppositions and illicitly privileges it as primal, grounding and fundamental, whereas deconstructive analysis can show that it is really derivative of – even inferior to – its opposite.[17] I mention this because the concepts which Baudrillard uses have become increasingly binary. Baudrillard's early writings contrast productivist societies with symbolic societies, exchange and use value with symbolic exchange, production with seduction, with the latter privileged over the former. One commentator, Douglas Kellner, states that a pervasive set of binary oppositions pervades Baudrillard's texts of the 1980s, and one of the binaries is claimed to be superior or preferable to the other. The fundamental binaries include subject/object, masculine/feminine, appearance/reality, depth/surface, production/sign.

As I said earlier, Baudrillard's early writings were neo-Marxian but, about 1970, he started to valorise symbolic exchange. He began to be interested in simulations and simulacra. Later, the concept of symbolic exchange was replaced by the concept of 'seduction'. The main value of his work lies in the fact that he draws our attention to the increasingly fundamental role of signs and images in consumer society. A post-Marxist, he argues that society has entered a new stage in which the theories and categories of the previous stage are no longer adequate or relevant to the new social conditions. Previous theories, like Marxism, are no longer useful or relevant to the new situation. He asserts that politics today is intrinsically equivalent to advertising, publicity, sports, fashion and special effects. It is not surprising that in his work the masses are weak and passive, almost completely determined, and there is an absence of any theory of political agency.

My father was the first Indian in the village to pass 'O'-level English. This enabled him to become a clerk in the Indian Civil Service. I've also been told that at one time he was a devout Hindu, and that he left his young family to go to the mountains to live there like a sadhu, but friends went and reminded him of his family duties and persuaded him to return .

My first memory of him is in our house in Simla. After he came home from work, he used to change his European clothes for Indian ones (a dhoti). He seemed to spend most evenings sorting out the many large tins which contained lentils and other foodstuffs. After my mother died, he lived alone. No-one ever came to the house. I have been told about the strong family ties in India, and so I have never understood this.

I remember very little about my father. A strong, well-built man,

I know he enjoyed walking. I also remember him showing me an electric gadget for making hot drinks: a little element that fitted into a light socket, which heated the water in a cup. Why do I remember such trivial things and not anything important ?

I cannot remember anyone telling me that I was going to England. I did not know where England was. I have learned that father and Bubi did not get along very well. In Bristol, on my first day at the primary school, he accompanied me and I felt embarrassed by him, I'm not sure why. When his six months' leave was over, he returned to India. I can't remember saying goodbye to him, but I can remember that after he left, people spoke to me and I did not reply. I think I did not hear them. I went deaf.

That was the last time I saw my father. Years later, I was told that he had died. As I had not seen him for years, and I did not know what death was, it did not seem to make much difference. I must have thought of him as a continuing absence. Now, of course, I realise that I did not, could not have mourned for him. There are two stories about his death. One is that he was last seen waiting at a railway station and that he died of cholera during the needless partition of India in 1947. The other story is that he, a Hindu living in the Muslim town of Sailkot, was killed and robbed in his house.

Looking back, I do wish I had known him. Having an English education was considered very prestigious, and I appreciate his sacrifice; but I often wonder about the emotional costs. It's pointless to think about what my life would have been like if I had stayed in India. I have not thought about that for some time.

When, a few years ago, my eldest brother Rashid stayed at my house for a night, he said to me: 'You are just like your father – your gestures, even your life-style'. I was astonished, and wondered how this could be, as I had not really known him. But I think he was right. I can feel my father's influence all around me. I am crying as I write this. My wish to do well, the desire to be educated, my compulsion to try and write, to study, is as if I were saying to him: 'Am I educated enough? Do I have your approval now, Father?

NOTES

1. Douglas Kellner, *Jean Baudrillard: From Marxism to Postmodernism and Beyond* (Cambridge: Polity Press, 1989), p. 3.
2. See, for example, Henri Lefebvre, *Everyday Life in the Modern World* (London: Allen Lane, 1971); Roland Barthes, *Mythologies* (London: Paladin, 1972); Roland Barthes, *Image – Music – Text* ed. Stephen Heath (London: Collins, 1977).
3. Baudrillard's first three books are: *Le système des objets* (Paris: Denoël-Gonthier, 1968); *La société de consommation* (Paris: Gallimard, 1970); *For a Critique of the Political Economy of the Sign* (St Louis: Telos Press, 1981).
4. Georg Lukács, *History and Class Consciousness* (London: Merlin Press, 1971).

5. Jean Baudrillard, *The Mirror of Production* (St Louis: Telos Press, 1975).
6. The imaginary is part of three linked terms: imaginary, symbolic, real. For Lacan, the imaginary was the register, the dimension of images, conscious or unconscious, perceived or imagined. The imaginary is not the opposite of 'real'. The image certainly belongs to reality. Jacques Lacan, *Ecrits: A Selection* (London: Tavistock, 1977), pp. 1–7.
7. The gift, though formally gratuitous, is in effect obligatory; the gift is never free. See Marcel Mauss, *The Gift* (New York: Norton, 1967). The work of Lévi-Strauss, in particular his studies of marriage exchange, was influenced by Mauss.
8. Jean Baudrillard, *L'échange symbolique et la mort* (Paris: Gallimard, 1976).
9. Quoted in Kellner, op. cit., p. 95.
10. This point is similar to Foucault's argument about the separation of reason and unreason in *Madness and Civilisation: A History of Insanity in the Age of Reason* (London: Tavistock, 1967).
11. Baudrillard was greatly influenced by the work of Marshall McLuhan. Indeed, there are so many references to it that one wonders: is Baudrillard's work a recycling of McLuhan? Originally a literary critic in Canada, he became a cult figure in the 1960s. He attacked humanists who focused on literature and were critical of modern technology, in particular the media. When his book *Understanding Media* came out, Baudrillard reviewed it from a Marxist point of view. The review is very critical, but one can see that he is fascinated by ideas. McLuhan tried to understand the stages of culture from that of primitive society, through printing, to electronic technology. He argued that the form of the media had a more significant effect on society and knowledge than the contents carried: the medium is the message. He fantasised a new type of global community, a new universal (media) consciousness, and he believed that the media could overcome the alienation produced by the abstract rationality of book culture. Baudrillard inverts McLuhan's thesis concerning the media as extensions of the human, and argued instead that people internalise the media and thus become terminals within media systems. See Marshall McLuhan, *Understanding Media* (New York: McGraw-Hill, 1964).
12. In Britain, in 1989, the average person watched twenty-four hours and forty-four minutes of television a week. See HMSO, *Social Trends* 21, reported in *The Guardian*, 17 January, 1991, p. 8. In my view, the Gulf War was presented as a media spectacle, a television entertainment, a video game. It was also used as an endless commercial for Western technology. We looked at Iraq from seven miles up; the reality of dead Iraqi people was not shown. Yet Baudrillard argued that this war would never happen, existing as it did only as a figment of mass-media simulation. Clearly, Baudrillard does not believe in the truth/falsehood, or fact/fiction dichotomy. In his view, we have long since lost any means of distinguishing 'reality' from its simulated counterpart. For criticisms of Baudrillard, see Christopher Norris, *Uncritical Theory: Postmodernism, Intellectuals and the Gulf War* (London: Lawrence and Wishart, 1992).
13. Jean Baudrillard, *Selected Writings*, ed. Mark Poster (Stanford: Stanford University Press, 1988), pp. 135–47.
14. Walter Benjamin, 'The Work of Art in the Age of Mechanical Reproduction', in idem, *Illuminations*, ed. Hannah Arendt (London: Fontana/Collins, 1973), p. 223.
15. Richard Nixon was the only US president to resign his office. He did this in 1972 to avoid impeachment on charges of conniving at illegal practices in the Watergate scandal and consistently misrepresenting the truth to Congress.
16. Foucault remarks that by 'power' he does not mean a group of institutions and mechanisms that ensure the subservience of the citizens of a given state. Power must be understood as the multiplicity of force relations. Power is everywhere; not because it embraces everything, but because it comes from everywhere. Power is not something acquired, seized or shared, something that one holds on to or allows to slip away; power is exercised from innumerable points. Power comes from below. And where there is power, there is resistance. See Michel Foucault, *The History of*

Sexuality, vol. 1, *An Introduction* (Harmondsworth: Penguin, 1981), pp. 92–4.

17. In his critique of Rousseau, Derrida attempts to show that a whole range of distinctions between the primitive and civilised, natural and non-natural, north and south, melody and harmony fail to retain their character as opposites. Thus Rousseau's assertion of the primacy of melody over harmony is shown to falter from the beginning, as melody, in order to be melody, must already implicitly involve harmony. Music is strictly unthinkable without the supplement of harmony. See Jacques Derrida, *Of Grammatology* (Baltimore: John Hopkins University Press, 1976), p. 199; Christopher Norris, *Derrida* (London: Fontana, 1987), p. 104.

9
·

CONSUMER IDENTITY AND
COMMODITY AESTHETICS

In this chapter, I will outline an argument which attempts to link social production with human psychology. It deals with some of the same themes that appear in the early work of Baudrillard: identity in consumer society, how advertising affects, for example, fashion and our concept of sexuality. It is argued that consumer identity is formed by commodity aesthetics.

COMMODITY AESTHETICS

In this section, I want to argue that our identity is moulded as consumers; that there is something we could call consumer identity. For my argument, I am going to draw on Wolfgang Haug's book, *Critique of Commodity Aesthetics*.[1] Though it explicitly deals with 'appearance, sexuality and advertising in capitalist society', I believe that his analysis makes a valuable contribution to an understanding of identity.

The term 'commodity aesthetics' refers on the one hand to beauty, an appearance which appeals to the senses, and on the other hand to a beauty developed in the service of the realisation of exchange value, whereby commodities are designed to stimulate in the onlooker the desire to possess and the impulse to buy. Haug believes that commodity aesthetics is not a phenomenon of luxurious prodigality in a 'satiated, abundant society', but a normal and necessary function inherent in every purchase or sale.

There is a contradiction of interests between buyer and seller, use value and exchange value (or valorisation). The buyer is concerned with the satisfaction of needs, thus aiming to achieve a certain use value, by means of exchange value in the form of money. For the seller, the same use value is merely a means to convert the exchange value of his or her commodities into money. From the point of view of needing the use value, the object of the exercise has been achieved if the purchased article is usable and satisfactory; from the exchange-value side, this is achieved when the exchange value is converted into monetary form. While one values the commodities as a means of survival, the other sees such necessities as a means of valorisation. Haug argues that the valorisation standpoint (which dominates in capitalist society) is diametrically opposed to what people are and want autonomously.

Not only are the ends and means for buyer and seller in opposition, but the same act also takes place at different times and with different meanings for each party. As far as the exchange value is concerned, the transaction is completed and the purpose realised with the sale itself. From the point of view of use value and need, the sale is only the start, and is the prerequisite to the buyer's realisation of the purpose in the use and enjoyment of the purchase.

Haug then makes a distinction between the use value and the appearance of use value. From the seller's (i.e. the exchange-value) position, until the sale is effected, the commodity's promise of use value is all that counts. Right from the start, therefore, because of its economic function, the emphasis is on what the use value appears to be. Appearance becomes just as important as – and practically more so than – the commodity's being itself. Something that is simply useful, but does not appear to be so, will not sell, while something that seems to be useful will sell. Within the system of selling and buying, the aesthetic illusion, the commodity's promise of use value, becomes crucial.

Whoever controls the product's appearance can control the fascinated public by appealing to it. The product's appearance is an aspect of commodity aesthetics. Commodity aesthetics is meant to trigger off the act of buying as forcefully as possible. What counts is the image, the impression, 'scoring a hit'. Haug then considers the domination over people that is effected through their fascination with technically-produced artificial appearances, how aesthetic images capture people's sensuality. The illusion which one falls for is like a mirror in which one sees one's desires and believes them to be real. The appearance of a commodity always promises more, much more, than it can ever deliver. In this way, the illusion deceives.

Commodity aesthetics determines the direction that an individual's being takes. First of all, new commodities make the necessary chores that much easier, and then the chores become too difficult to do unaided, without inevitably buying the commodities. Finally, what is necessary cannot be distinguished from what is unnecessary but which one can no longer do without. The ideal of commodity aesthetics is to deliver the absolute minimum of use value, disguised and staged by a maximum of seductive illusion. This is a highly effective strategy because it is attuned to the yearnings and desires of people.

Haug notes the tendency of all objects of use to assume a sexual form to some extent – a tendency towards a general sexualisation of the human condition. The general sexualisation of commodities also includes people. With the help of fashion, it is possible to advertise oneself as, above all, a sexual being.

Ever since the 1920s, there has been a demand from shopkeepers for the restyling of their employees. In the larger stores, there was a new standard of looks, behaviour and self-presentation. From here, further inroads were made into moulding the appearance and behaviour of the mass of the public. Haug describes in detail how the salesroom is designed as a stage, 'a stage for entertainment'. Clothes are advertised like packaging as a means of sales promotion. There is an emphasis on physical appearance, on how the skin feels and smells, the colour, sheen and cut of hair. Of course, by gaining a new face one simultaneously loses one's own. The body shares a similar fate. 'Health and beauty means happiness' is the new slogan. Capitalism homes in on fears and unsatisfied longings, redirecting action, and defining the body in a new way, both its look and its smell, as well as its tactile sense and self-perception. These are some of the ways in which commodity aesthetics takes possession of people. And maintaining the packaging is not only expensive, but it also keeps one occupied.

Propaganda for fashionable innovation is only effective if it influences the sensual being by playing on its desires and fears. What is being thrust on the public is a whole complex of sexual perception, appearance and experience. Marketing sets a new standard in men's relationship with their bodies. Men are now obliged to maintain a certain image as an attribute of their masculinity which, apart from the effort involved in cultivating the appearance, requires the continuous acquisition of a growing number of commodities.

The stress on youthfulness must also be mentioned. Youth becomes a stereotype not only for commercial success but also for sexual attraction, and thus for what appears to be happiness and success. Now, being young equals being sexually attractive. As a result, with the threat of sexual ageing and thus isolation, there spreads a universal compulsion for people to 'cosmeticise' both themselves and the interior of their homes.

Furniture companies have designed 'interior landscapes'. These landscapes are no longer decorated with single sexual symbols, but are surrounded by a whole complex of commodities which become the environment of one's sexual life. Once this sexual landscape has been purchased, because it promises the buyer sexual satisfaction, the owner's instincts will be inexorably drawn to populate this empty sexual stage with life. He or she will have to fill the scene with desirable sexual partners. However, while each commodity fills one gap, it opens up another; each commodity and sale entails a further one.

For Haug, capitalist society is one in which the vast majority of people can find no worthwhile goal. Many people, therefore, seek distraction from this aimlessness. The illusion industry populates the spaces left empty by capitalism, and people fall victim to the fascination of commodity aesthetics. Commodities breed modes of behaviour and structure perception, sensations and power of judgement, shaping our language, clothing and understanding of ourselves, our attitudes and above all our relationship to our bodies. Haug argues that, in a society in which crucial relationships are mediated by commodities, specific contradictory modifications in the sensuality of members of society take place. He writes that, insofar as these processes that mould sensuality happen, as it were, behind one's back, they seem to be natural, characterising history as natural history.

But aesthetics is not only used to sell commodities; it is used to sell politics as well. Walter Benjamin, in a famous essay, has shown what importance the aestheticisation of politics had for fascism. He writes: 'The masses have a right to change property relations; Fascism seeks to give them an expression while preserving property. The logical result of Fascism is the introduction of aesthetics into political life.'[2] Fascism attempted to organise the newly-created proletarian masses. It used big parades, monster rallies and sports events (all of which were captured by camera and sound-recording). What the fascists did was to make an aesthetic copy of the workers' movement, adding ingredients of petit-bourgeois and peasant nostalgia for the soil, blood ties, carnival, church and ceremonies of consecration.[3]

CONSUMER IDENTITY

I think that Haug's thesis is important because he tries to undermine the barrier between 'outside' and 'inside', between social production and human psychology. He successfully shows how the development of modern commodity forms, dominated by exchange value, intersects directly with the realm of human needs and the domain of sensuality. He does not use the terms 'identity' or 'identity formation', but everything he says implies them.

Though I regard Haug's thesis as valuable for thinking about certain aspects of identity, there are some criticisms that could be made: first of all, Haug bases his discourse on Marx's analysis of the commodity form in *Capital*, and some may say that this form of argument leads to economic reductionism. Second, it could be argued that his thesis is deterministic. Human agency seems to play no part in his ultimately pessimistic view of the workings of society. The role of interpretation is minimised, and there seems to be little scope for resistance to the ruthlessness of capital.

In this chapter, I have stressed the rather deterministic 'Haug' view of consumption. I should state that, in contrast to this, there are some writers who believe that shopping can be a subversive activity with revolutionary potential.[4]

Many writers have observed that the life-world of modern individuals has been subjected to the processes of Taylorisation and Fordisation.[5] Taylorisation consists, as it were, in the simplification of choices with which individuals who are engaged in direct productive operations are confronted. It removes uncertainty and hesitation. The process of Fordisation consists in removing the skills from the operator and investing them into the machinery which s/he operates. The combined effect of the two processes on the conduct of daily life is the shift of skill-demanding decisions away from the performers to the experts.

Since living with unresolved problems is uncomfortable, solutions are actively sought; choosing them is seen as an increase of personal freedom. And yet, as the personal skills needed to deal directly with the problems are no longer available, and the solutions appear solely in the shape of marketable implements or expert advice, each successive step in the endless problem-solving, while experienced as another extension of freedom, further strengthens the network of dependency.[6]

It has been argued by Zygmunt Bauman that one now relies not on one's own experience but on expert knowers.[7] It is the experts who set the standards of normality. No pain or suffering needs to be lived with. It is felt that any discomfort ought to be removed altogether; but, instead of achieving the promised reduction in the number of problems which beset us, the increasing refinement of expert skills rebounds in the multiplication of problems. Each problem-resolution begets new problems.

The irony is that most new developments in expertise and expertly-produced 'targeted' technology are aimed at the repairing of damage perpetrated by older technology and expertise. Damage done by expertise may be cured only by more expertise. More expertise means, in its turn, more damage and more demand for expert cure.

Experts promise individuals various means and abilities to escape uncertainty and ambivalence and thus to control their own life-world. Experts have created, for example, the shopping mall. In the shopping mall, the environment is carefully controlled and monitored.[8] Experts have created this world, and there are no mixed messages in it. The malls do not sell commodities only; they sell an alternative life-world. The contemporary consumer market does not adjust the level of supply to the existing demand, but aims at the creation of new demand to match the supply potential. There are now purchasable and consumable products imbued with totemic significance. They offer kits containing all the necessary symbols with which any life-style can be assembled.

The market puts on display a wide range of identities from which one can select one's own. Commercial advertisements often show the commodities which they try to sell in their social context (that is, as a part of a particular life-style), so that the prospective customer can consciously purchase symbols of such self-identity as he or she would wish to possess.

The market also offers tools of identity-making which can be used to produce results which differ somewhat from each other and are in this way customised or personalised. Through the market, one can put together elements of the complete 'Identikit' of a DIY self. These merchandised identities come complete with the label of social approval already stuck on in advance.

It has been suggested by Stuart Hall that greater and greater numbers of people (men and women) – with however little money – play the game of using things to signify who they are.[9] Let us consider the following.

> When I rummage through my wardrobe in the morning I am
> not merely faced with a choice what to wear. I am faced with a
> choice of images: the difference between a smart suit and a pair
> of overalls, a leather skirt and a cotton skirt, is not one of fabric

and style, but one of identity. You know perfectly well that you will be seen differently for the whole day, depending on what you put on; you will appear as a particular kind of woman with one particular identity which excludes others. The black leather skirt rather rules out girlish innocence, oily overalls tend to exclude sophistication, ditto smart suit and radical feminism. Often I have wished I could put them all on together, or appear simultaneously in every possible outfit, just to say, 'How dare you think any one of these is me. But also, see, I can be all of them.'[10]

One of the reasons why I like this little story by Judith Williamson is that it draws attention to how objects are actively used rather than passively consumed. I think we can assume at least two things about the writer/wearer: first, she lives in a society where the display of different self-images is possible and may even be encouraged. Second, she has considerable social and cultural knowledge, an understanding of the 'meaning' of different kinds of clothes. Williamson clearly makes the point that we can choose the image that we present to others – but this wonderful anecdote could only be told by someone who has a choice of what to wear and knows the symbolic consequences of her choices. The passage does not discuss how the clothes that we select may sometimes be read by people in different ways in different contexts. The question that it does raise, for me, is: does the image represent our identity? What the passage expresses are the ideas that persons are more than what they wear, that there is the possibility of multiple identities within the same individual. This leads me to wonder what would happen if Williamson mixed the clothes she wore. Perhaps, then, we would have to explore the range of meanings that a single object can acquire through its recontextualisation in a range of cultural settings. We would then have to focus on how people experiment, like bricoleurs, with common materials, to produce a range of new meanings.

There is a rapidly-growing literature that shows that personal identities are far more complex and shifting than is usually thought, that people have multiple, apparently contradictory, identities at any one time. Several authors have suggested that this is a characteristic of the transition from modernity to postmodernity.[11] Here is a typical statement that expresses such a view.

We are not in any simple sense 'black' or 'gay' or 'upwardly mobile'. Rather we carry a bewildering range of different, and at times conflicting identities around with us in our heads at the same time. There is a continued smudging of personas and life-styles, depending where we are (at work, on the high street) and the spaces we are moving between.[12]

I agree with this view, but I would say that in this area, as in the above passage, there is often a conflation between personas and life-styles. The question I want to ask is this: if people are living out quite fractured identities, representing themselves differently, feeling different in different spatial situations, what holds them together? From where do they get their sense of belonging?

I suggested earlier that there are many antithetical or bipolar terms, binary oppositions such as: public/private, centre/periphery, speech/silence, identity/difference, us here/you there. There are many difficulties with binary oppositions: they are always hierarchical, one term is always more powerful than the other. We may want to dissolve them, eradicate them, but we often seem to re-enact them. The role of these oppositions can be clearly seen in an increasingly important phenomenon: tourism.

Tourism is physical and metaphorical. Travel is a fascinating metaphor because it refers not to the fixed but to a journey, a crossing from the familiar centre to the exotic periphery. The nature of the centre and the periphery is of course changing. The centre is developing several Third World features, and urban areas of the periphery are beginning to have some postmodern features.

Tourism is also a metaphor for imposition of the Western gaze. There is enjoyment by the rich of the exotic difference of the Other – and exploitation too. Travelling has also become an increasingly popular way of 'discovering one's identity'.

CONCLUSION

I agree with Bauman's view that consumer freedom means orientation of life towards market-approved commodities and thereby excludes one crucial freedom: freedom from the market. Consumer freedom successfully deflects aspirations of human liberty from communal affairs and the management of collective life. Bauman writes:

> All possible dissent is therefore depoliticized beforehand; it is dissolved into yet more personal anxieties and concerns and thus deflected from the centres of societal power to private suppliers

of consumer goods. The gap between desirable and achieved states of happiness results in the increased fascination with the allurements of the market and the appropriation of commodities.[13]

It seems that, in the postmodern society of consumers, failure rebounds in guilt and shame, not in political protest.

The new values that inform postmodern mentality are those of liberty, diversity and tolerance. It could be said that, in postmodern practice, liberty boils down to consumer choice. To enjoy it, one must be a consumer first. This preliminary condition leaves out millions of people.

Freedom is now interpreted as freedom of the market, and communal needs are translated into individual acts of acquisition. There are, however, many social needs that cannot be met by personal purchases. One cannot, for example, buy privately one's way out of polluted air, or a broken ozone layer. As for diversity, it should mean more than a variety of marketable life-styles. What is to be fought for is the right to secure communal as distinct from individual diversity.

It has been suggested that postmodern values include novelty, rapid change, individual enjoyment and consumer choice. Under postmodern conditions, there is the exhilarating experience of ever-new needs rather than the satisfaction of the still-existing ones. But, as Bauman remarks, nothing merely ends in history, no project is ever finished and done with. Modernity is still with us – we still speak of it as a project. It lives as the pressure of unfulfilled hopes and interests. Postmodernity does not necessarily mean the end or the rejection of modernity. Postmodernity is no more than the modern mind taking a long, attentive and sober look at itself, at its condition and its past works, not fully liking what it sees, and sensing the urge to change.

NOTES

1. Wolfgang Haug, *Critique of Commodity Aesthetics* (Cambridge: Polity Press, 1986).
2. Walter Benjamin, 'The Work of Art in the Age of Mechanical Reproduction', in idem, *Illuminations*, ed. Hannah Arendt (London: Fontana/Collins, 1973), p. 243.
3. On the attempt of Italian Fascism to create new forms of subjectivity through its organisation of popular culture, see the articles by Colin Mercer and Victoria de Grazia in James Donald and Stuart Hall (eds), *Politics and Ideology* (Milton Keynes: Open University Press, 1986).
4. I am thinking of writers like Paul Willis, *Common Culture* (Milton Keynes: Open University Press, 1990) and Daniel Miller, *Mass Consumption and Material Culture* (Oxford: Basil Blackwell, 1987). For a thoughtful overview, see Peter Jackson, 'A

Cultural Politics of Consumption', in Jon Bird et al., *Mapping the Futures: Local Cultures, Global Change* (London: Routledge, 1993).

5. The best book on these processes is still Harry Braverman, *Labor and Monopoly Capital* (New York: Monthly Review Press, 1974).

6. See the work of Ivan Illich, whose main theme throughout his work has been the demystification through deprofessionalisation and deinstitutionalisation of secrets associated with religion, education and health. His belief is that people need to be more involved with those decisions and subsequent strategies which affect their lives. Ivan Illich, *Deschooling Society* (London: Penguin, 1973); idem, *Celebration of Awareness* (London: Calder and Boyars, 1971).

7. Zygmunt Bauman, *Modernity and Ambivalence* (Cambridge: Polity Press, 1991).

8. For an opposing view, the argument that the order of the system that builds and manages the shopping malls is consistently at risk of being turned into the disorder of those who use them, see John Fiske, *Understanding Popular Culture* (Boston, MA: Unwin Hyman, 1989), pp. 37–41.

9. Stuart Hall, 'The Meaning of New Times', in S. Hall and M. Jacques (eds), *New Times* (London: Lawrence and Wishart, 1989).

10. Judith Williamson, *Consuming Passions* (London: Marion Boyars, 1986), p. 91.

11. See, for example, Anthony Giddens, *Modernity and Self-Identity* (Cambridge: Polity Press, 1991); John Rutherford (ed.), *Identity: Community, Culture, Difference* (London: Lawrence and Wishart, 1990); Mike Featherstone, *Consumer Culture and Postmodernism* (London: Sage, 1991).

12. Frank Mort, 'The Politics of Consumption' in S. Hall and M. Jacques (eds), *New Times*, op. cit.

13. Bauman, op. cit., p. 262.

10

NATIONAL IDENTITY: 'ENGLISHNESS' AND EDUCATION

INTRODUCTION: NATIONALISM

The nation is difficult to define. It originated in eighteenth-century Europe, and, according to Benedict Anderson, is an imagined community.[1] A nation is a political arrangement of boundaries; it is a territorial space with a political centre which aims at unification. Nations foster a sense of belonging, a rootedness, a sense of sovereignty. What usually happens is that national states construe their subjects as 'natives'. States are engaged in incessant propaganda of shared attitudes. They glorify and enforce ethnic, religious, linguistic and cultural homogeneity. National states construct joint historical memories (called 'our common heritage') and do their best to discredit or suppress such stubborn memories as cannot be squeezed into a shared tradition. They preach the sense of common mission, common destiny. In other words, national states promote uniformity. This state-enforced homogeneity could be called the practice of nationalist ideology.

With the rise of nationalism, the state is regarded as legitimate; it represents the nation. It is said that nationalism 'works' only because it is based on national identity. We identify with others 'like ourselves'. We feel pride (or shame) about others who share our identity. National identity is an expression of a way of life, and it has a powerful appeal because it is a mode of self-fulfilment.

But what constitutes that identity? Let me mention some of the elements in the social construction of national identity. As Benedict Anderson has pointed out, nationalism links me with people in the past, with people elsewhere that I don't know, and with others in the future. Every nation has its own story. Every nation has its myths, myths that can exploit contradictions. Nations make claims to land, and they make appeals to blood, native soil, homeland, motherland, fatherland. It is not surprising that the discourse of the nation uses

'the family'.[2] And, of course, each nation has its culture. Collective
self-awareness is provided by culture. Culture is a complex concept;
it refers to the process, rather like acculturation, whereby persons are
inscribed; but culture also refers to, or is based upon, communication.
It is through language that a group becomes aware of itself.
Language and place are inextricably interconnected.

What is it about the modern world that brought about the emergence of nationalism? Some thinkers have provided a typology of
agrarian societies and have suggested that it was industrialisation
that provided the thrust that broke them down and pushed them
towards a homogenised mass culture.[3] The difficulty with this thesis
is that in some places nationalism arose before the Industrial
Revolution. One Marxist response to the above question is to stress
the emergence of the market. Others, like Benedict Anderson, stress
the emergence of the novel and the newspaper, but it could be argued
that his thesis assumes a level of literacy which did not exist at that
time.

Nationalism has a popular and powerful fascination because it
appeals to the real needs of people, their need for belonging. (This is
a point that socialists need to address. They have, perhaps, been
overly influenced by Hegel and Marx, who believed that the thrust
of modern life was cosmopolitan, and that the nation would not
survive.) But if some belong to the nation, others do not.
Nationalism, inevitably, excludes others from the ranks of the privileged group. Once nationalism gains momentum, others have to
assimilate – or to resist.[4]

THE CONCEPT OF 'ENGLISHNESS'

In recent years, I have attended several conferences where the speak-
ers have not made clear the distinctions between nation, nationalism,
national identity and nationality. Some people are not aware of the
differences between these concepts, while others know the terms
and, consciously or unconsciously, manipulate their listeners by
conflating the terms. Consider a simple example: there is a difference
between someone who belongs to a certain nation (James Joyce) and
someone who is a nationalist (W. B. Yeats). One can have British
nationality (a judicial category) without wanting to internalise all the
so-called characteristics of British 'national identity'.

I want to argue that national identity is a construct, fashioned by
particular people for particular reasons at a certain time. In different

historical periods, powerful groups have constructed a different national identity for their purposes. Certain elements are valued, others devalued. I think that the term 'national identity' has several meanings. It can refer to the identity of individuals within a nation; the views of individuals towards the nation in which they live; the identity of the nation itself.

The concept of Englishness has become central in the debates about national identity. Some of the major themes and images around which the traditionalist definition of Englishness is constructed and organised include respectability, work and the need for social discipline. First, there is the notion of respectability which is connected with self-respect, and the more 'Protestant' values of our culture: thrift, self-discipline, living the decent life. Second, there is work. Work is not only the guarantee of respectability, it is also a powerful image in its own right. (We know how much our personal and social identities are caught up with our work, and how men – especially men, given the sexual division of labour – who are without work feel not only materially abandoned but also emotionally decentred). And, third, there is the need for social discipline. Stuart Hall and his colleagues have pointed out that, as with other ideas, there are different versions of this very general social idea across the different class cultures.[5] The traditional idea of social discipline is closely linked with notions about hierarchy and authority. Fourth, a part of the traditional English ideology emphasises the practical and the concrete, the empirical. Particularly strong in English culture is a value which exalts common sense. English common sense is really an impatience with theory and reverence for 'sense experience'.

DEPRIVATION AND PRIVILEGE

I have a perception of E. M. Forster as being very 'English': a little, mild man in a crumpled suit, a 'civilised' liberal with the privileges of free food and lodgings in Kings College, Cambridge. When I read his 'Notes on the English Character', I was surprised by his sharp, acerbic remarks. He writes that, in his opinion, 'the character of the English is essentially middle-class':

> They gained wealth by the Industrial Revolution, political power by the Reform Bill of 1832: they are connected with the rise and organisation of the British Empire; they are responsible for the literature of the nineteenth century. Solidity, caution,

integrity, efficiency. Lack of imagination, hypocrisy. These qualities characterise the middle classes in every country, but in England they are national characteristics also, because only in England have the middle classes been in power for one hundred and fifty years.[6]

Forster then goes on to say that, just as the heart of England is the middle classes, the heart of the middle classes is the public-school system: 'with its boarding-houses, its compulsory games, its systems of prefects and fagging, its insistence on good form and an esprit de corps, it produces a type, whose weight is out of all proportion to its numbers'. His main criticism of public-school education is that it produces people with undeveloped hearts. For it is not that the Englishman can't feel; it is that he is afraid to feel. He has been taught at his public school that feeling is bad form.

Though I agree with Forster's points about public schools, I am surprised by one absence. He omits the fact that they inculcate patriotism. Patriotism is, of course, particularly associated with the middle classes and the public schools. George Orwell, who was educated at Eton, made the point that patriotism takes different forms in different classes, but it runs like a connecting thread through nearly all of them. In Orwell's view, England is the most class-ridden country under the sun. It is a land of snobbery and privilege, ruled largely by the old and silly. He sees England as a rather stuffy Victorian family – a family with the wrong members in control.[7] In these scathing terms, Orwell is referring to the English system of social stratification, which changed in the early nineteenth century from a system based on rank, order and degree to a system based on class. These are views of 'Englishness' of a certain period in the past, and I am well aware that contemporary ideas are not expressed here.

Reading an anthology on literature, I came across an extract on cricket. The author writes admiringly of a brilliant batsman. Spooner is natural, modest, 'the most lyrical of cricketers', 'the picture of swift, diving elegance':

> Spooner told us in every one of his drives past cover that he did not come from the hinterland of Lancashire, where cobbled streets sound with the noise of clogs and industry; he played always as though on the elegant lawns of Aigburth; his cricket was 'county' in the social sense of the term . . . If I have called his batsmanship that of manners, I do not mean it was ever

affected, every innings by Spooner was natural and modest, like the man himself. The pose was a consequence of an instinctive balance of cultural technical parts. What's bred in the bone comes out in an innings; I never saw Spooner bat without seeing, as a background for his skill and beauty, the fields of Marlborough, and all the quiet summertime amenities of school cricket.[8]

Neville Cardus's reminiscences about cricket, written in 1934, clearly express his view of the social world. There is the contrast of the noise of clogs and industry with the elegant lawns, the fields of Marlborough. He takes for granted, and so implicitly supports, a class system based on a certain type of elite education provided by the public schools. As a young schoolboy, Cardus stayed in the holidays with a fine cricketer, who was coaching him:

> Once I was writing a letter in the sitting room, and he watched me carefully. I dashed off my note home in a few seconds. Williams, when he had to write a letter, gave up a whole evening to it, and took off his coat. He gazed at me as I wrote rapidly, 'By Gow, if I'd been able to write like that I'd 'a' never wasted my life at a game.'[9]

The young man takes his education for granted and enjoys playing cricket. Old Williams appreciates education but has been deprived of it. His life has been limited to playing cricket professionally; he has 'prodooced nowt'. This incident illustrates the separation of mental and manual labour, the gulf between working-class and middle-class opportunity. For the author, old Williams's life is only an excuse for nostalgic romanticism. He describes but does not understand the poignancy of the situation, the injustice of the prevailing social system.

More recently, Marcia Pointon, in her article, argues that

> there is to this day a struggle to keep the game of cricket, a powerful symbol as an image of national survival. Following several national setbacks – 'Black Wednesday' when the pound reached an all-time low, IRA bombings, inner-city violence and the murder of an infant by two minors, on 28 February 1993 – the BBC programme *The World This Weekend* chose not to interview the Home Office, the Exchequer or the police force, but instead took its microphones and tape-recorders to rural Wiltshire. Here, reporters questioned members of the village cricket teams

and their wives on the state of Britain. Subsequently, on 22 April 1993, John Major made a speech invoking county cricket grounds and warm beer as a reassuring image of the survival of essential England.[10]

The mythic power of cricket as ideology is separate from the game as played. She makes her point that, 'though England may not necessarily win against Pakistani or West Indian teams, the fact that cricket is played is ample compensation for loss of any game, a perpetual and visible remainder of England's power to subordinate colonial nations'.

When John Bellany's portrait of Ian Botham, commissioned by the National Portrait Gallery, London, was 'unveiled' on 22 January 1986, it received coverage that was unusually widespread for an arts event. Newspapers from Worcester and Exeter to Liverpool and Darlington reported the occasion. Portraiture, the national art, was united with cricket, the national sport, the press release went on, 'in a large-scale popular icon as a folk hero of our times with a mirror-like panel emblazoned with the legends of the sitter's own allegiances, to the public, to England, Somerset'. This is repeated in the catalogue in which Robin Gibson further describes Botham as

> like some latter-day Siegfried, the golden boy of British cricket, emerging proud and unassailable, unbowed after sundry skirmishes with sporting opponents and the media alike. Cricket, as the national sport, symbolises orthodox masculinity and, through its participation in mythology of nationhood (which Tory rhetoric has reinforced), stands for the essence of Englishness.[11]

THE FUNCTION OF IDEOLOGY

I have briefly outlined above some of the characteristics of Englishness: the pervasive metaphor of cricket in English life; the dominance of the middle classes in England, and the socialising role of the public school; the emphasis on patriotism and class. I believe that our attitudes to cricket, public schools, feeling and nation are interconnected. To what extent are our views and beliefs about these things the effect of ideology?

The function of ideology, to put it very simply, is to legitimate the power of the ruling class in society; in the last analysis, 'the dominant ideas of a society are the ideas of its ruling class'. Of course, this is a simplification; ideology is never a simple reflection of a ruling class's ideas: on the contrary, it is always a complex phenomenon, which may incorporate conflicting, even contradictory, views of the world.

I would argue that national identity is an ideology. By ideology I mean the ways in which what we say and believe connects with the power structure and power relations of the society we live in. Ideology refers to those modes of feeling, valuing, perceiving and believing which have some kind of relation to the maintenance and reproduction of social power. Now, national identity is like 'social cement'; an effective form of ideological 'binding' and control. Like all successful ideologies, it works much less by explicit concepts or formulated doctrines than by image, symbol, habit, ritual and mythology. It is affective and experiential, entwining itself with the deepest unconscious roots of the human subject.

In any non-totalitarian society, certain cultural forms predominate over others, just as certain ideas are more influential than others; the form of this cultural leadership is what Antonio Gramsci has identified as hegemony. Here is a well-known example of the hegemony of dominant ideas over subordinate ones. For the middle classes, 'tea' in the afternoon means a leisured and unnecessary refreshment between lunch and dinner. You take it around four o'clock; the bread and butter will be cut thin. But tea to the majority of the population is the meal of the evening, eaten about five-thirty when father gets back from work. In this example, tea means, in fact, different things to different groups of people in England. Nevertheless, it is the first (minority), not the second (majority) meaning of tea which is thought 'characteristically English'. Stuart Hall has commented that a practice restricted to the English upper-middle classes has come to represent something universal for the English as a whole: a class custom has become 'hegemonic'. To put it in another way, the ruling classes have learned to give their ideas the form of universality and represent them as the only rationally, valid ones.[12]

I believe that the values and ideas mentioned above about cricket, patriotism, class and so forth are ideological. Ideology is not a set of doctrines. It refers to the imaginary ways in which men and women experience the real world. Ideology signifies the way in which subjects live out their roles in class-society, the values, ideas and images which tie them to their social functions and so prevent them from a true knowledge of society as a whole.

Let me give another example. We are often told that to be fully human we have to take on a 'balanced' identity. The idea of balance as something which proceeds from a position beyond the political is in fact a thoroughly political notion. The notion of a balanced identity bears a close resemblance to the political balance which, in England especially, is associated with the middle class. The concept of 'balance' has a crucial function in middle-class ideology, under-writing the political authority of 'consensus', or the 'middle ground', by representing as irrational extremism whatever refuses to be gathered into the middle ground.[13]

ON SCHOOLING AS AN IDEOLOGICAL FORM

It is important to see identity dialectically rather than mechanically, and I think we must try and understand identity in relation to history. The bourgeois class established its political, economic and ideological dominance under certain conditions. To achieve hegemony, it had not only to transform the base, the relations of production, but also radically to transform the superstructure. The school apparatus, argue Etienne Balibar and Pierre Macherey, is the means of forcing sub-mission to the dominant ideology. They have shown through their research in France that the division in schooling reproduces the social division of a society.[14] They argue that there is a contradiction between different practices of the same language. It is in and through the educational system that the contradiction is instituted – through the contradiction between the basic language as taught at primary-school level, and the literary level reserved for the few at the advanced level of teaching. At the primary level, there is a mere training in 'correct' usage and the reporting of 'reality'; at the advanced level of work, there is the so-called creative work which presupposes the incorporation of literary material.

Balibar believes that there has been a move to impose an 'inegali-tarian division' through education. There are class barriers so that everyone may not have the same access to language. This is an example of how a supposedly common language has been made to act as an 'instrument' which allows communication and non-com-munication. There are, in effect, differences in the access to and handling of the same language by the social classes. For the many there is incomprehension, and for the others there is mastery.

I would argue that, broadly speaking, this is the case in England too, but the contradiction occurs between the state secondary schools for the majority and public schools for the sons and daughters of a powerful elite. I am suggesting that different types of schooling produce different types of identity. It has been well documented that one of the main aims of public schools like Eton, Harrow and Winchester was to produce men with identities that could bear the burden of administering and governing the British Empire.

One of the most important aspects of 'Englishness', in my opinion, is its connections with Empire. The Empire, backed by military, naval and economic supremacy, became associated with certain beliefs. This includes the doctrine that the English are superior to other peoples in the world. This is often a quiet and unspoken assumption, but it is largely unquestioning. Secondly, there is the belief that the English possess special qualities as a people which keeps the country independent and secure. Thirdly, there is the view that the Englishman has a divine right to conquer 'barbaric peoples', a right which is then redefined, not as an aggressive economic imperialism, but as a 'civilizing burden'.[15]

Let me use the work of Rudyard Kipling, the national bard of imperialism. Kipling's White Man as an idea, a persona, appears in many of his works. He celebrated the 'road' taken by White Men in the colonies:

> Now, this is the road that the White Men tread
> When they go to clean a land –
> Iron underfoot and the vine overhead
> And the deep on either hand.
> We have trod that road – and a wet and windy road –
> Our chosen star for guide.
> Oh, well for the world when the White Men tread
> Their highway side by side![16]

Being a White Man was an idea and a reality. It meant – in the colonies – speaking in a certain way, behaving according to a code of regulations, and even feeling certain things and not others. It meant specific judgements, evaluations, gestures. It was a form of authority before which non-whites, and even whites themselves, were expected to bend. Being a White Man, in short, was a very concrete manner of being-in-the-world, a way of taking hold of reality, language and thought.[17]

Here is a brief description of an event some years after the First World War:

> A fortnight in advance of Empire Day we were asked to teach our classes Rule Britannia . . . We were given outline maps of

the world and the pupils coloured the British possessions red . . . Then came the day. Britannia led the way and was guarded by boys dressed as soldiers . . . Rule Britannia was sung by the school and the head gave a little speech between each verse: 'We are all proud of our flag because wherever it waves there is justice and freedom. In many countries there were slaves but the coming of the Union Jack meant the abolition of slavery.' Enter William Wilberforce, who was duly saluted.[18]

You will have noticed that the children's work consisted of activities (singing, colouring, acting) and that they are being socialised through art into certain role models. Though they are given some knowledge (a map of the world), really their attitudes are being formed.[19] National identity is being constructed through the ritual celebration of Empire Day (Rule Britannia, British possessions, our flag, the Union Jack). All these elements are articulated with the concepts of justice and freedom – the focus is not on Britain's participation in the slave trade, but on its abolition (when it was no longer profitable).[20]

CULTURE, NATIONALISM AND EDUCATION

I turn now to the present, the link between English education (the national curriculum), culture and nationalism. Members of the New Right believe that there is something unique about being British which unites the nation. Culture, in the discourse of the New Right, is deliberately associated with nationalism, and the exclusion from the nation of those who do not subscribe to its traditions. This can be clearly seen in the national curriculum. In my opinion, the national curriculum is a nationalist curriculum. Government ministers have made clear their views on the cohesive role of the national curriculum:

> In reality our proposals reflect a deep-seated conviction that a vital aspect of education is to pass on to our school children our common moral, cultural and spiritual heritage. We want all pupils to understand, love and value this. It seems to me that pupils are sometimes taught to be critical before they fully understand what it is that has been handed on to them, and I deplore the all-purpose cynicism which can result from this . . . Pupils should be able to absorb our national heritage and be prepared for adult life and citizenship.[21]

> I see the national curriculum as a way of increasing our social coherence. There is so much distraction, variety and uncertainty in the modern world that in our country today our children are in danger of losing any sense at all of a common culture and a common heritage. The cohesive role of the national curriculum will provide our society with a greater sense of identity.[22]

Well, I don't see the national curriculum like that at all. I believe that it reflects an imperialist and Eurocentric concept of a static Anglo-Saxon culture which no longer exists. My fear is that the current changes in the education system are leading to a closed and narrowly-defined nationalism. In England today, there is still a nostalgia for imperialist greatness. Why do so many people feel a need for nationalism and flag-waving patriotism? Is it not time that these aspects of Englishness were abandoned?

There is no doubt that the creation of a national identity is part of the political process of establishing the nation. National identity is a social construction, an invention. It is not generally understood, however, that there are many characteristics that people may be seen as having. Only some of them prevail. The question of which national characteristics prevail depends on the balance of social forces within this process. Those who have the power to create and rule a nation-state have the most influence in defining the 'national character'. The definition may embody abstract ideals ('liberty – equality – fraternity', for example), and it might satisfy a popular desire to 'belong'; but it is linked just as much to the economic and political interests of the definers.

One of the problems of the New Right is that in order to provide a unifying nationalism they have to presuppose a 'common culture'. The issue of a common culture, however, cannot be taken for granted; it is problematic and a matter for debate. There are sharp conflicts about culture between different classes, nations, regions and ethnic groups. Culture is not something fixed and frozen as the traditionalists would have us believe, but a process of constant struggle as cultures interact with each other and are affected by economic, political and social factors.

It is very important to realise that the reality-construction of a common culture or the national character is not something that happens once. Rather, there is a constant process of asserting, questioning and redefining national identity. We should remember that definitions are being repeated daily, hourly, of what the nation and society are – but there are also counter-definitions and alternative conceptions of personal and social identity.

CONCLUSION

Since the French Revolution, nationalism has spread everywhere in the world. All states everywhere legitimate themselves by using the ideology of 'the nation'. The nation has become the norm, the sole form. During the twentieth century, many people have struggled against the imperialist powers for their national independence. New nations and nation-states have been created, and so too have the subjects of these countries. In freeing themselves, they have had to create their own identity. There seem to be two views about national identity. One, you have to belong to a nation – and you can choose; two, you have to belong to a nation but you cannot choose – you are its national wherever you go.

The view that politics produces identities raises the question: to what extent are identities freely chosen – or are they constituted by social institutions (such as families, schools, the media and practices)? Nationalism can be both progressive and reactionary, sometimes at the same time. For many decades, the discourse of the nation has been used against the 'cultural other'. The nation, Britishness, is a representation which has successfully hegemonised other cultures. It is often assumed by the political Right that other cultures fragment Britishness, which is represented as a homogeneous, unitary formation.

I don't think that identity is nothing but ideology. Identities are not just expressions of the ideologies of their time. We are not merely prisoners of false consciousness. If this were the case, we would have to ask: why do so many people develop identities that transcend the ideological limits of their time, yielding us insight into the realities which ideology hides from view?

Some readers could argue that the picture which I have sketched in this chapter is no longer true. They could say that I have not described the loss of imperial power, the failure of economic nerve, the diminished influence of Britain and the effects of these changes on national identity. Has all this led to a new sense of shire, a new valuing of the native English experience, a certain nostalgia for Britain's imperial past that can be seen, for example, in the heritage industry?

Other readers may think that I have overemphasised the importance of the public school. In the stable world of prewar English life, the public schools provided fixed guide-marks. They had the confidence to judge events, the desire to impose 'our' civilisation or 'our' dominion upon other people. But not now. The changes, since the Second World War, have been so rapid that there is less confidence now. There is a shift from Newtonian mechanics to generalised relativity. We are now having to take part in this general shift. Some call it postmodernism.

The nation-state emphasised its boundaries and its institutions. We are constantly being told about national territory, the national government, the national army, even the national theatre. Many people hear the voice of the state as if it were in their head. How is this to be explained? Some thinkers have suggested that identity is about what you remember. Who you think you are is who you think you are. But does it necessarily follow that who you think you are is how you take yourself to be? While I think that people's sense of themselves should be respected, I believe, at the same time, that people's sense of who they are may be a misrecognition. People may be deluded about their self-conceptions. The vocabulary of identity may lead us to think that national identity, like personal identity, is real. In fact, aspects of national identity may be false – like the Lacanian 'ego'.

I think we should be thinking in terms beyond the nation-state. Internationalism is inadequate because it assumes the existence of the nation-state. I suggest that we try and discover a new form of world citizenship. Is it too idealistic to hope that, wherever you are, you are a citizen of that place? (After all, in most cultures there is a deep feeling that one must care for the visitor.)

The idea of belonging wherever you are, of being recognised by the people around you, implies the concept of multi-identities. Let me give an example. George Blake, the 1960s double agent who escaped to Moscow, was asked at a press conference to which country he felt loyalty, considering that one of those for which he spied, the Soviet Union, is no more. "I feel attached to four nations", said Mr Blake. They are Holland because his mother was Dutch, Israel because his father was a Jew, Britain because he once had an English wife and family, and Russia because he now has a Russian wife and a son.'[23] He added that these countries should not necessarily be considered in that order.

But in what sort of society would the concept of multi-identities be valorised? At this point, it may be useful to remind ourselves of

Julia Kristeva's commitment to cosmopolitanism.[24] She contends that we are still living with the inheritance of the Enlightenment and the French Revolution. The French Enlightenment laid down, at the same time, two opposing ideas: nationalism and cosmopolitanism. What is a cosmopolitan? A cosmopolitan is a word used to refer to one 'who has no fixed abode' or one 'who is nowhere a foreigner'. The word 'cosmopolitan' often had a pejorative meaning; nationalists, in particular, have never liked it. Kristeva believes that the explosion of nationalism in the nineteenth and twentieth centuries has meant that cosmopolitanism has been ignored and undervalued.

Kristeva writes enthusiastically of Anarcharsis Clootz, who ceaselessly proclaimed his cosmopolitan ideas. Clootz and his friends supported the idea of a universal republic and challenged the very notion of 'foreigner'. The cosmopolitan trend was powerful at the beginning of the French Revolution and found concrete fulfilment in many decrees, but was defeated by the forces of nationalism.

Clearly, Kristeva believes in the principle of the rights of man as embodied in the Enlightenment. She states that it fell to Immanuel Kant to formulate the Enlightenment's moral universalism, its internationalist spirit, in political, legal and philosophical terms. In Kant's view, 'Hospitality means the right of a stranger not to be treated as an enemy when he arrives in the land of another'.[25]

Kristeva remarks that the reasoned hymn to cosmopolitanism, which runs through Kant's thought as a debt to Enlightenment and the French Revolution, appears today still, like an idealistic Utopia, but also as an inescapable necessity. She raises the question:

> Could cosmopolitanism as moral imperative be the secular form of that bond bringing together families, languages, and states that religion claimed to be? Something beyond religion: the belief that individuals are fulfilled only if the entire species achieves the practice of rights for everyone, everywhere?[26]

In her view, there must be an ethics, the fulfilment of which would depend on education and psychoanalysis. Such an ethics would reveal, discuss and spread a concept of human dignity, of cosmopolitanism.

Let me summarise some of the main points of this chapter. I have tried to reflect on national identity by examining 'Englishness'. Drawing on the work of Forster, Orwell and others, I suggested that the characteristics of Englishness might include, for example, certain attitudes to cricket, public schools, patriotism and class. I believe that in England there is a major difference between the public schools and the state secondary schools and that different types of schooling produce different types of identity. Public schools teach certain attitudes. The values of the public school are widely admired, and they permeate downwards through the grammar schools to the state schools. The type of identity produced by the public schools has become the 'norm' of Englishness. There are, of course, other definitions of Englishness, but the definition of the public school has become the dominant one. Thus a particular view of national identity is fostered.

I focused particularly on the connections between 'Englishness' and Empire; how an aggressive economic imperialism was redefined, by the work of Kipling and others, as a 'civilizing burden'. Turning to the present, it was argued that, in New Right discourse, culture is being articulated with nationalism and that black people are being excluded from the nation. It was suggested that the English national curriculum was a nationalist curriculum, and that one of its purposes was to increase 'social coherence' by a stress, a common culture, a common heritage. In conclusion, it was stated that national identity is a construct and that there are many characteristics that people may be seen as having. But only some of them prevail. Moreover, we need to remember that the definition of national identity, of the 'norm' of Englishness, is not something that happens once, but is a constant process of ideological struggle.

> *My first memory of my eldest brother is when, as a young man, he returned from his studies in England. (Perhaps this visit was because of my mother's death? I do not know.) He was showered with garlands and surrounded by a large group of people as he climbed up the hill to Simla.*
>
> *Some years later, I remember him in Karachi, where he used to take me to the seaside in the evenings and buy me ice cream. We were together for a while in Bristol, but he was soon posted away. He was so many years older than I was that I didn't think of him as a brother. During my schooldays, he (and my father) supported me by paying for my digs. I should be grateful for this, but what I can remember is that his cheques often 'bounced', and I felt embarrassed by this in my dealings with the landlady.*
>
> *On his return, after the war, he married a Pakistani woman, became a Muslim and called himself 'Rashid'. He bought a posh house to impress his wife. I left school and was given a room in his house while I was trying to work out what I was going to do. I wanted to*

go to university, but I needed to pass a Latin examination. My brother's advice was to get a job.

And so I got a dead-end job. I failed my Latin exam. Rashid criticised my dress and my politics. His wife did not want me living in their house, and he asked me to leave. On a cold, rainy, dark night, I got on a bus, got out half an hour later, looked at some cards in a tobacconist's shop-window and, again, found some digs.

It was at this time that my elder (middle) brother Roshan contacted me. He began to advise me about my health and my career problems. I used to to Rugby, where he worked, and stay with him at weekends and vacations. We had a close relationship. We talked, and, later on, when I could afford it, we went on holidays together to India. He too was hurt by Rashid. When Roshan got married, for example, Rashid did not go to his wedding, and I know that this hurt Roshan very much. For many years, Roshan tried to meet and talk with Rashid, but he was always rebuffed. Finally, Roshan gave up trying.

Years later, it became clearer that when Rashid married he had changed his identity. When he became a Muslim, he had to hide the fact that he had a family, and that that family was (originally) Hindu. Moreover, he was Indian, not Pakistani.

After Rashid's rejection, I didn't see him for many years. He became involved in his own family affairs and returned to develop his business. After this, there were only a few, two or three, superficial meetings: at my wedding, and our brother Roshan's death. Perhaps as an elder brother he wanted me to 'respect' him, but I did not understand this, and as a younger brother I wanted him to look after me. I always felt that, after he married, he was not interested in me. Perhaps he did not know that I needed his support; but, in any case, he could not give it to me.

Some years ago, he must have had a premonition that he was going to die. He sent me a brief note in which he said 'I am old now', and he wished me well. The note was signed 'Ronnie'. When I received a telegram, five months later, to say that he had died, I was not sad. After all, I did not know him. I have not been able to forgive him.

NOTES

1. Benedict Anderson, *Imagined Communities: Reflections on the Origin and Spread of Nationalism* (London: Verso, 1983).
2. In the years after the Second World War, BBC programme executives and planners created out of a large number of diverse audiences one large and unitary one. They evolved modes of addressing their growing number of listeners and, needless to say, there was a struggle over whether a public-service institution like the BBC should speak in the national or in the public interest. The radio helped the British nation to form a family. The formation of this mass audience depended on planning,

regular timings, continuity provided by a series of programmes, and the construction of a kind of almanac of national events in which the seasons of the years were defined by Wimbledon, the Cup Final, the Boat Race and royal occasions. This led to the creation of a totality, a social whole; but the concept of the nation as a unitary family clearly ran counter to regionalism and favoured central, metropolitan control. See Paddy Scannell and David Cardiff, *A Social History of British Broadcasting*, vol. 1, *1922–1939: Serving the Nation* (Oxford: Basil Blackwell, 1991).

3. Ernest Gellner, *Nations and Nationalism* (Oxford: Oxford University Press, 1983).
4. See the superb play about the British occupation of Ireland, with its cultural and linguistic domination, which is full of insights about this process: Brian Friel, *Translations* (London: Faber, 1981).
5. Stuart Hall et al., *Policing the Crisis* (London: Macmillan, 1978), pp. 140–2.
6. Dennis Walder (ed.), *Literature in the Modern World* (Oxford: Oxford University Press, 1990), p. 176.
7. Ibid., p. 189.
8. Neville Cardus, 'Good Days', in Walder (ed.), op. cit., pp. 172–3.
9. Ibid., p. 175.
10. Marcia Pointon, 'A Latter-day Siegfried: Ian Botham at the National Portrait Gallery, 1986', in idem, *Post-Colonial Insecurities* (London:Lawrence & Wishart, 1994), p. 131.
11. Ibid., p. 135
12. Stuart Hall et al., op. cit., p. 156.
13. See John Barrell, *Poetry, Language and Politics* (Manchester: Manchester University Press, 1988).
14. Etienne Balibar and Pierre Macherey, 'On Literature as an Ideological Form', in Robert Young (ed.), *Untying the Text: A Post-Structuralist Reader* (London: Routledge, 1981). It is also in Walder (ed.), op. cit., p. 223.
15. Stuart Hall et al., op. cit., p. 147.
16. Edward Said, *Orientalism* (London: Penguin, 1985), p. 226.
17. This extract from *Orientalism* is in Walder (ed.), op. cit., p. 241. The themes of culture and imperialism are taken up again and discussed in Chapter 11 below.
18. *Educational Worker*, June 1927, quoted in Ken Jones, *Beyond Progressive Education* (London: Macmillan, 1983), p. 23.
19. For essays on the varied forms in which Englishness was constructed, see Robert Colls and Philip Dodd (eds), *Englishness, Politics and Culture 1880–1920* (London: Croom Helm, 1986).
20. See Robin Blackburn, *The Overthrow of Colonial Slavery 1776–1848* (London: Verso, 1988).
21. Angela Rumbold, in *The Sunday Times*, 22 November 1987.
22. Kenneth Baker, in *The Times Educational Supplement*, 25 September 1987.
23. *The Independent*, January 1992, p. 1.
24. Julia Kristeva, *Strangers to Ourselves* (London: Harvester Wheatsheaf), 1991.
25. Ibid., p. 172.
26. Ibid., p. 173.

11

·

IMPERIALISM AND CULTURE

In this chapter, I want to explore the connections between culture and imperialism. The latter has influenced the lives and identities of millions of people throughout the world. I do this through a study of what has come to be known as 'postcolonial criticism'.

THE WORK OF EDWARD SAID: *ORIENTALISM*

Edward Said has rightly observed that the literary–cultural establishment has declared the serious study of imperialism and culture off-limits. To give an example, Raymond Williams's influential *Culture and Society* (1958) and *The Long Revolution* (1967), which spanned the years of colonial conquest and the consolidation of Empire, have nothing to say about the functioning of imperialist ideology in Britain. Very few 'great' novelists deal with colonialism and imperialism, and most literary critics, too, have remained silent.

But things are gradually changing. In a publisher's catalogue of new books, after 'Literary and cultural theory' and before 'Feminist theory', there is a new classification. It is called 'Postcolonial criticism' and lists books on, for example: *Europe and the Native Caribbean, 1492–1797*; *British Women Writers and Slavery, 1670–1834*; travel writing and 'transculturation'. They are by 'the theorists of colonialism': Edward Said, Homi Bhabha and Gayatri Spivak.

I begin by looking at Edward Said's enormously influential book, *Orientalism*. I will then consider Said's book which appeared fifteen years later: *Culture and Imperialism*. This is followed by an introduction to the views of two leading discourse analysts, Homi Bhabha and Gayatri Spivak. (Spivak, in recent years, has become particularly interested in imperialism and how the 'Third World' has been created as a representation.) But why is there a section on colonial discourse in a book on identity? I am writing this chapter about colonialism and imperialism because they were not only a territorial and economic but inevitably also a subject-constituting project. The imperial project of educating the natives has influenced the identities of millions of people, all over the world, who realised that they remained subordinate dependants of an authority based somewhere other than in their lives.

In a previous chapter, I mentioned 'Englishness' and its relationship with Empire; but we should not limit the discussion to the English. The European nations had their imperial adventures too. It could be argued that the major component in European culture is precisely what made that culture hegemonic both in and outside Europe: the idea of European identity as a superior one in comparison with all the non-European peoples and cultures. The French and British have had a long tradition of what Edward Said calls 'Orientalism', a way of coming to terms with the Orient that is based on the Orient's special place in European Western experience.[1] The Orient is the place of Europe's greatest, richest and oldest colonies, the sources of its civilisations and languages, its cultural contestant, and one of its deepest and most recurring images of the Other. In addition, the Orient has helped to define Europe (or the West) as its contrasting image, idea, personality, experience.

By 'Orientalism', Said means several things. Anyone who teaches, writes about or researches the Orient is an Orientalist. Secondly, Orientalism is a style of thought based upon an ontological and epistemological distinction made between 'the Orient' and 'the Occident'. Many poets, novelists, philosophers, political theorists and others have accepted the basic distinction between East and West as the starting point for elaborate theories, epics, novels and social descriptions. Thirdly, Orientalism can be discussed and analysed as the corporate institution for dealing with the Orient – dealing with it by making statements about it, authorising views of it, describing it, teaching it, ruling over it; in short, Orientalism as a Western style for dominating and having authority over it. The relationship between Occident and Orient is a relationship of power, of domination.

Orientalism is not an airy European fantasy about the Orient, but a created body of theory and practice in which, for many generations, there has been a considerable material investment. Continued investment made Orientalism, as a system of knowledge about the Orient, an accepted grid for filtering through the Orient into Western consciousness.

Said draws attention to the culturally-sanctioned habit of deploying large generalisations by which reality is divided into various collectives: languages, races, types, colours and mentalities, each category being not so much a neutral designation as an evaluative interpretation. Underlying these categories is the rigidly binary opposition of 'ours' and 'theirs', with the former always encroaching upon the latter.

This opposition was reinforced not only by anthropology, linguistics and history but also, of course, by the Darwinian thesis on survival and natural selection, and by the rhetoric of high cultural humanism. European values were (let us say) liberal, humane and correct, and were supported by the tradition of belles-lettres, informed scholarship and rational inquiry.

But these cultural values excluded as much as they included. There was a system of rule whose principle was simply to make sure that no Orientals were ever allowed to be independent and rule themselves. This was a principle that was to be challenged by a growing nationalism.

Most of the resistance to Occidental-white rule has been conducted in the name of nationalism. Nationalism, as we now know, is a deeply contradictory enterprise. It has been successful in ridding many countries of imperialist rule, but the problem is that many of the nationalist struggles were led by bourgeoisies that were partly formed, and to some extent produced, by the colonial power. These bourgeoisies replaced the colonial force with a new class-based exploitative force. Instead of liberation after decolonisation, one simply gets old colonial structures in new national terms.[2]

There is another problem with nationalism: the cultural horizons of nationalism are fatally limited by the common history of coloniser and colonised assumed by the nationalist movement itself. Imperialism, after all, is a cooperative venture. Both the master and the slave participate in it, and both grew up in it, although unequally. Imperialism, in most places, set out quite consciously to modernise, instruct and 'civilise' the natives. As Edward Said has said, a massive chapter in cultural history across five continents grows up out of it. The annals of schools, missions, universities and scholarly societies in Asia, Africa, Latin America, Europe and America fill its pages.[3]

In the era of nationalist anti-imperialism, there was, then, an acute awareness of European and Western culture as imperialism. Europe's claim to guide and instruct the non-European was challenged by prophets and priests, poets and visionaries. In this period, there is a pressing need for the recovery of the land which, because of the presence of the colonising outsider, is recoverable at first only through the imagination.[4] Many writers have noted the importance of the geographical: imperialism, after all, is an act of geographical violence through which virtually every space in the world is explored, charted and finally brought under control. For the natives, the history of their colonial servitude is inaugurated by this loss to an outsider of the local place, whose concrete geographical identity must thereafter be searched for and somehow restored.[5]

With the new territoriality, there are other developments: the search for authenticity, for a more congenial national origin than that provided by colonial history, for a new pantheon of heroes and myths, and a redevelopment of the native language.

One of the heroes of the anti-imperialist struggle is Frantz Fanon, who analysed the impact of white colonialism on blacks in studies which, influenced by Sartre's existentialism as well as by psychoanalysis, showed the deforming effect on both peoples.[6] The theoretical elements of Fanon's thinking were phenomenology, existentialism and Hegelian Marxism, and the aim of his writing was to liberate the consciousness of the oppressed. One of his main concerns was the constitution of self-identity. His writings promote the construction of a politically-conscious, unified, revolutionary self that is in struggle against the oppressor. In his view, decolonisation is the meeting of two forces, opposed to each by their very nature. Colonisation constructed white as the sovereign law, and black as its transgression; white was good and beautiful, black was evil and ugly.[7]

Colonialism, writes Frantz Fanon, is not simply content to impose its rule upon the present and the future of a dominated country. It is not satisfied with holding a people in its grip. By a kind of perverted logic, it turns to the past of the oppressed people and distorts, disfigures and destroys it.[8] Colonialism tried to plant deep in the minds of the native population the idea that before the advent of white rule their history was one which was dominated by barbarism. Europe brought the blessings of civilisation, but the colonised returned only ingratitude.

What effects does imperialism have on black identity? Frantz Fanon noted three phases. In the first phase, there is unqualified assimilation. The black intellectual's inspiration is European, and he gives proof that he has assimilated the culture of the occupying power. In the second phase, we find that the black writer is disturbed; he decides to remember what he is. Past happenings of the bygone days of his childhood will be brought up out of the depths of his memory; old legends will be reinterpreted. In this period of creative work, the native writer is not a part of his people, since he only has exterior relations with his people.

Finally, there is the third, fighting phase in which the native writers turn themselves into awakeners of the people. A great many people feel the need to speak to their nation. Hence comes a revolutionary, national literature. The colonised now wish to change the role and identity fashioned for them.

Since the Second World War, the slow and painful decolonisation of the European empires has taken place; there has been, at the same time, an attempt to decolonise European thought. This is where Edward Said's book *Orientalism* fits in. He argues that a complex set of representations was fabricated which, for the West, effectively became the Orient and determined its understanding of it. Disclosing a web of writings that stretch from literary, historical, scholarly accounts to political, military and imperial administrative ones, Said suggests that the former produced the Orient for the eventual appropriation by the latter. Said's book demonstrates, above all, the deep complicity of academic forms of knowledge with institutions of power.

The main argument is that the texts of Orientalism can create not only knowledge but also the very reality which they appear to describe. On the one hand he suggests that Orientalism merely consists of a representation that has nothing to do with the real Orient, while on the other hand he argues that its knowledge was put in the service of colonial conquest, occupation and administration. To put it in another way: Said asserts that the Orient is just a representation, and yet he also claims that Orientalism provided the necessary knowledge for colonial conquest, that Orientalism justified colonialism in advance.

The book, therefore, falls into two halves: the first concerned with the invention of the Orient by Europe, and its construction as a representation; the second with the moment when this representation, and the academic knowledge that was fabricated around it, became an instrument in the service of colonial power. Said's analysis of the Orientalists takes the form of a series of judgements, according to which each writer is identified in turn as complicit in the process of intellectual subordination of the East by the West. One critic comments:

> Said's remorseless drive to judge the texts of Orientalism into a straightforward 'for' and 'against' leads him to conclude that it

is therefore correct that every European, in what he could say about the Orient, was consequently a racist, an imperialist, and almost totally ethnocentric.[9]

Said's salient point is that Islam has been fundamentally misrepresented in the West. And yet, as he says, 'the real issue is whether indeed there can be a true representation of anything or whether any and all representations, because they are embedded first in the language and then in the culture, institutions, and political ambience of the representer'.[10] This raises all the problems about truth and reality that are being discussed in intellectual circles. If all knowledge is being produced within institutions of various sorts, there is always a determined relation to the state and to its political practices.

The problem that Said faces is that, if Orientalism as a discursive structure is so determining on writers about the East, how can he escape himself? How does Said separate himself from the coercive structures of knowledge that he is describing? In fact, there are critics who do say that Said's analysis ends up by repeating the same structures of knowledge and power that he censures.[11] Robert Young has suggested that Said's difficulty is that his ethical and theoretical values are so deeply involved in the history of the Western culture that he criticises. Said's culture is exclusively European high culture, and it is a pity that he is not aware of the tradition that derives from Brecht, Benjamin and the Frankfurt School. An objection to *Orientalism* has always been that it provides no alternative to the phenomenon which it criticises. Ultimately, we are all left with the question: how can knowledge that is non-dominative and non-coercive be produced in a setting that is deeply connected with the politics and strategies of power?

IMPERIALISM

Fifteen years after *Orientalism*, Said produced his book on *Culture and Imperialism*.[12] It lays out a huge literary and political map. He demarcates the main areas, he puts up many signposts, and he is generous in that he mentions the most important books which we should consult. It is a big book of synthesis. In academic life, at the present time, there is a strong tendency to separate and divide; to specialise. In contrast, what is interesting about Said is that he wants to understand the national and international context, the connections between fiction and the historical world.

Said extends Raymond Williams's concept of 'structures of feeling' by using the phrase 'structures of attitude and reference'. Said gives the example that in British culture there may be a consistency of concern in different authors that fixes socially desirable ideas. And with these references come attitudes about control. These attitudes create a virtual unanimity that there are subject races and that they should be ruled. These structures are bound up with the development of Britain's cultural identity.

Said deliberately abstains from advancing a completely worked-out theory of the connection between culture and imperialism. He believes that 'no one theory can explain or account for the connections among texts and societies. But reading and writing texts are never neutral activities: there are interests, powers, passions, pleasures entailed no matter how aesthetic or entertaining the work.'[13]

Said argues that in any serious study of contemporary literature we cannot postpone discussions of slavery, colonialism or racism. We should begin by acknowledging that the map of the world has no dogmatically-sanctioned spaces, essences or privileges.

He proposes a contrapuntal method of global analysis, in which texts and worldly institutions are seen working together. He wants to look at the comparative literature of imperialism, to consider metropolitan and formerly colonised societies with their intertwined histories.

Apart from an emphasis on history, Said focuses on geography. Imperialism and the culture associated with it affirm both the primacy of geography and an ideology about control of territory. The actual geographical possession of land is what empire in the final analysis is all about. We have become so used to thinking about temporality that we often overlook the function of space, geography and location.

Said's earlier, path-breaking book *Orientalism* focused only on the Middle East. In *Culture and Imperialism*, he has widened his concerns to include India, Africa and South-East Asia. He has also expanded his argument; he is now more aware that 'Orientalism' is an outcome, an effect of Imperialism. Compared with the earlier book, he is more aware that we belong to the period of colonialism and of resistance to it. Said begins by noting that, though we must try and understand the pastness of the past, there is no way in which the past can be separated from the present. How we formulate or represent the past shapes our understanding of the present. How do the past and present of the imperial encounter interact with each other? The meaning of the imperial past is not totally contained within it, but has entered the reality of hundreds of millions of people. Imperialism is the practice, theory and attitudes of a dominating metropolitan centre ruling a distant territory. Said reminds us that, by 1914, Europe controlled roughly 85 per cent of the earth. Hardly anyone alive today has not been touched by the empires of the past. Little attention, however, has been paid to the privileged role of culture in the modern imperial experience.

Imperialism was not a simple act of acquisition and accumulation; Western men and women believed that they had an obligation to rule inferior peoples and that these peoples should be subjugated. In other words, the enterprise depends upon the idea of having an empire. When most European thinkers celebrated humanity or culture, they were mainly celebrating ideas and values that they ascribed to their own national culture. World literatures were organised as a hierarchy with Europe and its Latin Christian literatures at the top. European pre-eminence seemed natural; after all, Europe did command the world.

Said believes that there was a coherent, fully mobilised system of ideas about gaining overseas territory towards the end of the eighteenth century. This was before the systematic conquests under Napoleon, the rise of nationalism and the European nation-state. He emphasises that almost all colonial schemes begin with an assumption of native backwardness and general inadequacy.

It is well known that, wherever they went, Europeans began to change the local habitat; their conscious aim was to transform territories into images of what they had left behind. The process was never-ending, as a high number of plants, animals, crops and building methods gradually turned the colony into a new place, complete with new diseases, environmental imbalances and traumatic dislocations for the overpowered natives.

But how does culture participate in imperialism and yet is somehow excused for its role? It is argued that novels have authority. There is the authority of the author, the narrator and the community. Novels confirm and highlight an underlying hierarchy of family, property, nation. Our world is always validated; other worlds are devalued. This can be seen in the racist writings of Carlyle, Macaulay and Ruskin. Said places them in the context of a staggering range of British overseas war campaigns which led to territorial gain. And, with the active domination of the non-Western world by the West, there is a codification of difference ranging from primitive to subject races and finally to superior or civilised peoples.

THE NOVEL AND IMPERIALISM

Said argues that literature makes constant references to itself as somehow participating in Europe's overseas expansion. Novels (and other art-forms) create structures of feeling that support, elaborate and consolidate the practice of Empire. He does not say that the novel 'caused' imperialism. The argument is that the novel and imperialism fortified each other to such a degree that it is impossible to read one without in some way dealing with the other. Said's 'contrapuntal reading' suggests that in reading a text one must open it out both to what went into it and to what its author excluded. Moreover, we must connect the structures of a narrative to the ideas, concepts and experiences from which it draws support.

Let me now briefly present a few of Said's comments on the work of three novelists: Rudyard Kipling, Edward Forster and Albert Camus. Though compressed, these remarks may be useful in indicating the general approach. In Said's view, Kipling's *Kim* (1901) deals with a masculine world dominated by travel, trade, adventure and intrigue. The novel celebrates the friendship of two men in an Orientalised India. Kipling assumes an uncontested empire. The conflict between Kim's colonial service and loyalty to his Indian companions is unresolved not because Kipling could not face it, but because for Kipling there was no conflict. In *Kim*, no-one challenges British rule; it is India's destiny to be ruled by England. It is not surprising that Kipling gives us the British view of the Mutiny. The novel describes an India of the imagination which contains no elements of either social change or political resistance.

Another novel set in India that Said discusses is *A Passage to India* (1924). E. M. Forster's achievement is to show how the moral drama of contemporary Indian mysticism (Godbole) and nationalism (Aziz) unfolds against the older clash between the British and Mogul Empires. Said comments:

> Almost by virtue of its liberal, humane espousal of Fielding's views and attitudes, *A Passage to India* is at a loss, partly because Forster's commitment to the novel exposes him to difficulties in India he cannot deal with. The sense that India and Britain are

opposed nations . . . is played down, muffled, frittered away . . . The novel's helplessness neither goes all the way and condemns (or defends) British colonialism, nor condemns or defends Indian nationalism.[14]

Said also discusses Algerian nationalism and the work of Camus. Why was Algeria the setting for so many of Camus's novels? To what extent does his work consolidate the nature of the French enterprise in Algeria? Camus's narratives of existential confrontation, which had once seemed to be about opposing both mortality and Nazism, can now be read as part of the debate about culture and imperialism.

Most readers tend to associate Camus's novels with French novels about France. Moreover, his novels are usually read as parables of the human condition. Said disagrees with this view, and argues that Camus's work is informed by a colonial sensibility. He usually ignores Algerian history, and it is well known that in the last years of his life Camus publicly opposed the demands for Algerian independence. Both the novels *The Outsider* and *The Plague* are about the deaths of Arabs. In the former, there is a famous incident in which Meursault kills an Arab but he is not named, his mother and father are not mentioned. Why is he without a history? Said does not doubt that Camus's fiction incorporates French imperial attitudes.

RESISTANCE

This brings us to the question of resistance. To become aware of one's self as belonging to a subject people is the founding insight of anti-imperialist nationalism. Said believes that peoples being conscious of themselves as prisoners in their own land is one of the main themes in the literature of the imperialised world.

There are some important themes in theorising cultural resistance. There is, for example, the insistence on the right to see the community's history coherently and integrally. The role of the national language is central here, because it is through language that national culture organises and sustains communal memory.

When anti-imperialist struggles begin to take place, nationalism begins to grow. All nationalist cultures depend heavily on the concept of national identity, and nationalist politics is a politics of identity.

It should also be mentioned that there is the idea that resistance, far from being merely a reaction to imperialism, is an alternative way of conceiving human history. We must make a distinction, writes Said, between nationalism and liberation. Liberation by its very nature involves a transformation of social consciousness beyond national consciousness.

Said also makes the point that Europeans could not have conquered and ruled their empires without indigenous collaboration, without the voluntary or enforced cooperation of their governing elites. Many of the individuals collaborating with imperialism began by trying to emulate modern European ways. The many colonial schools throughout the Empire taught generations of the native bourgeoisie. Out of that learning, millions grasped the fundamentals of modern life, yet remained subordinate dependants of a foreign imperial power. The indigenous bourgeoisie formed a powerful elite, 'the Nehrus and the Gandhis', who, in leading the various nationalist independence movements, had authority handed on to them.

The scenario, then, seems to be like this: a cultural war against imperialism occurs in the form of resistance in the colonies. The first phase of this dynamic produces nationalist independence movements, the later and more acute phase produces liberation struggles. Fanon was the first major theorist, argues Said, to realise that orthodox nationalism followed along the same track hewn out of imperialism, which while it appeared to be conceding authority to the nationalist bourgeoisie was really extending its hegemony. Fanon makes the case for liberation as a process and not as a goal contained automatically by the newly independent nations.

Said contrasts the roughly contemporary work of Michel Foucault and Frantz Fanon. Fanon's work seeks to treat colonial and metropolitan societies together, as discrepant but related entities, while Foucault's work moves further and further away from serious consideration of social wholes. In his last years, Foucault swerved away from politics altogether.[15]

Said also criticises the Frankfurt School for being silent on racist theory and anti-imperialist resistance. Reacting against French theory and Western Marxism, which have ignored the question of imperialism, Said argues for a contrapuntal analysis of history that sees Western and non-Western experiences as belonging together, connected by imperialism. Said's method in *Culture and Imperialism* is to rejoin experience and culture, to read texts from the metropolitan centre and from the peripheries contrapuntally. He gives the following example:

> Jane Austen's *Mansfield Park* is about England and about Antigua, and the connection is made explicitly by Austen. It is

therefore about order at home and slavery abroad, and ought to
be read with Eric Williams and C. L. R. James alongside the
book. Similarly, Camus and Gide write about precisely the same
Algeria as Fanon and Racine'.[16]

In other words, Said wants the experiences of domination and being
dominated to be studied together. Imperial domination and resistance
to it is a dual process and both sides of the contest should be interpreted not only hermeneutically but also politically.

The contrapuntal method goes beyond the reified polarities of
East versus West. To read not univocally but contrapuntally is to
have a simultaneous awareness of the metropolitan history that is
narrated and of those other histories against which the dominant
discourse acts. Said gives as an example Gauri Viswanathan's work,
which has uncovered the political origins of modern English studies.
What has conventionally been thought of as a discipline entirely by
and for British youth was first created by early nineteenth-century
administrators for the ideological pacification and reformation of a
potentially rebellious Indian population, and then imported into
England for a very different but related use there.[17]

Another example of the contrapuntal method is the book alluded
to earlier, James's *Black Jacobins*, which treats the Santo Domingo
slave uprising as a process within the same history as that of the
French Revolution.[18] Events in Haiti criss-cross and refer to one
another like voices in a fugue. In other words, we cannot deal with
the literature of the peripheries without also attending to the literature
of the metropolitan centres.

Furthermore, Said argues that it is impossible to write of liberation
and nationalism, however allusively, without also declaring oneself
for or against them. As far as imperialism is concerned, there can be
no neutrality; one is either on the side of empire or against it.

Most accounts of European cultural history still take little notice
of empire. The great novelists are analysed as if they were completely
aloof from it. But now, changes are taking place. Thirty years ago,
few universities studied African literature; now an interest is being
taken in the works of Bessie Head, Wole Soyinka, Nadine Gordimer,
J. M. Coetzee and many others. No longer does the logos dwell
exclusively in London and Paris. There is now an interesting variety
of hybrid cultural work.

CROSSING BOUNDARIES

Our age has produced more refugees, migrants, displaced persons and exiles than ever before in history – most of them as consequences of great imperial and postcolonial conflicts. Said writes that he is thinking of the migrant, the stranger, 'the intellectual and artist in exile, the political figure between domains, between forms, between homes, and between languages'.[19] Exile, far from being the fate of nearly-forgotten unfortunates who are dispossessed and expatriated, becomes something closer to a norm, an experience of crossing boundaries and charting new territories in defiance of the classic economic enclosures.

Crossing boundaries is often associated with transgression. In fact, Said refers to the French urban sociologist Paul Virilio, who has suggested that the fundamental transgressive act is to inhabit the normally uninhabited (factories, churches, empty buildings).[20] Virilio's notion of counter-habitation is to live as migrants do in habitually uninhabited but nevertheless public spaces.

Later, Said remarks that 'It is not only tired, harassed, and dispossessed refugees who cross borders and try to become acculturated in new environments; it is also the whole gigantic system of the mass media that is ubiquitous, slipping by most barriers and settling in nearly everywhere'.[21] The new media have the power to penetrate more deeply into a receiving culture than any previous manifestation of Western technology.

It is clear that Said has been deeply influenced by Gramsci's work, and is sympathetic to his approach. This is not surprising, since Gramsci had a profound understanding of culture, the workings of capital and the role of intellectuals. Said argues that comparative literature, English studies and cultural studies have contributed to the maintenance of Western ascendancy over non-Western natives, the ongoing contest between north and south, metropolis and periphery, white and native.

Besides Gramsci, Said draws on the work of Frantz Fanon – not the Fanon of *Black Skin, White Masks*, a psychic study, but of *The Wretched of the Earth*.[22] Said often cites Fanon because he expresses the immense cultural shift from the terrain of nationalist independence to that of liberation.

It is clear that Said is very concerned about the role of intellectuals in modern life. There has been a fantastic explosion of specialised and separatist knowledge. Critical of this trend, Said is antagonistic to all forms of professionalism that divide material into fields, subdivisions, specialities, accreditations and the like. Consider history as a discipline, for example. He believes that many orthodox, authoritatively national and institutional versions of history tend to freeze provisional and highly contrastable views of history into 'official versions'. What Said tries to do in his work is to focus on the disparate but intertwined and interdependent, and above all overlapping streams of historical experience. Said, in short, wants to make connections between the past and present, between imperialiser and imperialised, between culture and imperialism. He does this not to reduce differences but rather to convey a more urgent sense of the interdependence between things.

One of the reasons why I have focused on Said's work is that he has brought together a lot of the intellectual work that is being done all over the world about culture and imperialism. As he says, it is clear that hardly anyone alive today has not been touched by the empires of the past. The identities of millions of people have been deeply affected, in many different ways, by imperialism.

Said is especially interested in questions of national identity and exile, and does not write much about personal identity or the psyche. Nevertheless, he has some profound things to say about identity. An important, basic point is: no-one today is one thing. Labels like Indian, or woman, or Muslim or American, are no more than starting points. He does not regard national identities as God-given essences. He sees them as contrapuntal ensembles, for it is the case that no identity can ever exist by itself and without an array of negatives. (Did not the Greeks always require barbarians?) While identity is crucial, just to assert a different identity is never enough. The main job facing the cultural intellectual is not to accept the politics of identity as given, but to show how all representations are constructed, for what purpose, by whom, and with what components.

Said concludes his book with a quotation from a twelfth-century monk: 'The person who finds his homeland sweet is still a tender beginner; he to whom every soil is as his native one is already strong'.[23] The strong person achieves independence not by rejecting imperial national and provincial attachments, but by working through them. Perhaps this is what Said is trying to do.

POSTCOLONIAL CRITICISM: AN INTRODUCTION

Homi Bhabha

Said's *Orientalism* has been criticised for its reductive simplification from a postmodernist position by Homi Bhabha. He has written that Orientalism is not a single homogenising perspective but a polarity.[24] It is a discipline – of encyclopaedic learning and of imperial power – and yet on the other hand it is also a fantasy of the Other. Said posits a binary opposition between power and powerlessness, which requires the supposition of an exterior controlling intention and leaves no room for negotiation or resistance.

What Bhabha has done in a series of essays is to shift Said's perspective, which emphasises the representation of the Orient for consumption within a dominant Western culture, to focus on Orientalism's role when used as an instrument of colonial rule.[25] In Bhabha's view, though the representation may appear to be hegemonic, actually it carries within it a hidden flaw invisible at home but increasingly apparent abroad.

Focusing on the colonial stereotype, Bhabha argues that it is a complex, ambivalent, contradictory mode of representation. In racial stereotyping, 'colonial power produces the colonized as a fixed reality which is at once an other'.[26] In his view, colonial discourse does not merely represent the other so much as simultaneously project and disavow its difference. Bhabha has stressed the need to examine colonial discourse in psychoanalytical as well as historical terms. He writes that colonial discourse is an apparatus of power and goes on to suggest (against Foucault) that the colonial subject who is the object of surveillance is also the object of paranoia and fantasy on the part of the coloniser. Bhabha contends that there is a narcissistic demand for colonial objects and that when the narcissistic demand is refused, paranoia occurs: the coloniser perceives that the colonised hates him.

Bhabha tries to show (against Said) that the authority of colonial power was not straightforwardly possessed by the coloniser. Although there is surveillance, fixity is not achieved. He demonstrates this by developing Lacan's remarks on mimicry.[27] Mimicry is a form of stereotyping of the colonial Other. It refers to a colonial subject who will be recognisably the same as the coloniser but still different: 'not quite/not white'.

Bhabha refers to Macaulay, who conceived of a 'class of interpreters between us and the millions whom we govern – a class of persons Indian in blood and colour but English in taste, in opinions, in morals and in intellect' – in other words a mimic man (such people can be traced through the works of Kipling, Forster, Orwell and Naipaul).[28] If it is in some sense reassuring for the colonisers that Indians become in certain respects 'English', the production of mimic Englishmen also becomes disturbing, for mimicry is at once resemblance and menace. The mimic man, insofar as he is not entirely like the coloniser, white but not quite, constitutes only a partial representation of him: far from being reassured, the coloniser sees a grotesquely displaced image of himself. Mimicry, then, is the displacement of authoritative discourse where ambivalence shifts to fantasies of menace. To put this another way, the surveillant eye is suddenly confronted with a returning gaze of otherness and finds that its mastery, its sameness, is undone.

The coloniser performs certain strategies in order to maintain power, but the ambivalence which inevitably accompanies the attempt to fix the colonised as an object of knowledge means that the relation of power becomes much more equivocal. This process simultaneously stabilises and destabilises the position of the coloniser, and the identity of the coloniser and colonised becomes curiously elided.

We should remember that there is never a simple distinction between coloniser and colonised. Bhabha believes that there is always an ambivalence at work within the discourse of colonial instruction. For example, he shows how in the instructions of the East India Company, as the directions from London are transported for implementation in India, there is a slippage between their Western and colonial significance in the space between their initial enunciation and their destined address.

One of the main themes of the book edited by Homi Bhabha, *Nations and Narration*, is that 'the idea of nation is inseparable from its narration; that narration attempts interminably, to constitute identity against difference, inside and outside, and in the superiority of inside over outside, prepares against invasion and for enlightened colonialism'.[29] Bhabha writes that the margins of the nation displace the centre, the peoples of the periphery return to rewrite the history and fiction of the metropolis. It seems to me that he is interested in living and theorising in the interstices, in and between cultures. In his view, these intervening spaces have a strategic importance. Working on the borderlines, he is very aware of the cultural incommensurability that has to be negotiated. He has drawn attention to hybridisation, the process whereby two cultures retain their distinct characteristics and yet form something new. He has also suggested that when we think of power-knowledge we should also consider the role of anxiety. Anxiety can be a sign of danger, but it can also be a sign that something new is emerging.

Gayatri Spivak

Another writer, like Homi Bhabha, who is questioning Western canons and is trying to deconstruct the texts of colonialism is Gayatri Chakravorty Spivak. One of the most influential cultural theorists working today, she has referred to herself as 'the post-colonial diasporic Indian who seeks to decolonize the mind'.[30] A literary critic, her work can be considered deconstructionist, feminist and Marxist. She was born into an upper-class Brahmin family in metropolitan Bengal, had a postcolonial education, went to the USA as a student, and became a university teacher and an authority on Derrida and deconstruction. She sees herself as bicultural, but it is clear that she is not at home in either India or America. However, she doesn't feel that she is an exile either; an exile is someone who is obliged to stay away, and she doesn't feel that. She has strong views on the search for roots: 'If there's one thing I totally distrust, in fact more than distrust, despise and have contempt for, it is people looking for roots'.[31] She believes that everyone has roots. Why look for them? I can understand her view that it is important for people not to feel rooted in one place, but I wonder: why is she so unnecessarily emphatic?

She believes that the task of the critic is to ask: who is represented and who is not? It is to utilise the methods of literary analysis, to demonstrate the indeterminacy of the distinction between truth and fiction in imperialist histories, as well as to construct counter-narratives.

In her work, she has focused on the relation of history to pedagogy, and criticised the way in which nineteenth-century literary history is taught without any consideration of imperialism and its cultural representation.[32] She argues that analyses of colonial discourse demonstrate that history is not simply the disinterested production of facts, but is rather a process of 'epistemic violence'. For her, the epistemic violence of the discourses of the Other include: imperialism, the colonised, Orientalism, the exotic, the primitive, the anthropological and the folkloric. Nor surprisingly, a concept with which Spivak has often been associated is 'marginal'.

From an interest in the metaphor of margins, she has moved onto an interest in the history of margins. She believes that, in a sense, there is nothing that is central. The centre is always constituted in terms of its own marginality. She makes the interesting point that textual criticism in the premodern period was much interested in marginalia. In the early print culture of the West, marginalia were in fact rather important, because it was in the margins that the so-called argument of the paragraph was written.

Spivak is very interested in subject-positions and has drawn attention to the way in which the factors of class and, particularly, gender create a heterogeneous field. She is particularly concerned with the apparently monolithic and ubiquitous signifier 'Third World Woman'.

Spivak is often asked to speak as a spokeswoman for the Third World point of view. She questions the portmanteau description of herself as a 'Third World Woman' because she was, as I mentioned earlier, born in Calcutta in the 1940s into a metropolitan, professional family. She argues that the idea of the Third World is a monolithic entity and that people should fight against such labelling. Perhaps such labelling reflects a desire of First World people to have a manageable other?

From a Marxist point of view, one can argue that the worker produces capital because the worker, the container of labour power, is the source of value. By the same token that it is possible to suggest to the so-called 'Third World' that it produces the wealth and the possibility of the cultural self-representation of the 'First World', Spivak argues that the US educational system is able to make itself technically and qualitatively well endowed because a lot of it is produced by the 'Third World'. In short, it is the manipulation of Third World labour that sustains the resources of the US academy which produces the ideological supports for that very manipulation.

Some Western scholarship constitutes women of the Third World as a homogeneous group, which it then uses as a category of analysis on the basis of certain sociological and anthropological universals which crush out specific cultural, historical and economic contexts. This paternalistic assumption of an identical cross-cultural universal subordination unquestioningly privileges the values of Western feminism. Not only is much of Western feminism ethnocentric, but also in certain contexts it can itself be shown to be a contemporary form of colonial discourse.

Spivak states that the native is constructed into a narcissistic, self-consolidating other for the Western feminist. In her view, theorists must work out the heterogeneous production and constitution of women as sexed subjects, not according to the schemas of psycho-analysis but in terms of the diversity of subject-positions which each individual is obliged to take up or refuse. The subaltern as gendered subject has a subject-position different from the subaltern as class-subject.

As an example of the process by which the colonial subject functions only to consolidate the self of the coloniser, she considers the career of Bertha Mason, the white Jamaican Creole wife of Rochester in *Jane Eyre*:

> In this fictive England, Bertha must play out her role, act out the transformation of herself into that fictive Other, set fire to the house and kill herself, so that Jane Eyre can become the feminist individualist heroine of British fiction. I must read this as an allegory of the general epistemic violence of imperialism, the construction of a self-immolating colonial subject for the glorification of the social mission of the colonizer.[33]

The moment when Jane achieves her independence by inheriting a fortune from the West Indies is also the moment in which she becomes complicit with the history of slavery.

The 'Third World Woman' is not allowed to speak; she is caught between patriarchy and imperialism, subject-constitution and object-formation, between tradition and modernisation. She is rewritten continuously as the object of patriarchy or of imperialism. Spivak is aware of the ways in which radical critiques of patriarchy can themselves become oppressive or imperialist when seen in a different context. But there is also the in-built colonialism of First World feminism towards the Third which means that Western liberal feminism validates forms of behaviour which, possible only for the elite, can at the same time serve to oppress sub-proletarian women.

By changing the question from 'who am I?' to 'who is the other woman?', Spivak offers a heterogeneity and discontinuity which demonstrates the extent to which – although, as women, women may be said to share a common situation – each instance of being a woman is historically specific.

In the same way as with the 'Third World Woman', Spivak argues that the concept of the Third World has itself to be retrieved from its role as convenient but hegemonic signifier that homogenises the Third World into questions of nationalism and ethnicity. Most arguments, whether from coloniser or colonised, tend to revolve around the terms which the colonisers have constructed. To reverse an opposition of this kind is to remain caught within the very terms that are being disputed. Nationalist resistance to imperialism, for example, itself derives its notion of nation and of national self-determination from the Western culture that is being resisted. Nationalism is a product of imperialism and often only succeeds in changing the situation from territorial imperialism to neo-colonialism.[34]

Spivak has noted that the heterogeneity of one's own culture is protected because one sees oneself as outside of the cultural construction of gender and race or as a victim of it, whereas the homogeneity of other cultures is implicitly taken for granted. In short, Spivak has accused First World academic feminists of a double standard: of ignoring, reducing or explaining away the otherness of other women. She has also challenged the phallic metaphors through which gender roles are constructed, and has discussed the oppression of women under patriarchy in terms of the effacement of the clitoris, of women's sexual pleasure, whereby clitoridectomy can be considered a metonymy of women's social and legal status.

Before concluding this section, I must refer briefly to the debate about the relative merits of the 'universal' and the 'specific' intellectual. Sartre, a universal intellectual, was attacked by Foucault who argued for the specific intellectual. Specific intellectuals are those who work only 'within specific sectors at the precise points where their own conditions of life or work situate them (housing, the hospital, the asylum, the laboratory, the university, family and sexual relations)'.[35] Spivak, to my surprise, remarks: 'I cannot in fact clean my hand and say "I'm specific". In fact I must say that I'm an essentialist from time to time.' She criticises those who keep themselves clean by not committing themselves to anything. In her view, many people protect their theoretical purity by repudiating essentialism. But it is not possible, within discourse, to escape essentialising somewhere. Since one cannot not be an essentialist, why not look at the way in which one is essentialist, carve out a representative essentialist position, and then do politics according to the old rules while remembering the danger in this? 'Strategically, one can look at essentialisms, not as descriptions of the way things are, but as something one must adopt to produce a critique of anything.'[36] One can use terms such as 'essentialism' strategically without necessarily making an overall commitment to them.

Spivak has described herself as a deconstructionist feminist Marxist. She believes that the feminist and Marxist projects cannot be thought of as operating together, although they do relate. Marxism and feminism are extremely heterogeneous, and she argues that these discourses must bring each other to crisis all the time because that is the relationship between theory and practice. As for deconstruction, she defines it more as a way of looking than a programme for doing. She values Derrida's critique of phallocentrism and anthropomorphism, but she argues that there is no deep coherence between deconstruction and Marxism. In her view, the relationship between a reading of Marxism enhanced by deconstruction, and the extraordinary richness of the Marxian project, is a much more interesting one than a mere coherence. Though she is not interested in privileging the class struggle, she finds in Marx's analysis of capital the most powerful way of understanding what's going on in the world. She knows that there is a tense relationship between deconstruction, feminism and Marxism, but rather than look for an elegant coherence, or produce a continuist narrative, she wants to preserve the discontinuities within these discourses. She argues that deconstruction, feminism and Marxism must critically interrupt each other and be brought into a productive crisis.

CRITICISM

Having given valorising expositions of Bhabha's and Spivak's projects, I want to express briefly another, more critical, point of view about their work. Recently, a new edition of Fanon's *Black Skin, White Masks* has been published with a foreword by Homi Bhabha. It is a poststructuralist reading of Fanon's text in which Bhabha is critical of Fanon's use of Hegelian concepts, the phenomenological affirmation of self and other, and the Marxist dialectic. This sort of critique is very fashionable among poststructuralists and postmodernists. Bhabha writes: 'it is through image and fantasy – those orders that figure transgressively on the borders of history and the unconscious – that Fanon profoundly evokes the colonial condition'.[37] Bhabha praises Fanon for shifting the focus of cultural racism from the politics of nationalism to the politics of narcissism.

I am critical of Bhabha's stance and want to ask: what is the politics of a criticism that focuses not on ideology but 'discourse'? In Bhabha's account, relations of power are theorised in terms of psychoanalytic categories. In deconstructing the anti-colonialist text, the voice of the oppressed native is erased.

The other theorist associated with colonial discourse analysis,

Gayatri Chakravorty Spivak, has theorised the silence of the doubly-oppressed subordinate woman. She has written that the European agent induces the native to collude in its own subject(ed) formation as other and voiceless. Spivak's work, broadly speaking, disparages the nationalist discourses of resistance, and exaggerates the role of the postcolonial woman intellectual. As Benita Parry has pointed out, in this sort of work colonial power is theorised as something textual.[38] Analysts like Bhabha and Spivak overstress discourse and tend to ignore the 'counter-discourse' of liberation movements. For them, critical practice is to disclose the construction of the signifying system and thereby to deprive it of its mandate to rule. In brief, colonial discourse analysis has failed to engage with the range and effectivity of imperialism's oppressive and exploitative practices.

It is clear that the work of Said, Bhabha, Spivak and others is important in showing that colonialism was not a marginal activity on the edges of English life, but fundamental in its own cultural self-representation. There are, however, some matters for concern. Indebted to poststructuralist thought and influenced by postmodernism, there is a shift in their work from politics to psychoanalysis, from ideology to discourse, to textuality. I believe that colonial criticism should now try and develop a form of discourse that tries to wipe out negative and derogatory images portrayed by European literature, valorise native traditions and affirm the radical potential of historical memory.

NOTES

1. Edward W. Said, *Orientalism* (London: Penguin Books, 1985); idem, 'Orientalism Reconsidered', *Race and Class*, 27:2 (autumn 1985), 1–15. For a discussion of Said's book, see Madan Sarup, *Education and the Ideologies of Racism* (Stoke on Trent: Trentham Books, 1991), pp. 68–75.
2. Edward Said, 'Nationalism, Colonialism, and Literature', Field Day Pamphlet no. 15, Field Day Theatre Company, Derry, 1988.
3. An extract from the above, 'Yeats and Decolonization', is in Dennis Walder (ed.), *Literature in the Modern World* (Oxford: Oxford University Press, 1990), p. 35.
4. See Benedict Anderson, *Imagined Communities: Reflections on the Origins and Spread of Nationalism* (London: Verso, 1983).
5. One example of recent 'geographical' thinking is David Harvey, *The Condition of Postmodernity: An Enquiry into the Origins of Cultural Change* (Oxford: Basil Blackwell, 1989).
6. David Caute, *Fanon* (London: Fontana/Collins, 1970).
7. Some theorists are critical of binary oppositions; they argue that the two poles of an opposition are complicit with one another. I think Jacques Derrida is right to remind us that binary oppositions are really a violent hierarchy where one of the two terms forcefully governs the other.
8. Frantz Fanon, 'On National Culture', in Walder (ed.), op. cit., p. 265. This is an extract from *The Wretched of the Earth*.

9. Robert Young, *White Mythologies: Writing History and the West* (London: Routledge, 1990), p .204.
10. Said, *Orientalism*, op. cit., p. 272.
11. Young, *White Mythologies*, op. cit., p. 127.
12. Edward W. Said, *Culture and Imperialism* (London: Chatto and Windus, 1993). Henceforth *C and I*.
13. Ibid., p. 385.
14. Ibid., p. 243.
15. Ibid., p. 336. See also Edward W. Said, 'Foucault and the Imagination of Power', in David Hoy (ed.), *Foucault: A Critical Reader* (Oxford: Basil Blackwell, 1986), pp. 149–55.
16. *C and I*, p. 313.
17. Gauri Viswanathan, *The Masks of Conquest: Literary Study and British Rule in India* (New York: Columbia University Press, 1989).
18. C. L. R. James, *Black Jacobins: Toussaint L'Ouverture and the San Domingo Revolution* (New York: Vintage, 1963).
19. *C and I*, p. 403.
20. Ibid., p. 395.
21. Ibid., p. 374.
22. Frantz Fanon, *Black Skin, White Masks* (London: Pluto Press, 1986). This edition contains a foreword by Homi Bhabha. Frantz Fanon, *The Wretched of the Earth* (New York: Grove, 1968).
23. *C and I*, p. 407.
24. Homi Bhabha, 'Difference, Discrimination, and the Discourse of Colonialism', in Francis Barker et al. (eds), *The Politics of Theory* (Colchester: University of Essex Press, 1983).
25. Bhabha's essays include: 'The Other Question', *Screen*, 24:6 (1983); 'Of Mimicry and Man: The Ambivalence of Colonial Discourse', *October*, 28 (1984); 'Sly Civility', *October*, 34 (1985); 'Signs Taken for Wonders: Questions of Ambivalence and Authority under a Tree Outside Delhi, May 1817', in Francis Barker et al. (eds), *Europe and its Others*, 2 vols (Colchester: University of Essex Press, 1985).
26. What does it mean to use Western psychoanalytic theory to analyse the colonial condition? Bhabha discusses some of these issues in his 'Foreword' to Frantz Fanon, *Black Skin, White Masks* (London: Pluto Press, 1986).
27. For Jacques Lacan's discussion of 'mimicry', see *The Four Fundamental Concepts of Psycho-Analysis* (London: Penguin Books, 1979), pp. 98–100. He reminds us that mimicry is like camouflage as practised in warfare, not a harmonisation. For Bhabha, colonial mimicry is 'the desire for a reformed recognizable Other, as a subject of a difference that is almost the same but not quite. Which is to say that the discourse of mimicry is constructed around an ambivalence; in order to be effective mimicry must continually produce its slippage, its excess, its difference.' See Homi Bhabha, 'Of Mimicry and Man: The Ambivalence of Colonial Discourse', in James Donald and Stuart Hall (eds), *Politics and Ideology* (Milton Keynes: Open University Press, 1986), p. 199.
28. Sara Suleri argues that from Forster's *A Passage to India* onwards, books about India have been more accurately books about the representation of India. These acts of representation are a mode of recolonisation; there is an impulse to empty the area out of history and to represent India as an amorphous state of mind. She sees Forster's novel as a humanely liberal parable for imperialism. In her view, Forster provides Western narrative with its most compelling image of India, the figure of India as a hollow or cave. He is obsessed with representing India as a figure of both an erotic yet a sterile duplicity. That the Orient has traditionally been represented as a figure of seduction, duplicity and rape is a commonplace that is clearly established by European historical and travel narratives from the seventeenth century onwards. She notes that Naipaul's *An Area of Darkness* repeats Forster's model. Both fictions share in that Western project which represents India as an empty site that

is bounded only by an aura of irrationality. See, for example, Sara Suleri, *The Rhetoric of English India* (Chicago: University of Chicago Press, 1992); Rob Nixon, *London Calling: V. S. Naipaul, Postcolonial Mandarin* (Oxford: Oxford University Press, 1992).

29. Geoffrey Bennington, 'Postal Politics and the Institution of the Nation', in Homi K. Bhabha (ed.), *Nation and Narration* (London: Routledge, 1990), pp. 121–37 (p. 132).
30. Gayatri Chakravorty Spivak, *The Post-Colonial Critic: Interviews, Strategies, Dialogues*, ed. Sarah Harasym (London: Routledge, 1990), p. 67.
31. Ibid., p. 93.
32. Gayatri Chakravorty Spivak, *In Other Worlds: Essays in Cultural Politics* (New York: Methuen, 1987).
33. Spivak, 'Three Women's Texts and a Critique of Imperialism', *Critical Inquiry*, 12:1 (1985). Note the reference to *sati*, the practice in India of the self-immolation of widows on the funeral pyres of their husbands.
34. Spivak, *In Other Worlds*, op. cit., p. 245.
35. Michel Foucault, *Power/Knowledge: Selected Interviews and Other Writings, 1972–1977*, ed. Colin Gordon (Brighton: Harvester Press, 1980), p .126.
36. Spivak, *The Post-Colonial Critic*, op .cit., p. 51.
37. Fanon, *Black Skin, White Masks*, op .cit., p. xiii.
38. Benita Parry, 'Problems in Current Theories of Colonial Discourse', *Oxford Literary Review*, 9 (1987), p. 43.

12

·

'RACE', ETHNICITY AND NATION-NESS

In previous chapters, I have argued that identities do not remain static, but that they change according to the strength of social forces, the dynamics of class, nation, religion, sex and gender, 'race' and ethnicity. In this chapter I want, first, to focus on 'race'. I am particularly concerned about racism because I believe it has many effects, in different ways, on the identity of black people. I will consider some psychoanalytical aspects of the analyst–analysand and the white–black relationship, and then Kristeva's thesis on the 'foreigner within'.

In the second part of the chapter, I move from 'race' to questions of ethnicity. After making some connections between ethnic groups and nationalism, there are some reflections on the purpose of tradition, and the role of psychoanalysis in understanding identity. But, first, a note about 'race'.

It is assumed in this chapter that 'race' as a scientific fact does not exist. 'Race' in the biological sense does not exist – it has no scientific status.[1] Of course, there are still many people who believe that there is a valid biological concept of 'race' (I always put the term in inverted commas to indicate that we should question it, make it problematic), and we know how dangerous politically this view can be. In my view, when most people use the word 'race', they are either using it to refer to some physical characteristic like skin colour, or they are using it metaphorically.

BLACK IDENTITY: A PSYCHOANALYTIC VIEW

How do we acquire knowledge of our identity? Clearly, our identity is influenced by the experiences of our parents and what they tell us. But when listening to the views of other in the family, friends, the community, why do we accept some views and reject others? It is often the case that discrepancies between what we expect and what we actually experience (disconnections, or contradictions) make people aware of themselves and their identity.

More specifically, how is it that colonised people are made to feel inferior? Human subjects appropriate and transform aspects of different cultures with which they are in contact. But it must be remembered that white structures (I mean the structures in which, and through which, white people have power) propagate and impose their ideas. Certain images, representations, are imposed on black people by the cultural apparatuses. (In the media, for example, Asian women are depicted as if they are passive and victims of customs such as arranged marriages, the dowry system, purdah.)

We all know that in society there are hierarchies of power. But it is not often admitted that many of the hierarchies are based on notions of racial superiority. The whites represent the colonisers, the blacks the colonised. Some thinkers have argued that these hierarchies exist not only in the outside world but also in the inside, in the psyche. How does the outside get into the inside? Perhaps the values of parents are introjected in non-verbal ways. With the development of the superego, it seems that certain codes are internalised. It must be remembered that it is not the parents that are internalised but the parents' superegos.

The superego is the vehicle for the passing-on of tradition and, on the whole, traditions which are white. Frantz Fanon makes this quite clear in *Black Skin, White Masks*.[2] To succeed, black people have to repress aspects of their own culture and have to become 'white'. It has been speculated that the superego of some black people is doubly ferocious because it has been colonised by white rulers. This may help explain why some blacks are more severe on other blacks than they are on whites. (For example, I was with an Indian driver the other day, and he reacted much more aggressively to being overtaken by another black person than by a white man.)

I want now to consider the relationship between psychoanalysis and the identity of black people. Let me tell you three stories.

One: a 'Chinese' boy was adopted by a white family. Now an adult, many people see him as 'odd' because 'he goes on about foreigners, but he himself is a foreigner'. He has been brought up as English, he sees himself as English, but he is seen by others as Chinese. Here, 'race' has become culture. I could ask: what is the 'real' identity of this person? I think that that would be a wrong type of question to ask because there is no core or 'essence': there is a split between how he sees himself and how others see him.

Two: a black father, who had worked very hard all his life, used to reiterate to his son: 'we are third-class citizens here'. The son introjected his father's views and, in time, became a lowly clerk. And then he began to notice that to get on he had to work twice as hard as his white colleagues. How did the white analyst see this situation? If, as is often the case, the white person has a more comfortable life, would the analyst understand the situation? Would he or she feel guilty? In short, what is the general attitude of analysts to the external reality of their black analysands?

Three: a white analyst says to his black analysand (I don't like using the word patient): 'you've got a chip on your shoulder'. Yes, this could be the case. On the other hand, it could be that the analyst is not aware of the extent of personal, institutional and state racism experienced by black people. The analyst argues that what the analysand experiences as racism is really not to do with the external world, but the inner world; it is really to do with lack, loss, separation. The analysand replies: 'That is what the analyst would say, isn't it? Those who have a vested interest deny the existence of social oppression – they marginalise the issue of racism, they push it to the periphery.'

One of the problems encountered in therapy is that of personal antagonism. What happens when analyst and analysand don't like each other? Most analysts are white and middle-class, and there is an enormous power imbalance between analysts and analysands, white and blacks – just as there is in everyday life. Many analysts have no knowledge of how black people live, and impose their interpretations on them.

When considering the interactions between black and white people, we must bear in mind the effects of transference and countertransference. Transference occurs where the analysand transfers unconscious ideas on to the analyst. These are often fantasies in which the analyst replaces some other person. The analysand makes the analyst play the role of loved or feared parental figures. The analyst may, for example, find himself placed in the position of the superego. The subject's relationship to parental figures is once again lived out in the transference. Freud thought that the mechanism of transference on to the analyst is triggered off precisely at the moment when particular important repressed contents are in danger of being revealed.[3] The signs of the transference become more and more insistent the closer one gets to the pathogenic complex. Freud believed that the patient is obliged to repeat the repressed material.

Transference, then, involves two dimensions – actualisation of the past and displacement on to the person of the analyst.

Counter-transference is the result of the patient's influence on the analyst's unconscious feelings. It is the reaction to the other's transference. Some analysts believe that, in considering the analysis as a whole, we have to ascertain the part of transference and counter-transference in each of the two people present.[4]

Let me describe the situation in another way. The analysand has ideas about the analyst, and the analyst has his own ideas about himself. The analyst has ideas about the analysand, and the analysand has his own ideas about himself. If the analyst accepts the psychotic analysand's definition, he will be crushed. If the patient rejects the analyst's interpretation, he will not be helped. How can such a situation be contained? How can there be a bridging of such gaps between people?

We often think that it is the other person who distorts; we do not like admitting that we have agendas for them. And we are often deaf because others' views challenge our own. I think that a part of the problem is to do with disavowal and negation. Disavowal (*Verleugnung*) is a mode of defence which consists in the subject's refusing to recognise the reality of a traumatic perception. It is a primal defence mechanism for dealing with external reality. Sometimes, for example, a person can hold two incompatible positions at the same time. Inasmuch as disavowal affects external reality, Freud sees it as the first stage of psychosis, and he opposes it to repression; whereas the neurotic starts by repressing the demands of the id, the psychotic's first step is to disavow reality.[5]

Negation (*Verneinung*) has been defined as the procedure whereby the subject, while formulating one of his wishes, thoughts or feelings which have been repressed hitherto, contrives, by disowning it, to defend himself against it. It means denial or rejection of a statement which I have made or which has been imputed to me. Freud wrote that there was no stronger evidence that we have been successful in our efforts to uncover the unconscious than when the analysand reacts to it with the words 'I didn't think that'.[6]

ON REPRESENTATION

There are many problems associated with the representation of personal and social identity. There are times when people feel insecure; they have feelings of ambiguity, undecidability. There is a need for such groups to represent something about themselves and to others. In the process of representation, there is a transition from one stage to another.

Jacques Lacan's work is useful here. He argues that the human subject has a split identity, and that we all have a lack.[7] The group or entity seeking representation is not full in itself; it is not 'pure' because it needs something else. A 'lack' is a precondition for representing oneself. But the representation is never full, never complete. And if not everything can be represented, what is left over?

I would like to be able to say that our sense of identity must not be limited to being either 'white' or 'black' – there has always been an intermingling of the two – and that we must try and go beyond these narrow definitions. Much as I believe this (in the long term), to think this at the present time would be Utopian. While blacks are being attacked every day by right-wing groups, and discriminated against by institutions and national states, they will inevitably cling to their own community and culture. Some may even become more 'black' as an act of collective solidarity.

This reminds me of a similar argument in social theory, where there is a fierce debate between those who want to uphold a modernist notion of identity and those who argue for a postmodernist identity. The modernists stress the unitary subject and the view that identity must have some 'core' or essence that must remain the same. The postmodernists believe in dispersed identities. They say that we play different 'language games' and have a different identity in each language game. Some theorists believe that we are subjects with contradictions and that these bring about changes – our identities are processual.[8] I support those who say that we must create a viable position beyond current definitions of modernist and postmodernist identity. Moreover, I believe that if racism is a cultural projection, that if we have learned it, we should be able to unlearn it. If racism is constructed, there must be possibilities of deconstructing it.

Finally, I wonder if some sorts of racism involve desire and whether hatred is the other side of desire. Perhaps the Other is the Same, and is a part of us? Let me explain.

FREUD, AND THE FOREIGNER WITHIN

Some of the traditional theories of subjectivity are well known. They include the Cartesian view of the self (the cogito model) which stresses the conscious mind: 'I think, therefore I am'. One of the main objections to this view is that it ignores the pervasiveness and the powerful influence of the unconscious in everything we say and do.

According to a Freudian viewpoint, there is no one self. There are, at least, two selves: besides the conscious there is the unconscious. I think we should remember that the subject is not the ego. For Freud there was the id, the ego and the superego. Our identity is not just a matter of how we see ourselves. We are (partly) dependent on the other.

According to Julia Kristeva, the Bulgarian psychoanalyst writing in French, Freud wanted to show on the basis of a semantic study of the German adjective *heimlich* and its antonym *unheimlich* that a negative meaning close to that of the antonym is already tied to the positive term *heimlich*, 'friendly, comfortable', which would also signify 'concealed, kept from sight', 'deceitful and malicious', 'behind someone's back'. Thus, in the very word *heimlich*, the familiar and the intimate are reversed into their opposites, brought together with the contrary meaning of 'uncanny strangeness' harboured in *unheimlich*.[9]

Such an immanence of the strange within the familiar is considered as etymological proof of the psychoanalytic hypothesis according to which 'the uncanny is that class of the frightening which leads back to what is known of old and long familiar'.[10] Freud noted that the archaic, narcissistic self projects out of itself what it experiences as dangerous or unpleasant in itself, making of it an alien double, uncanny and demoniacal. In this instance, the strange appears as a defence put up by a distraught self.

Freud writes:

> We can understand why linguistic usage has extended *das Heimliche* into its opposite, *das Unheimliche*; for this uncanny is in reality nothing new or alien, but something which is familiar and old-established in the mind and which has become alienated from it only through the process of repression.[11]

The repetition that often accompanies the feeling of uncanny strangeness relates it to the 'compulsion to repeat' that is peculiar to the unconscious. The feeling of uncanny strangeness is an instance of anxiety in which the frightening element can be shown to be something repressed which recurs.

Uncanniness occurs when the boundaries between imagination and reality are erased. In a way, *das Unheimliche* is a crumbling of conscious defences, resulting from conflicts which the self experiences with an other – the strange – with whom it maintains a conflictual bond: at the same time 'a need for identification and a fear of it'. To recapitulate: the clash with the other, the identification of the self with that good or bad other that transgresses the fragile boundaries of the uncertain self, is the source of an uncanny strangeness.

Freud himself did not speak of foreigners; nevertheless, Kristeva argues that his work teaches us how to detect foreigners in ourselves. She argues that in the fascinated rejection that the foreigner arouses in us there is a share of uncanny strangeness in the sense of the depersonalisation that Freud discovered in it, and which takes up again our infantile desires and fears of the other. With the Freudian notion of the unconscious, the foreigner is neither a 'race' nor a nation. The foreigner is neither glorified nor banished. Uncanny, foreignness is within us. We are divided; we are our own foreigners. And when we flee from or struggle against the foreigner, we are fighting our unconscious.[12]

It is through unravelling transference – the major dynamics of otherness, of love/hatred for the other, of the foreign component of our psyche – that, on the basis of the other, we become reconciled with our own otherness-foreignness. Kristeva says that it is because of Freud that we have learned that we are foreigners to ourselves, and it is with the help of that sole support that we can attempt to live with others. In this view, psychoanalysis becomes 'a journey into the strangeness of the other and of oneself, towards an ethics of respect for the irreconcilable'. The ethics of psychoanalysis implies a politics: it would involve a cosmopolitanism of a new sort that, cutting across governments, economics and markets, might work for a mankind whose solidarity is founded on the consciousness of its unconscious.[13]

ETHNICITY AND ITS CONSTRUCTION

In this section, I want to move on from talking about 'race' to ethnicity. Why? As I said earlier, 'race' is often thought of as biological. But many people nowadays are not crude racists but are instead rather sophisticated. Not wanting to be seen as racist, they disguise their views by saying that their objection to black people is not because of their 'race' but because of their culture. And so it is often said that the heterogeneous cultures of ethnic groups threaten the homogeneity of English culture.

There is, at the same time, an intellectual tendency ('we mustn't be essentialist') to think that the term 'black' denied differences by subsuming people from different cultures into one reductionist category. As a consequence, the terms 'ethnic' and 'ethnic minorities' came to be increasingly used. (Sometimes these terms are used, it seems to me, as a euphemism for 'Asians' or 'blacks').

But what is ethnicity? Ethnicity is polysemic, it has many meanings. I would describe it as the shared, cultural, historical features of a group. Ethnicity is to do with place, with shared historical experience. How is ethnicity constructed? The process seems, broadly, to be like this: bards and prophets create legends which describe their 'origins' and their heroic deeds. These cultural workers are the myth-makers of ethnicity. Later, religious and educational institutions are created. In this process, there is considerable cultural borrowing: many external influences are absorbed and assimilated. The 'lower' castes/classes are incorporated into the belief system. It is emphasised that the community, the ethnic group, or nation, has been 'chosen'. These myths of ethnic 'election' encourage survival and renewal. Sometimes, of course, this is the myth of the dominant ethnic group of the emerging 'nation'.

In this construction, poetry, painting and music are used to build cultural values. Culture and politics are interwoven; there is a continual emphasis on flags, symbols and rituals; there are parades, plays and operas, music, films. Ethnic groups have heroes and myths which the group thinks are primordial. The ethno-history gives dignity to the people. Through art and ritual, memories are evoked and aspirations organised.

Ethnic identity is based on an identification with a group conscious of its language, religion, history, tradition and ways of life. In Raymond Williams's *Keywords* (a history of a society through the study of its changing concepts), which doesn't give the 'correct' meanings of words but shows how the meanings of words have shifted,[14] he writes, for example: 'Ethnics came to be used in the United States as what was described in 1961 "a polite term for Jews, Italians and other lesser breeds" . . .' Ethnicity seems to have, on the whole, rather negative connotations.

At the present time, there is a proliferation of ethnic identity movements. There are the Bretons, Basques, Catalans, Armenians, Kurds, Palestinians, Sikhs, Tamils. The list could be greatly extended. As national states are moving towards forms of interdependence and globalisation, there are astonishing developments taking place all over the world such as the resurgence of ethnic violence. There are conflicts between Arabs and Jews in the Middle East, Hindus and

Muslims in India, Tamils and Sinhalese in Sri Lanka, Serbs, Croats and Muslims in Bosnia.

Ethnicity, like nationalism, is Janus-headed; it can be progressive and regressive. It can unify a group of people in their struggle against oppression, but it can also lead to persecution of other ethnic groups, 'ethnic cleansing', massacres, long-lasting hatreds and wars. The boundaries of nation-states do not coincide with the presence of ethnic groups. Each nation-state has within it many ethnic groups, and some ethnic groups (like the Kurds and the Palestinians), having no national homeland, live in many countries. In each national state, there seems to be a dominant ethnic group which emphasises its ethnos: it stresses its purity, invents its privileged historic past. The dominant group sees other groups as 'ethnic' – but not itself. There are white ethnic groups and 'non-white' ethnic groups, but the former are not seen as a problem. In the United States, people with single identities (for example, the English) are regarded as superior to those who have what are called 'hyphenated' identities (for example, Spanish-American).

The term 'ethnicity' has no necessary 'belonging' – by that I mean that ethnicity does not have one, inherent, fixed meaning. It is not one thing; it is always, to use a Lacanian term, sliding. Ethnicity is, of course, a social construction, but it presents itself as 'natural'. That is to say, it gives the impression of disinterestedness. It implies that some ties such as birthplace, region, religion or language are not chosen. Ethnicity appears natural and inevitable. We are made ethnic subjects. We acquire an ethnic identity.

In the discourse of 'race', there has always been a strong element that has insisted on biological arguments. Many right-wing scientists have wanted to prove through genetics that black people are inferior. As they have not been successful in proving this, they have moved their focus on to skin-colour as a signifier. I want to make the point that, just as 'race' can be culturalised, ethnicity can be biologised.

I believe that in Britain the term 'ethnicity' has been appropriated, like so many others, by the political Right. It has been used to divide black people into different constituent groups ('divide and rule'): Indians and Pakistanis, Sikhs and Hindus, Asians and Afro-Caribbeans, Greeks and Turks. The divided, fragmented ethnicities of the minorities can then be contrasted to the apparently homogeneous, unified 'British way of life' which is not seen as ethnic at all! This is a strategy that stresses the differences between groups rather than the similarities. Differences divide, similarities unite. But if one stresses only unity, then there may well be valuable differences which are not noticed. But even within differences there are differences. There are, for example, many fundamentalisms: Islamic fundamentalism in Iran is different from that in Egypt. It is often forgotten that there is also a Christian fundamentalism; perhaps we even say that there is a 'Western' fundamentalism.

In recent years, there has been a greater understanding of the role of the symbolic, how language works. There has also been a renarrativisation of the history of Africa. One example that comes to mind is Martin Bernal's huge, scholarly work on the relation between Egypt and Greece.[15] He argues that the version of the history of Ancient Greece which he had been taught was a recent invention. This dominant history, 'the Aryan model', stressed Greek civilisation as the pure and uncontaminated origin of European civilisation. Actually, this model only emerged in the 1840s and 1850s when, mainly in Germany but also in Britain and in other European countries, counter-revolutionary intellectuals saw the study of the Greeks as a way of reintegrating people alienated by modern life, and even of re-establishing social harmony in the face of the French Revolution. Gradually, the previous view, 'the Ancient Model' of Greek civilisation – that the Greeks were merely pupils of the Egyptians – was eroded by hostility to the French Revolution. In short, 'the Ancient Model' was accepted until the late seventeenth century. With the spread of European imperialism and the rise of racism, the ancient notion that Greece was a mixed culture that had been civilised by Africans was thought of as not only abominable but also unscientific.

This reference to Bernal's *Black Athena* reminds me that another important development has been the construction of the term 'black' (like 'green' or 'red') as a political category. There was a need for minority groups to come together, to create a unity that stressed their commonality. 'Black' referred to diverse types of people; it ignored certain differences, but nevertheless it was a useful concept at the time. This was a time when young Afro-Caribbeans used language, music and culture to popularise Rastafari, a belief that increased black pride and cohesion. As you know, the movement stressed the impulse to return to Africa – not physically but in consciousness.

Now, it is fashionable to say that the term 'black' is reductionist, it reduces people with many different cultures to one flat category. It is also modish to argue against essentialism – everyone is against it. One exception is Gayatri Spivak, who has said that, in their need to create new political identities, dominated groups will often appeal to bonds of common cultural experience in order to mobilise their constituency. Spivak's point, I think, is that the term 'black' can be seen as a useful essentialism, if one thinks of it strategically.[16] It is strange that at the same time that there is an acknowledgement of difference in society, (it looks as if) the field of antagonisms is proliferating in it.

I have stressed the point that identity is not fixed, but we should remember that it is not free-floating either. It is important to know where we come from. All people construct a home, all people have a place to which they feel an attachment, a belongingness. This is in contrast to some postmodernist writers who stress the subject as nomad, a wanderer roaming from place to place. We have to understand the power and pull of home. How do we imagine ourselves in relation to an (imagined) place? One of the problems is that there are so many axes of identification, so many specificities that constitute subjects, that have to be considered: language, class, gender, sexuality, 'race', ethnicity, religion and nation. In the next section, I want to make some remarks on the nation and nationalism.

NATION AND NATIONALISM

The word 'nation' is often used to mean the whole people of a country, often in contrast to some group in it. It is often used to refer to the nation-state, a form of identification that subsumes local loyalties such as tribe, city, region. The development of nation-states has occurred within the historical phase called modernity; there have been powerhouses of modernisation.

The nation has been both progressive and regressive at different periods. If one considers the process of decolonisation, or the liberation movements, the struggle to create a new nation, nationalism, was absolutely necessary. In the postwar period, nationalism has been vital in the creation of independent nation-states. It should be noted, however, that nationalism has no necessary political belonging. The meaning of the word varies according to context. Nationalism consists of many varied and often contradictory elements that vary at different times. Another way of saying this is to say that nationalism (like ethnicity) has no essence; it is a 'sliding' or 'floating' signifier.

But what is the link between the nation and nationalism? It must be remembered that nationalism is not the awakening of nations to self-consciousness; it invents nations where they do not exist. As

Ernest Gellner has said, 'The cultural shreds and patches used by nationalism are often arbitrary historical inventions. Any old shred would have served as well. But in no way does it follow that the principle of nationalism . . . is itself the least contingent and accidental.'[17] But it is not only nations that are invented; even historic continuity has to be invented, for example, by creating an ancient past. Traditions are invented by governments to give permanence and solidity to a transient political form.

Tradition, it has been remarked, is akin to memory; their functions are often the same. Tradition, usually said to be received, in reality made, is an activity of selection, revision and invention. Its function is to defend identity against the threat of heterogeneity, discontinuity and contradiction. The purpose of tradition is to bind and necessarily, therefore, to exclude. It tends to represent itself as custom, as continuity. In this way, tradition becomes a usable past, and the evocation of deep, sacred origins becomes a means of creating a people.

Modern nationalism creates a people by emphasising three key notions: the idea of a chosen people, the emphasis on a common stock of memory of the past and hopes for the future, and national messianism. It was in Germany that the mystical idea of the nation and national messianism acquired its full scope. According to Herder, a supreme value, such as nation or national genius, is not biological, 'scientific' or even political, but essentially moral. With Herder, there is a burst of national feeling anchored in language.[18] Moreover, in opposition to universalist abstraction, there is a romantic withdrawal into the mystique of the past. Within this irrational pouch, there was room both for national withdrawal in times of defeat and difficulties, and national pride during periods of aggression. Henceforth the supreme good was no longer the individual but the nation as a whole. The path was thus open to irrationalism, to fascism.

In recent years, there has been considerable discussion about the negative, regressive aspects of both ethnicity and nationalism. Questions of ethnic identity always arise in times of crisis; problems always flare up in moments of danger. The civil war between warring factions in former Yugoslavia is considered by many people as regressive; it appears as a return to the past.

How can we put a brake on nationalism's destructive force? Some people have suggested that the idea of citizenship could, perhaps, be used as an antidote to nationalism. This is particularly relevant at the present time, when many European countries still deny the rights of citizenship to their black inhabitants. Their freedom of movement is restricted, their right for education, for permanent residence is limited. The concept of citizenship could be radicalised and foregrounded – but it has, unfortunately, an abstract quality. In contrast with citizenship, there is something about the nation which is very powerful. It is so dynamic and vigorous that people are willing to die for it. How can the concept of citizenship have the magnetic pull of the nation?

I feel that something is missing in the above account: the psyche. In discussions such as this, about nation and nationalism, 'race' and ethnicity, I often wonder about the role of psychoanalysis. I know that many people are asking some trenchant questions about psychoanalysis. To what extent is psychoanalysis Eurocentric? Is psychoanalysis being used as an apparatus of social control of blacks and ethnic minorities? We know that theory is not neutral. In this chapter, I have suggested that the discourse of psychoanalysis filters out some of the experiences of black people. I have heard people say 'well, we are all human' (or something similar) while they are deliberately ignoring or excusing the specific effects of a racist society. There seems to be a universalism about psychoanalysis which often denies the specificity of different ways of life. If a psychoanalytic account of racism is difficult to give, perhaps it is because it is not specific enough?

On the other hand, I am convinced that psychoanalysis has a lot to say, for example, about how identification works, how subject-positions are constructed. Some people assume that if identification works in a particular way in the case of individuals, then it must work in the same way with, say, nations. This would be using psychoanalysis analogically. But to draw psychoanalytical insights from one sphere and to transfer them to another sphere is reductionist. There are many types of identification, and one cannot just transfer what happens in one scenario to another, larger, scenario. There are many differences between one scenario and another, and, to avoid the charge of reductionism, much more theoretical work will have to be done. Perhaps there will always be a tension between the psychic and the social and we may have to learn to live with that tension?

Though I want to stress the usefulness of psychoanalysis, there is no doubt in my mind that the pivotal concept in these discussions is culture. It is culture that forms us; without culture there would be no identity at all. National cultures are systems of representation. Discourses of the nation always seem to override class, gender and other social dynamics. By the use of representation, nations recognize and represent the differences between people and make them into a unity. In this way, we are subjected and made into subjects.

> *Roshan and I came to England at the same time. I was nine years of age and he was sixteen. There were not many Indians in Bristol at that time, and there must have been considerable pressure on us to speak English well. Some people do not believe me when I tell them that I've forgotten how to speak my mother language, Punjabi. You can imagine how embarrassed I feel when people speak to me in Punjabi and receive no reply. In India it's painful when I can't respond, and I can see that other people are puzzled.*
>
> *In contrast with me, Roshan never forgot his mother tongue. While I still speak with a Bristolian accent, Roshan never lost his Indian accent. One day, he surprised me by saying: 'Don't think I don't know that I speak with an Indian accent. It's something I've never wanted to give up.'*
>
> *Some years ago, Roshan told me he had angina. I met him several times in London, and I noticed that he had difficulty in walking even short distances. He often used to ring me at bedtime to talk. He would suggest meeting in London to see a play, a film or an exhibition. He was always keen to plan our next visit to India together. I often postponed our meetings with the excuse that I had to finish my writing. I remember our few short holidays in India together and they seem so wonderful, so vibrant. Why didn't I start travelling earlier and more often? Years have passed, and yet when I'm in bed I sometimes still think, and remember his phone-calls. The most painful aspect is that I never used to think about death. It never occurred to me that he could possibly die before me. And now I miss him, I have no-one to talk to about the things I am writing about. There is no-one in the world who knows about our shared experiences.*

NOTES

1. Robert Miles, *Racism* (London: Routledge, 1989), p. 70.
2. Frantz Fanon, *Black Skin, White Masks* (London: Pluto Press, 1986).
3. J. Laplanche and J. B. Pontalis, *The Language of Psycho-Analysis* (London: The Hogarth Press, 1973), p. 458.
4. Ibid., p. 93.
5. Ibid., p. 118.
6. Ibid., p. 261.
7. Madan Sarup, *Jacques Lacan* (Hemel Hempstead: Harvester Wheatsheaf, 1992). If, as Lacan says, the subject is constituted through language, how does it know that alternatives are possible? Perhaps a migrant's journey, a change of spatio–temporal location, can provide a different view of possibilities.
8. It is usually taken for granted that the active construction of identity is 'progressive'. But there is no such guarantee; the active construction of identity can produce, in certain circumstances, a 'reactionary' identity.

9. *Das Unheimliche* comes out in French as 'l'inquiétante étrangeté'; but this is different from 'the uncanny'. The translator tries to bridge the gap between French and English words by rendering the French phrase as 'uncanny strangeness'.

10. 'The Uncanny' (1919), in Sigmund Freud, *Art and Literature*, vol. 14, The Pelican Freud Library (London: Penguin Books, 1985), p. 339.

11. Julia Kristeva, *Strangers to Ourselves* (London: Harvester Wheatsheaf, 1991), p. 184.

12. Ibid., p. 191.

13. Ibid., p. 192.

14. Raymond Williams, *Keywords: A Vocabulary of Culture and Society* (Glasgow: Fontana, 1976), p. 119.

15. Martin Bernal, *Black Athena* (London: Free Association Books, 1987).

16. Gayatri Chakravorty Spivak, *The Post-Colonial Critic: Interviews, Strategies, Dialogues*, ed. Sarah Harasym (London: Routledge, 1990), p. 11.

17. Ernest Gellner, *Nations and Nationalism* (Oxford: Basil Blackwell, 1983), p. 56.

18. To what extent do books determine our identities? How has literature influenced the attitudes, beliefs, customs and language of people? Our national identity has certainly been influenced by the novel. According to Ben Anderson, the newspaper and the novel were crucial in defining the nation as an imagined community. Socially, the novel joined the newspaper as the major vehicle of the national print media, helping to standardise language, encourage literacy and remove incomprehensibility. Its manner of presentation allowed people to imagine the community that was the nation. Read in isolation, the novel was a mass ceremony; one could read alone with the conviction that millions of others were doing the same, at the same time. See Benedict Anderson, *Imagined Communities: Reflections on the Origin and Spread of Nationalism* (London: Verso, 1983).

Good friends
Died
of Drug
overdoses.

Ryan Killduf — learn your lesson Dale

Matty Davis

Arse

Rondeen

INDEX

The way surgs are mixed

Note: 'n.' after a page reference indicates the number of a note on that page.